STAGING THE LYRIC

Sarah Berry is an assistant professor of English at the University of Dallas, USA. She has published articles in *Literature/Film Quarterly*, *Journal of Modern Literature*, *Christianity and Literature,* and *Twentieth Century Literature* as well as reviews in *Modern Drama* and *Modernism/Modernity*.

Also available in the Critical Companions series from Methuen Drama:

THE DRAMA AND THEATRE OF ANNIE BAKER
Amy Muse

THE THEATRE OF PAULA VOGEL: PRACTICE, PEDAGOGY, AND INFLUENCES
Lee Brewer Jones

THE THEATRE OF SIMON STEPHENS
Jacqueline Bolton

CRITICAL COMPANION TO NATIVE AMERICAN AND FIRST NATIONS THEATRE AND PERFORMANCE: INDIGENOUS SPACES
Jaye T. Darby, Courtney Elkin Mohler, and Christy Stanlake

THE DRAMA AND THEATRE OF SARAH RUHL
Amy Muse

THE THEATRE OF AUGUST WILSON
Alan Nadel

THE THEATRE OF EUGENE O'NEILL: AMERICAN MODERNISM ON THE WORLD STAGE
Kurt Eisen

THE THEATRE AND FILMS OF CONNOR MCPHERSON: CONSPICUOUS COMMUNITIES
Eamonn Jordan

IRISH DRAMA AND THEATRE SINCE 1950
Patrick Lonergan

For a full listing, please visit https://www.bloomsbury.com/uk/series/critical-companions/

STAGING THE LYRIC

MODERN AND CONTEMPORARY EXPERIMENTS WITH VERSE DRAMA

Sarah Berry

Series Editors: Patrick Lonergan and Kevin J. Wetmore, Jr.

methuen | drama

LONDON • NEW YORK • OXFORD • NEW DELHI • SYDNEY

METHUEN DRAMA
Bloomsbury Publishing Plc
50 Bedford Square, London, WC1B 3DP, UK
1385 Broadway, New York, NY 10018, USA
29 Earlsfort Terrace, Dublin 2, Ireland

BLOOMSBURY, METHUEN DRAMA and the Methuen Drama logo are trademarks of
Bloomsbury Publishing Plc

First published in Great Britain 2025

Copyright © Sarah Berry, 2025

Sarah Berry has asserted her right under the Copyright, Designs and Patents Act, 1988, to be
identified as author of this work.

For legal purposes the Acknowledgments on p. ix constitute an extension of this copyright page.

Cover image: The Cure at Troy, 2022 © Linda Johnson / Quintessence Theatre,
Philadelphia, PA, USA

All rights reserved. No part of this publication may be reproduced or transmitted in any form or
by any means, electronic or mechanical, including photocopying, recording, or any information
storage or retrieval system, without prior permission in writing from the publishers.

Bloomsbury Publishing Plc does not have any control over, or responsibility for, any third-party
websites referred to or in this book. All internet addresses given in this book were correct
at the time of going to press. The author and publisher regret any inconvenience
caused if addresses have changed or sites have ceased to exist, but can accept
no responsibility for any such changes.

A catalogue record for this book is available from the British Library.

Library of Congress Cataloging-in-Publication Data

Names: Berry, Sarah (College teacher) author. | Lonergan, Patrick series editor. |
Wetmore, Kevin J., Jr. series editor.
Title: Staging the lyric : modern and contemporary experiments with verse drama /
Sarah Berry; series editors: Patrick Lonergan and Kevin J. Wetmore, Jr.
Description: London ; New York : Methuen Drama, 2025. | Series: Critical companions; vol 35 |
Includes bibliographical references and index.
Identifiers: LCCN 2024020149 (print) | LCCN 2024020150 (ebook) |
ISBN 9781350420380 (hardback) | ISBN 9781350420465 (paperback) |
ISBN 9781350420397 (ebook) | ISBN 9781350420403 (pdf)
Subjects: LCSH: Verse drama, English–History and criticism. |
Verse drama, American–History and criticism. | Theater–Great Britain–History. |
Theater–United States–History.
Classification: LCC PR635.V4 B47 2025 (print) | LCC PR635.V4 (ebook) |
DDC 822.009–dc23/eng/20240607
LC record available at https://lccn.loc.gov/2024020149
LC ebook record available at https://lccn.loc.gov/2024020150

ISBN: HB: 978-1-3504-2038-0
ePDF: 978-1-3504-2040-3
eBook: 978-1-3504-2039-7

Series: Critical Companions

Typeset by RefineCatch Limited, Bungay, Suffolk

To find out more about our authors and books visit www.bloomsbury.com
and sign up for our newsletters.

For my father, Kevin Casey

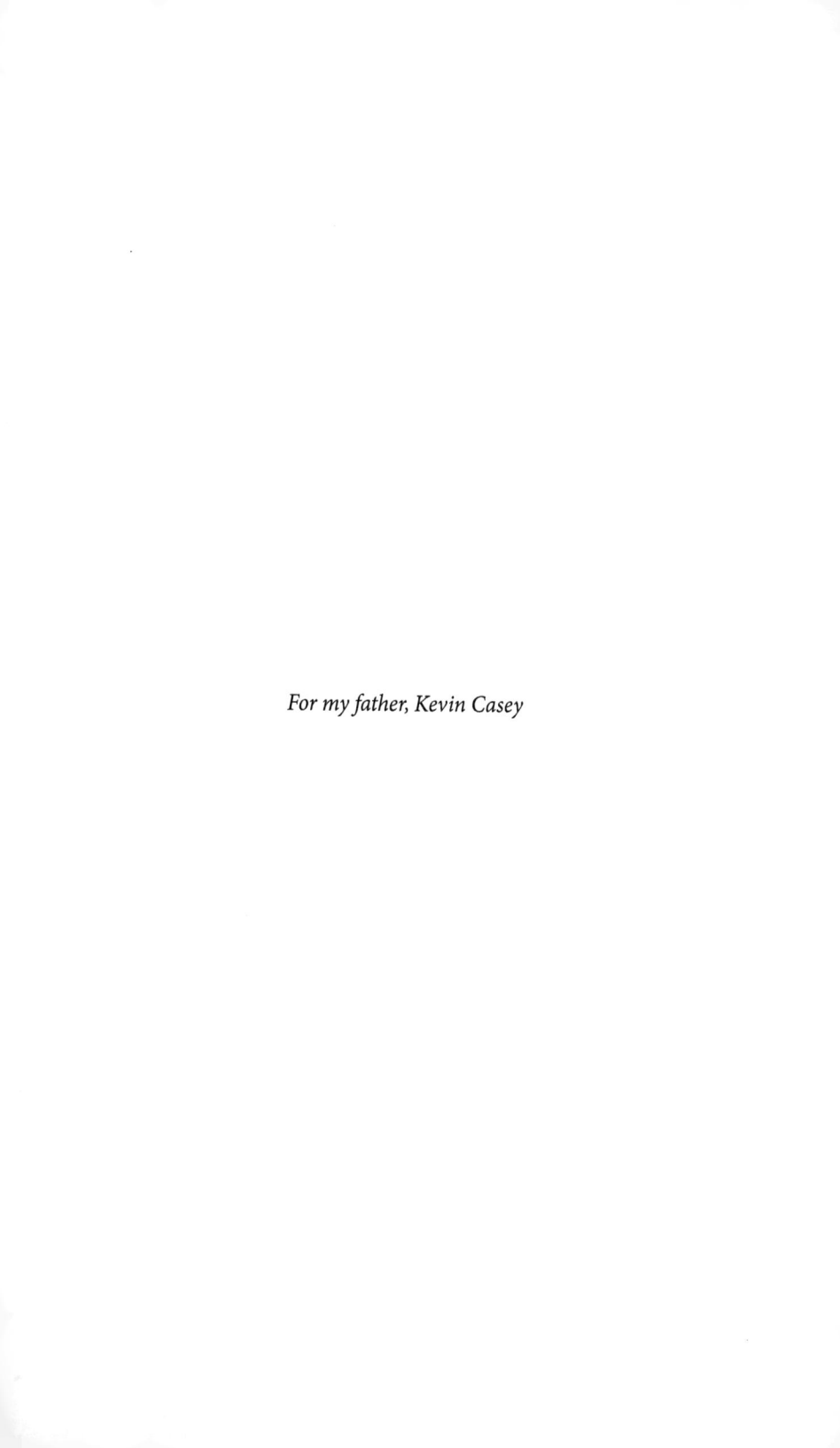

CONTENTS

List of Figures — viii
Acknowledgments — ix

Introduction: Verse Drama after the Lyric — 1

Part I: Voice

1 The Chorus — 23

2 Radio Drama — 49

Part II: Words

3 Counted Meter — 73

4 Language as Material — 101

Part III: Time

5 Temporality — 131

6 Anachronism — 155

Conclusion: Verse Drama after the Internet — 175

Notes — 181
Bibliography — 209
Index — 219

FIGURES

1. Costume plates for *The Just Vengeance* (1946) by Norah Lambourne. Reproduced by permission of the Dorothy L. Sayers Society.   33
2. *for colored girls who have considered suicide when the rainbow is enuf* (1976). Pictured l-r: Rise Collins, Trazana Beverly, Paula Moss, Seret Scott, Aku Kadogo, Laurie Carlos, Janet League. Photograph by Martha Swope © New York Public Library for the Performing Arts.   37
3. Frontispiece of *Leviathan* by Thomas Hobbes, engraving by Abraham Bosse (1651).   42
4. Linocut by Stanislaw Gliwa, from Turret Books edition of *Three Women* (1968).   62
5. Sylvia Plath, "Triple-Face Portrait" (1951). Courtesy of Lilly Library, Indiana University, Bloomington. © 2022 Estate of Sylvia Plath. Reproduced by permission of Faber and Faber Ltd.   63
6. *Nayatt School* (1978). Pictured (l-r): Ron Vawter, Spalding Gray, Joan Jonas. © Bob Van Dantzig.   107
7. *Nayatt School* (1978). Pictured (l-r): Erik Moskowitz, Ursula Easton, Ron Vawter, Tena Cohen, Spalding Gray. © Nancy Campbell.   108
8. *Rockaby* (1982). Pictured: Billie Whitelaw. Reproduced with permission from photographer, Irene Ikner Haupt.   142

ACKNOWLEDGMENTS

Like the Airman in *The Just Vengeance*, I have been picked up and carried along by community. So, let me start by thanking the Dorothy L. Sayers Society, especially Seona Ford, for sharing her knowledge and archival materials related to this play. The same goes for Clay Hapaz, with the Wooster Group. I am also grateful to playwright Joanna Laurens and directors Kimberley Lynne and Robert McNamara for sharing their experiences with me.

I am indebted to my mentors at the University of Connecticut, especially Mary Burke, Penelope Pelizzon, Charles Mahoney, Yohei Igarashi, and Brenda Murphy, who shaped this project in its earliest days. Some of this book was written during my year as a fellow at UConn's Humanities Institute (2017–2018), and I am grateful for the support of Michael Lynch, Alexis Boylan, and the rest of the team, as well as my cohort. More recently, I received a Haggar Grant from the University of Dallas that subsidized this project in its final stages—thank you to the Provost's office for that! And thank you to my colleagues at UD, especially in the English department and the Faculty Writing Group. Special thanks to Michael West, Bernadette Waterman Ward, Theresa Kenney, Debra Romanick Baldwin, Katie Davis, Dan and Kim Burns, Fr. Joseph Van House, Christi Ivers, Anne Jeffrey, Kerri Farrell, Kate Gross, and Eleanor Reeds for offering feedback and encouragement along the way.

I am grateful to and for my parents, Kevin and Angie Casey; my sister, Anna Casey; my Berry and Koch in-laws; and my four children, Daniel, John, Margaret June, and Thomas. I also want to thank the women who helped take care of those children: Lee, Pam, Shanitta, Denise, Jamie, Joanna, Kathleen, Maggie, Gabi, Angela, Emily, and Jeanna. Their efforts have made this book possible. And finally, to Matt—the babysitter, barista, Greek translator, loyal opposition, word-count decimator, and snowstorm chauffer behind the scenes—thank you for all of these efforts, and a lot more besides.

A version of Chapter Two appeared as "(Re)Embodying the Disembodied Voice of Lyric: The Radio Poems of Derek Walcott and Sylvia Plath" in

Acknowledgments

Twentieth Century Literature. I thank the journal as well as the publisher, Duke University Press, for permission to reprint portions of this article.

The author and publisher gratefully acknowledge the permission granted to reproduce the copyright material in this book:

"This Room" from *Your Name Here* by John Ashbery. Copyright © 2000 by John Ashbery. Reprinted by permission of Georges Borchardt, Inc., on behalf of the author's estate. All rights reserved.

"I Catch Sight of the Now" from *To 2040* by Jorie Graham. Copyright © 2023 by Jorie Graham. Reprinted with the permission of The Permissions Company, LLC on behalf of Copper Canyon Press, coppercanyonpress.org.

Every effort has been made to trace copyright holders and to obtain their permission for the use of copyright material. However, if any have been inadvertently overlooked, the publishers will be pleased, if notified of any omissions, to make the necessary arrangement at the first opportunity.

INTRODUCTION

Verse Drama after the Lyric

Verse drama in the twentieth century is the literary equivalent of the living dead. Its critics denigrate it as a kind of zombie, shamming life but lacking real vitality, while its advocates prefer to cast it as a cryptobiotic lifeform, surviving in a state of suspended animation until conditions are favorable for revival. Up until the eighteenth century, things were different: verse was the primary form of drama in the West from classical Greece to early modern England. At that point, it began to fall out of fashion on the English-language stage, a process that continued through the nineteenth century. Since then, it has been subject to a cycle of alternating decline and revival, shaped by movements in theater and literature as well as trends in audience reception and theater scholarship.

Its most recent resuscitation was heralded by Kasia Lech in an article prophetically titled "Five Reasons Why Verse is the Language for Theatre in the 2020s."[1] In this piece, Lech observes a "resumed interest in verse and its hybrid forms" in contemporary theater, citing examples from around the world, from Nigerian-born British writer Inua Ellams's *An Evening with an Immigrant* (2017) to Polish playwright Marta Górnicka's *Hymn to Love* (2018). According to Lech, verse is well-suited to theatrical experimentation with new media, and conducive to writers from marginalized groups giving expression to their experiences. Lech is not alone in promoting renewed interest in verse drama. In October 2020, Turn to Flesh Productions, a New York-based theater company, released the first season of a podcast called *Hamlet to Hamilton: Exploring Verse Drama*. The program, hosted by Emily C.A. Snyder, bills itself as an educational podcast, with the goal of teaching its listeners how to write and perform verse drama.

This characterization of verse drama as the wave of the future will come as a surprise to those who are familiar with the story of verse drama in the twentieth century, when it seemed all but extinct. Most scholars concur with the summary given by Harley Granville-Barker in 1937:

> The vulgar history of it would still perhaps run thus: that it rose to great heights with Shakespeare and the Elizabethans; so rapidly

declined in quality that when the Puritans closed the theatres in 1642 it was already moribund; that it was reformed by Dryden and his school, and maintained a respectable if dull existence throughout the eighteenth century; that what the nineteenth chiefly saw was its divorce from the theatre, despite the efforts of the well wishers of both parties to bring them together again. Sporadic efforts these, and sparsely rewarded [...][2]

Granville-Barker refers to the fact that dramatic verse was still being written during the nineteenth century, but not for the stage. And certainly during this period, the plays of Shakespeare were still being performed. J.C. Trewin goes as far as to declare nineteenth-century verse drama "a haunted ruin"—haunted, it would seem, by the legacy of Shakespeare, the foremost verse dramatist in English.[3] Glenda Leeming puts it this way: "verse drama continued to be written and revived after the seventeenth century" but "its dominance as a creative force declined."[4]

Either way, by the beginning of the twentieth century, the matter was settled: verse was out and prose was in. Turn-of-the-century scholars like Wilfrid Wilson Gibson describe verse drama as having "a past—a superb and unsurpassable past—but no possible future."[5] The few verse dramas from this period—such as Thomas Hardy's three-part epic *The Dynasts*—were often subject to critical scorn. Even the practitioners of verse drama admit that it can be awkward and anachronistic. Christopher Fry, in a 1955 interview with *Vogue* magazine, acknowledges that many people find verse drama "an irritating, or boring, or distracting, or pretentious flight of fashion."[6]

And yet, this was precisely the moment when verse drama was revived. In Ireland, W.B. Yeats began writing verse plays for the Abbey Theatre in Dublin as part of the Irish Literary Revival. Across the Atlantic, the Provincetown Players, whose membership included Alfred Kreymborg, Edna St. Vincent Millay, Mina Loy, and William Carlos Williams, staged their experiments with verse in Provincetown, Massachusetts, and later Greenwich Village, between 1915 and 1922.[7] While these plays have not enjoyed the same canonical status among scholars as Yeats's do, Sarah Bay-Cheng and Barbara Cole harvested enough examples from American modernist writers to fill an anthology called *Poets at Play*.

After the Second World War, a group that included Mary Manning, Richard Wilbur, John Ashbery, and Frank O'Hara, staged plays in Cambridge, Massachusetts. Unlike their English counterparts who tend to invoke Elizabethan antecedents, these writers did not claim Shakespeare or his contemporaries as their own national tradition. In fact, their stated goal, according to Nora Sayre, was "the emergence of an American verse theater."[8] Reflecting on their heyday, Sayre describes the group "seeth[ing] with confidence," believing that "the Poets' Theatre was the institution that would unite prophecy and literature with performance."[9] The Poets' Theatre declined in the 1960s and eventually disbanded in 1968, but the project was revived in 1986 (with a two-evening celebration billed as "a wake") and still stages plays from time to time.[10] In England after the war, there was a distinct movement, a revival of religious verse drama; plays by John Masefield, T.S. Eliot, Charles Williams, and Dorothy L. Sayers were written and performed for the Canterbury Festival, and later at the Mercury Theatre under the direction of E. Martin Browne. At the same time, Rupert Doone's Group Theatre staged work by Eliot, W.H. Auden, Christopher Isherwood, Stephen Spender, and Louis MacNeice. And then there is Fry, who does not properly belong to any of these movements but is probably the most popular verse dramatist of the period, with his hit play *The Lady's Not For Burning* (1948). In the decades following these mid-century revivals, several scholarly monographs were published: Denis Donoghue's *The Third Voice: Modern British and American Verse Drama* (1959), William Spanos's *The Christian Tradition in Modern British Verse Drama* (1967), Arnold Hinchcliffe's *Modern Verse Drama* (1977), and Leeming's *Poetic Drama* (1989). Donoghue is particularly sanguine about the future of verse drama; he thinks of it as an essential part of Modernism and crucial to understanding the movement.

But almost as soon as these books were published, other critics began bemoaning verse drama's decline once more. In 1980, William McCollom asked, "The declining visibility of verse drama in this century"—a trend he believes began in the 1950s—"raises the question whether the verse medium can again attract a large number of playgoers."[11] Even some of the monographs betray a degree of wistfulness. Leeming, for her part, presents her book as a kind of *post-mortem*. She dates the first signs of decline to the 1940s, claiming the movement was eclipsed by the likes of Osborne, Wesker, Arden, and Pinter in the 1950s. By the 1980s, Leeming insists, there were no longer any "serious plays" being written in verse. In 1990, Derek Walcott would observe, "we now speak of the poetry of the theatre as if it were an archaic visitor, an unwanted aunt."[12] This critical consensus persists in the early twenty-first century. Writing in 2004, Charles Martin laments that verse drama has "virtually disappeared from the stage" and "seems to have only a great past."[13] This refrain is eerily reminiscent of that of the century before. In fact, Joel Brouwer presents his own diagnosis of the situation in

Staging the Lyric

2009 as a kind of update to Eliot's 1920 essay "The Possibility of a Poetic Drama," averring: "if there was no poetic drama then, I guess there's something like less than none now."[14]

And yet, even in this period, we find a persistent interest in verse drama. Plays like Caryl Churchill's *Serious Money* (1987) and more recently Mike Bartlett's *King Charles III* (2014) have fared well with audiences on both sides of the Atlantic. One explanation for these apparently contradictory narratives about verse drama is the difference of opinion among verse drama's stakeholders—that is, the playwrights, the audiences, and the critics. For example, Fry's plays enjoyed popular success, but have not maintained their status among theater scholars—and the inverse could be said of Yeats. But another factor contributing to the confusion is the lack of a consistent definition or clear criteria to distinguish verse drama from other forms of theater. John Arden, whom Leeming names among the British New Wave dramatists, wrote several plays in verse or in a combination of verse and prose; so, it can hardly be said that his plays undermined verse on the stage. The critical consensus of Leeming et al. also ignores the scattered examples of verse plays that do not belong to an identifiable movement, like those written by Steve Berkoff and William Alfred, or "one-off" verse plays like Churchill's *Serious Money* and Terry Eagleton's *Saint Oscar* (1989). Irene Morra's recent monograph, *Verse Drama in England, 1900–2015*, argues for verse drama's persistent presence on the English stage as a kind of "loyal opposition" to mainstream theater, rather than a unitary movement in its own right. Scholars also tend to overlook translations and adaptations written in verse, as well as verse drama written by writers like Walcott and Wole Soyinka from outside the United Kingdom and the United States. As Walcott observes, a great deal of verse drama is being written outside of the mainstream: "without any academic urging, without any sense of siege or nostalgic aggression, verse ignores the centre and continues exuberantly in provincial or ghetto theatre, in rap, in rock music, and in that second-rate expression of exuberance—the stage musical".[15] And indeed, the popularity of Lin-Manuel Miranda's *Hamilton* (2015) would seem to confirm Walcott's hunch that audiences tolerate verse more readily in the context of a stage musical, even when some of that verse is spoken. All this suggests that the story of verse drama in the twentieth century, when you consider the outliers and limit cases, is more complicated than the dominant narrative admits—not a straightforward story of rise and fall. It can—and has—survived in various forms and contexts, especially when it is mixed with prose, as it is in Shakespeare, or song, as it is in musical theater.

Introduction

I want to suggest that the insistence on verse drama's disappearance persists, in spite of evidence to the contrary, because this narrative is useful to verse dramatists. As R.C. Churchill observes, "poetic drama is being constantly revived, it exists in a perpetual state of convalescence."[16] Hence my claim that it has never been dead—because it is *undead*, persisting in a state of cryptobiosis until the time is right for reanimation. The decadence narrative allows writers to insert themselves into a myth of recovery in which their plays are the descendants of an illustrious tradition, without being encumbered by competition from immediate predecessors. As Octavio Paz observes, modernity does not set itself up in opposition to all things past, but only the "immediate past"; in fact, "The very old can be adopted by modernity if it rejects the tradition of the moment and proposes a different one [...] what is very old is not a past but a beginning."[17] In the case of modern verse dramatists, the denial of immediate predecessors frees them up to reinvent verse drama—not a stuffy or clumsy imitation of Shakespeare, but something new.

So, what exactly is new about twentieth-century verse drama? I will argue that it is reconceived at this time as a hybrid of lyric and drama, rather than genre in its own right. If, as Michael Goldman claims, plays always "imply the existence of a set of genre rules from which they depart," then verse dramas take as their point of departure a bespoke selection of conventions from both theater and poetry.[18] What is new is not the departure from convention, but the cross-pollination of conventions, especially those conventions that seem contradictory or mutually exclusive. This new way of thinking about verse on the stage is possible because of two changes, one in theater and one in literature, that take place between the mid-eighteenth century and the mid-twentieth. One is the extraction of verse from stage drama, a process which began before the 1800s, but reached its apotheosis with realism at the end of that century. The other is the introduction of a new genre, the lyric, which necessitated a renegotiation of existing literary taxonomies, and the subsequent expansion of that category to include more verse forms. The combined effect of these parallel changes is that verse is detached from its association with theater and cemented in its (now nearly exclusive) association with the lyric.

Stage Histories and Page Histories

The verse drama's unsteady retreat from English-language theater began with the emergence of bourgeois tragedy in the mid-eighteenth century.

Staging the Lyric

These plays drew on the precedent set by the domestic tragedies a century prior—*Arden of Faversham* (1592) and Thomas Middleton's *A Yorkshire Tragedy* (1608), for instance—in their choice of middle-class protagonists, but differed in their use of prose. The earliest example in English is George Lillo's *The London Merchant* (1731). Around the same time, French playwrights like Paul Landois and Denis Diderot began to write bourgeois tragedies of their own. The French version of this movement is called *tragédie domestique et bourgeoise*—a term that points to the continuity between its two distinct English analogues. One of these bourgeois tragedians, Edward Moore, offers a justification for his use of prose in the preface to *The Gamester* (1753):

> [A]s it struck at a vice so universally prevailing, it was thought proper to adapt its language to the capacities and feelings of every part of the audience: that as some of its characters were of no higher rank than Sharpers, it was imagined that [...] speaking blank verse upon the stage would be unnatural, if not ridiculous. But though the more elevated characters also speak prose, the judicious reader will observe, that it is a species of prose which differs very little from verse: in many of the most animated scenes, I can truly say, that I often found it a much greater difficulty to avoid, than to write, measure. I shall only add, in answer to this objection, that I hoped to be more interesting, by being more natural [...][19]

Moore suggests that it is "unnatural" for low-born characters to speak in verse. Conversely, it is so natural for "more elevated characters" to speak in verse that he must fight against the pull of "measure" even as he writes these parts in prose. Perhaps it goes without saying, but these associations are not self-evident: in real life, aristocrats do not go around speaking in verse any more than "Sharpers" do. It is this particular convention, class-inflected meter, and not verse itself, that eighteenth-century playwrights take issue with. The convention dates back at least to Shakespeare, who often uses blank verse for noble characters and prose for common people. There are some exceptions: in *Henry IV*, Prince Hal speaks in prose with characters like Falstaff and speaks in verse with characters like Hotspur. Such characters, dubbed "adaptable nobles" by Jason Tootalian, expose the fluidity of the classification of characters, but they also show how strong the associations are between commoners and prose, and between nobles and verse.[20] Reacting to this hierarchy without challenging the underlying associations, eighteenth-century playwrights reject verse as part of their movement away from the noble tragic hero and toward more average subjects.[21]

Donoghue, after tracing a direct line from the domestic tragedies of Middleton and Heywood to the bourgeois tragedies of Lillo and Moore, insists that prose drama remains a "minority tradition" during the eighteenth century.[22] But by the nineteenth century, it became the norm. Stendhal gives voice to this consensus in *Racine and Shakespeare* (1853), where on the first page he declares, "henceforth tragedies should be written for us, the young people of the year of grace 1823" and that "those tragedies should be in prose."[23] Later on, he identifies two problems with verse. One is political: verse is associated with nobility and courtiers. The other is formal: while poetry derives its effects from beauty of expression, drama gets its effects from "an exact rendering of the emotions and events of life."[24] For Stendhal, then, clarity and simplicity are more important than beauty. He explains:

> We must always remember that the dramatic action takes place in a room, one wall of which has been removed by the magic wand of Melpomene and replaced by the orchestra and box-seats, thanks to the magic wand of a fairy. The characters do not know there is an audience. From the moment they make *apparent* concessions to that audience, they are no longer characters: they are rhapsodists reciting an epic poem that may be more or less beautiful.
>
> Inversion is a great *concession* in French, an immense privilege of poetry, in this language friendly to truth and clear before it is anything else.
>
> The dominance of rhythm, or of the poetic line, begins only when inversion is allowed.

The problem with verse is that it draws attention to itself, through word order inversions and other poetic techniques. By contrast, the modern and contemporary verse dramatists, especially those discussed in Chapters Three and Four, embrace verse precisely because it draws attention to itself.

There is also in Stendhal's manifesto an implicit association of verse with the past and prose with the future. Joseph Wood Krutch has argued that the defining feature of modern drama in Europe and North America is an emphasis on a break with the past.[25] The key figure for this new kind of theater, one who rejected verse and embraced realism, is Henrik Ibsen. Ibsen did not invent realism, nor was he the first to write modern realist plays, but he has earned the title of "exemplary realist in the theatre," according to

Derek Miller, because of "his ability to synthesize realism's multiple representational techniques with more subtlety and sophistication."[26] Over the course of his dramatic career, Ibsen moved away from Romantic tragedies depicting the struggle between good and evil and toward tragedies of middle-class domestic life, eventually succeeding in imbuing a bourgeois domestic story with the seriousness of high tragedy in *A Doll's House* (1879). As he transformed from Romantic to realist, he became "increasingly ambivalent about verse," according to Stine Brenna Taugbøl.[27] His early plays, like *Brand* (1866) and *Peer Gynt* (1867), are in verse. But after his move to Germany in the late 1860s, he began to write exclusively in prose, even as he tested the waters of realism in plays like *The League of Youth* (1869). When translator Edmund Gosse observed that *Emperor and Galilean* (1873), the last of his epic plays, should have been written in verse, given its subject, Ibsen claimed, "only prose allowed him to situate the tragedy among real human beings."[28] By 1883, Ibsen would assert:

> Verse has been most injurious to the art of drama [...] It is improbable that verse will be employed to any extent worth mentioning in the drama of the immediate future since the aims of the dramatists of the future are almost certain to be incompatible with it. Consequently it is doomed. For art forms become extinct, just as the preposterous animal forms of prehistoric times became extinct when their day was over.[29]

Notice Ibsen's repeated emphasis on future theater, all of which will presumably be written in prose. Verse, he implies, is antiquated, even regressive.[30]

It is worth asking where this association comes from, although that question could generate a book of its own. Walcott attributes the break with verse to the prevailing irony of our age. In "The Poet in the Theatre," he argues that verse drama is the "first victim" of modern cynicism because it is too sincere, too "exuberant" for modern audiences.[31] Greek and Elizabethan tragedies, he says, aimed for sublimity, a sense of awe in the face of tragedy. Verse played a key role in rendering tragic action sublime, as in Ibsen's early plays. But now, Walcott claims, we no longer believe that that suffering is fated. Now every tragic event seems random, and so, there is no reason to attribute to these events any nobility or even meaning. Verse assumes an order to the universe, which makes it a tough sell in an age convinced of existential randomness. The reaction to this loss of meaning is irony. Walcott explains, "irony is the furthest point of tragedy in modern theatre. Not true irony, but sarcasm. This sarcasm mocks literature, scuttles the articulate, deepens chasms."[32] In light of this communicative failure, playwrights resort to either absurdism or minimalism, both of which are more compatible with prose. Verse, on the other hand, "carries the greatest conviction," Walcott says.[33] Too exuberant, it must be consigned to the good old days, when it was still possible to believe in things like fate and nobility, or relegated to places and peoples who are considered "primitive" or "provincial." Either way, there is no longer a place for poetry in the modern, mainstream theater, Walcott believes.

But changes on the stage make up only half of the story. There are also, at the same time, changes taking place in the world of print which play a role in the decline of verse drama in theater. In *Print and the Poetics of Modern Drama*, W.B. Worthen observes the various ways that drama began to take on a "bookish shape" in the nineteenth century, thanks to new editions of Shakespeare's plays and the "novel-like design" of George Bernard Shaw's plays.[34] For my purposes, it is worth noting that Shaw's literary aspirations led him to approximate the appearance of prose, filling the page with text, and to embrace the realist conventions of the nineteenth-century novel. Also during this time, Romantic poets began to write closet dramas. Examples include Coleridge's *Osorio* (1797, later *Remorse*), Goethe's *Faust* (1808), Byron's *Manfred* (1817), and Shelley's *Prometheus Unbound* (1820). In the second half of the century, Tennyson, Browning, and Swinburne conducted their own experiments with closet drama and dramatic monologue. The Romantic and Victorian interest in literary verse forms contributed to the growing association of verse with the page, rather than the stage.

At the same time, a parallel development in literary history cemented this association. As verse drama disappeared from the stage, the lyric, only recently introduced as a genre in its own right, came to be understood as the primary, and eventually the only, type of literature in verse. Virginia Jackson has given the name "lyricization" to the process by which the lyric expanded to subsume all other forms of verse. The first step in this process, during the eighteenth century, involves the "federation"—to use Gerard Genette's metaphor—of various verse forms, such as eclogues, ballads, sonnets, elegies, and odes, into a single genre called the lyric. By the Romantic period, the lyric is a category large enough and distinct enough to qualify as one of the three major genres of poetry, along with epic and dramatic. Genette traces this Romantic taxonomy of genres back to 1746, when Abbé Charles Batteux developed a taxonomy based on the content represented rather than a difference in form or mode of enunciation. Similarly, Friedrich Schlegel, in an unpublished note from 1797, divides the three major genres of poetry on the basis of what they represent: the objective, the subjective, and a mixture of objective and subjective. Although his application of these categories to specific genres is not always consistent, the lyric is always the subjective one. For Hegel, lyric poetry differs from epic and dramatic insofar as "Its content is not the object but the subject, the inner world, the mind that considers and feels, that instead of proceeding to action, remains alone with itself as inwardness, and that therefore can take as its sole form and final aim the self-expression of the subjective life."[35] Notice that in all of these taxonomies, the lyric is still only one of three types of poetry.

The second phase of lyricization occurs in the twentieth century, when the definition of the lyric narrows considerably to the norm we know today. In *Dickinson's Misery*, Jackson argues that lyric is not itself a form but rather a "modern mode of literary interpretation"; in other words, "to be lyric is to be read as lyric."[36] Taking Dickinson's writings as her case study, Jackson traces the way that "the lyric takes form through the development of reading practices in the nineteenth and twentieth centuries that became the practice of literary criticism."[37] These reading practices, codified in the mid-twentieth century by the New Critics, defined the lyric poem according to an attenuated version of a certain kind of Romantic poem. According to this paradigm, the lyric poem is a "temporally self-present or unmediated" expression of subjectivity.[38] It does not need to be mediated because it expresses a truth or subjective experience that any reader can access, without any requisite background knowledge of historical, social, or literary context. The lyric, according to this approach, is a universal, ahistorical expression of self to self, across time, space, and culture.

This lyric ideal is far from what happens in a typical verse drama, in which characters speak to other characters in specific settings. It might, in some cases, involve the expression of self to self, but more likely it would be an argument, a proclamation, a confession, or some other speech act. It would certainly not be the expression of pure "self-present" subjectivity. Even in the rare cases of lyric ventriloquism, when the poet puts the words of a lyric meditation in the mouth of a dramatic character, the speech must still be staged in some context, and the poet is expected to make some concessions to the identity and personality of the character. In that case, it is not an expression of the poet's subjectivity, but a lyric meditation mediated through dramatic character. This is why, by the way, so many lyric passages are written for the chorus: it is the character that can most easily step outside of the diegetic world of the play and serve as a mouthpiece for the writer. But more about that in Chapter One!

Introduction

Experimenting with a Hybrid Genre

As a result of lyricization, which has rendered all poetry a species of lyric, any use of verse, even in drama, now carries with it the conventions and assumptions of lyric poetry. Rather than reject these lyric associations as a misguided approach to verse drama, many poets and playwrights take advantage of the lyricization of verse drama, treating it as a hybrid form that draws on the conventions of the lyric as well as the dramatic. As early as 1921, Eliot characterizes the Francophone verse drama of Maurice Maeterlinck and Paul Claudel as hybrid: they enact, he says, "the mixture of the genres in which our age delights."[39] Although Eliot did not embrace either of these dramatists as his model when he began to write his own verse dramas a few years later, his characterization of their work reveals that he was thinking about the hybrid potential of verse drama as early as 1921.

The same year, in *The Old Drama and the New*, William Archer advanced the theory that all theater emerges from two impulses: "imitation" and "passion." "Imitation" refers to the tradition, going back to Plato and Aristotle, of conceiving of drama as *mimesis*, that is, an imitation of life. Archer uses it more narrowly to designate a particular kind of realism. And by "passion," he means "the exaggerated, intensified—in brief, the lyrical or rhetorical—expression of feeling."[40] Archer's definition of the "lyrical" reflects the influence of lyricization, as Jackson describes it, in its emphasis on the straightforward, unmediated communication of subjective experience. Later on, Archer equates the lyrical with the "rythmic" [sic], his word for self-expression at its most primitive: communicating *via* something deeper and more fundamental than the semantic meaning of words.[41] He distinguishes between these two elements, imitation and passion, only to insist on their hybridity in drama. Interestingly, he thinks this hybridity obtains in all forms of drama, not just verse. Or at least, it did, until it was "cast out" of theater in the nineteenth century.[42] It seems to me that Archer is imputing modern categories—that is, nineteenth-century notions of realism and the post-Romantic paradigm of the lyric—onto earlier drama of the fifteenth to the eighteenth centuries. The hybridity he discerns there, I would argue, is an artifact of his twentieth-century vantage point. More simply: not all drama is hybrid in the way he describes, because these two impulses can be distinguished only after the lyric is distinguished from other forms of poetry as privileged form of intense self-expression. And this lyric ideal does not exist—or, at least, it was not theorized as such—until the nineteenth century.

So, the kind of hybridity Archer prizes is possible only in so-called "new" drama, after lyricization.[43]

A few decades later, Eliot attempted to theorize the hybridity of his own plays in *The Three Voices of Poetry* (1953). Here Eliot identifies three different "voices," distinguished by mode of address. The first is "the voice of the poet talking to himself—or to nobody"; it is essentially "non-dramatic".[44] Poetry written in this voice eschews didactic, narrative, and political ends; it is "concerned solely with expressing."[45] Although the reader might be tempted to equate this category with the lyric, Eliot rejects the term lyric as "unsatisfactory," preferring to call it "meditative verse."[46] The second voice of poetry, which Eliot calls "quasi-dramatic verse," is "the voice of the poet addressing an audience."[47] The clearest example of this voice, according to Eliot, is the dramatic monologue. The distinction he is making here seems to be that quasi-dramatic verse is rhetorical, rather than meditative. Yet it is difficult to imagine a poem, no matter how meditative, that eschews rhetoric entirely. The third voice—the true dramatic voice—is "the voice of the poet when he attempts to create a dramatic character speaking in verse; when he is saying, not only what he would say in his own person, but only what he can say within the limits of one imaginary character addressing another imaginary character."[48]

These "voices" then are not discrete genres of writing but closer to what Northrop Frye would later call "radicals of presentation." As Martin observes, Eliot "had in mind an older idea of voice as a poet's mode of relating (or not relating) to an audience, rather than the contemporary sense of poetic voice as a means of individuation."[49] And because they are modes rather than genres, a writer is free to use more than one in the same text. This is exactly what Eliot does in his verse plays like *Murder in the Cathedral*.

The challenge of writing poetic drama, according to Eliot, is writing compelling poetry in this third voice, the voice of a dramatic character, without lapsing into the first or second voice—in other words, without turning the character into a lyric speaker. Looking back on his first verse play, *The Rock*, he laments that the only discernible voice in this text is "the second voice, that of myself addressing—indeed haranguing—an audience."[50] He explains that the chorus "members were speaking *for me*, not uttering words that really represented any supposed character of their own."[51] Eliot calls this challenge the "problem of speech in verse." He accuses himself of lapsing back into a voice that is "unindividuated"—that is, general or universal—one that expresses his thoughts and feelings rather than the thoughts and feelings of an individual character. What he seems to be describing here, although he does not use these words, is the difficulty of disentangling "poetry"—that is, poetic language—from lyric, here understood as a mode of enunciation, in order to write poetry in the voice of a dramatic character. Understood this way, Eliot's project is a kind of recovery work: an attempt to go back in time to access a no-longer-extant way of thinking about poetry in order to write poetry in the voice of a dramatic character rather than a lyric speaker. We will see if he succeeds in Chapter One.

This spirit of experimentation unites all the plays in this book. When I call them "experimental," I mean something broader than the technical usage—designating Language poets like Lyn Hejinian and Charles Bernstein—and something narrower than the general "disposition or attitude" Natalia Cecire diagnoses in her book on experimental poetry.[52] My own meaning is the commonsensical one: that the playwright is conducting an experiment, testing what they can accomplish when they combine the techniques and conventions associated with these forms in new ways. As Fry quipped, "It is almost true to say that I write plays in verse to find out why I write plays in verse."[53] Fry, like Eliot, is trying to figure something out: what it means to write in verse for the theater after writing in verse has been redefined in opposition with theater. These investigations allow writers to test the limits of the dramatic as well as the lyric, uncovering new things about each of these genres in the process. And these are not dry, academic exercises either; from the perspective of the practitioners, at least, they are a vital and rejuvenating force in a theatrical world otherwise in decline. Tony Harrison explains, "my obsessive concern with Greek drama isn't about antique reproduction, but part of a search for a new theatricality and also a way of expressing dissatisfaction with the current theatre where I work as a poet."[54]

What makes such investigations interesting is that many aspects of lyric poetry are at odds with the conventions of modern realist drama, or even performance itself. Eliot raises several of these issues in *The Three Voices of Poetry*: for instance, is it possible to put the voice of a universal "I" into the mouth of a dramatic character? This would seem to undermine the norms of characterization according to the conventions of realist theater. There are other difficulties related to voice and enunciation. Many of the speech acts that populate lyric poems—including apostrophe, elegy, and other paradoxical forms of address—do not work on the stage. Beyond these issues of enunciation, there is the tendency of lyric poems to resist communication, sometimes on purpose, an impulse that seems to be at odds with the goals of theater. Verse dramatists, like lyric poets, often cultivate this lyric privacy by prioritizing the material properties of language—the way the words look, sound, and feel—over semantic properties, even at the expense of clear communication. As Heidi Bean observes, the language of Poets' Theater—her preferred name for experimental verse drama—a language "thickened by a poets' sense of sound, rhythm, and layers of meaning" has led to its characterization as "antitheatrical."[55] A third complication is that lyric poetry and theater are associated with two competing notions of time: the seemingly suspended moment of lyric temporality versus the stage time in which the action of the play transpires. These various lyric elements are not as much antitheatrical as they are antimimetic; that is, they do not make the play unperformable, they make it resistant to interpretation according to the traditional dramatic conventions. Rather than shying away from these points of seeming incompatibility, modern and contemporary verse dramatists take advantage of them, thereby discovering new possibilities for lyric poetry and for the theater.

Reading these plays with attention to the interplay of lyric and dramatic features, one observes a surprising continuity between early twentieth-century verse drama written by Modernist poets and their contemporaries and the avant-garde and postmodern experiments with verse drama in the late twentieth and early twenty-first centuries. As Claire Warden argues, "many of the most celebrated experiments of 1956 onwards" were "preceded and anticipated by" Eliot, Yeats, and Auden. So as to uncover these unseen continuities, I have cast a wide net by defining verse drama capaciously, to include plays written in counted meter and free verse, plays that alternate between verse and prose, and plays that mix spoken and sung verse. Some were intended for theatrical performance, while others were written as closet dramas—and in some cases, like Djuna Barnes's *The Antiphon*, the author's intention is unclear. While they do not share the same ideology or make use of the same forms, all of the writers in this book conceive of verse drama in terms of lyric and dramatic elements. They are interested in many of the same domains of experimentation—the questions and tensions I mention above. Joyelle McSweeney poses the same paradoxes of lyric voice and physical embodiment in her plays about the digital age that Walcott and Sylvia Plath raise in their midcentury radio plays. Joanna Laurens, in 2000, uses the same strategies as Auden did in 1947: foregrounding the way that words look and sound, at the expense of their meaning, to underscore the failures of communication between characters. And there are many verse dramatists that play with temporality, from Yeats at the turn of the twentieth century to David Greig, a century later. What emerges, then, is a living tradition, throughout the twentieth century and into the twenty-first, despite the rhetoric of decadence that crops up in the scholarship and criticism. Within this paradoxically experimental tradition, one can find postmodern and avant-garde writers, different from one another and from antecedents, engaged in the same kind of investigations of voice, language, and temporality in lyric and drama.[56] In the chapters that follow, I trace a series of genealogies from twenty-first-century experiments with verse back to their twentieth-century antecedents. These genealogies indicate that the questions and tensions that animate verse drama have stayed the same, even as the strategies for staging them have evolved.

Here my argument runs somewhat counter to the consensus in theater history, which, following Martin Puchner, perceives an opposition between Modernist antitheatricality and avant-garde antitextualism.[57] As Erika Fischer-Lichte observes, theater "always fulfills a referential and a performative function" (in other words, it is always somewhere between literature and performance); in fact, she says, the whole history of theater "can be understood as a record of the shifting dominance and corresponding restructuring of the relations between these two functions."[58] Amid such shifts, verse drama manages to find a place in modernist theater as literature—with its lyric elements sometimes serving the antitheatrical strain in these plays—and in avant-garde theater as performance—by drawing on the lyric's rituality. This goes to show the degree to which verse drama becomes a shape-shifter in the twentieth century, thanks to bespoke arrangements and combinations of lyric and theatrical elements playwrights and practitioners have at their disposal.

In the chapters that follow, however, readers may notice my tendency to say more about texts than performances. This may come as a surprise in a book called *Staging the Lyric*, but there are several reasons for this asymmetry. One is a matter of literary history: the rise of print has changed the way we think and write about performance, making it difficult to understand or evaluate any form of theater without reference to a text. Verse drama in particular, given its attention to visual as well as aural properties of language, prizes the text in a special way. As Bay-Cheng and Cole observe, "the textual form of poetic drama is always self-consciously evident, even in performance."[59] This is, by the way, why I prefer the term "verse drama" to other monikers: it allows me to keep the textual form in view. For the purposes of this book, my definition of verse drama comprehends any theatrical performance with lineated spoken dialogue, whether in counted meter or free verse, insofar as that lineation manifests in performance as an

Staging the Lyric

attention to the material properties of language. I include plays written in verse as well as plays that mix prose and verse, and even some that use song too. Worthen argues that the interrelation between text and performance is the essential feature of modern drama.[60] In the postdramatic theater that has emerged since the 1960s, the "perpetual conflict between text and scene" becomes a "consciously intended principle of staging," according to Hans-This Lehmann.[61]

There is also a logistical challenge: some of these plays have not been staged very many times. In fact, some of the plays were originally conceived, or received, as closet drama. But all of them have staged at least once—in the case of these pseudo-closet dramas, the tension between text and performance is even higher. My approach, in all cases, is a dramaturgical one, attending to the way these formal features and tensions might be staged. I include production histories, supplemented by interviews and audience accounts, whenever possible, but my primary interest, by necessity, remains the playwright's experiments with the lyric and the dramatic.

Staging the Lyric

The book is divided into three sections that correspond with three domains of experimentation: Voice, Words, and Time. They correspond with the three features used to distinguish the lyric from other genres of literature: lyric's mode of enunciation, its emphasis on the material properties of language, and its unique sense of time.

The first section begins with Eliot's three voices and moves to questions of enunciation, identity, and embodiment in subsequent verse plays. Over and over, in different ways, modern verse drama prompts us to reconsider our understanding of the relationship between voice and character. Can we assume a one-to-one correlation between character and voice, as it is represented on the page or enunciated on the stage? In this respect, verse drama targets many of the same conventions as postdramatic theater does. One of the defining features, in fact, of postdramatic performance is, according to Lehmann, the "autonominization" of language; he observes that in these plays, "language appears not as the speech of characters—if there are still definable characters at all—but as an autonomous theatricality."[62] But verse drama got there first. As early as 1916, Gertrude Stein started experimenting with techniques like unassigned speech, in *Ladies Voices*; this same technique would be adopted by Sarah Kane almost a century later, in her 2000 play *4.48*

Introduction

Psychosis. Verse turns out to be especially useful for these experiments because of the ambiguity that line breaks introduce into a play. In *Ladies Voices* and *4.48 Psychosis*, line breaks (or stanza breaks) might indicate a switch from one character's voice to that of another—and some directors interpret them this way—but they could just as easily be part of one continuous speech spoken by a single actor. In fact, Stein's collection *Geography and Plays* is full of plays and portraits that exhibit different ways of avoiding attributing speech to human persons: in "The King or Something," for example, each line is credited to a page in a book, as if "Page I," "Page II," "Page III," and so on, all the way up to "Page XCVII," were names of human characters with their own experiences and opinions. This technique of Stein's anticipates a play like Khadijah Queen's *Non-Sequitur* (2015), where the lines are attributed to abstract and virtual entities such as "The Online Payments," "The Hoped-For Aftermath," and "The 40% Discount."

Another way to trouble the audience's assumptions about voice and character is to write lines for a collective voice. Does a chorus count as one character? Does it speak in one voice, or many? In Chapter One, I take as my point of departure Eliot's decision to abandon the chorus in his later plays, in light of his alleged failure to craft a voice that is both lyrical and convincingly dramatic. There is a formal difficulty here: the tension between the universality of the lyric speaker and the particularity of a dramatic character. But there is also a related political problem: the chorus, which purports to speak for the people, is worryingly reminiscent of the rhetoric of the fascist regimes that come into power in the first half of the twentieth century. After the Second World War, Sayers, Ntozake Shange, and Seamus Heaney pick up where Eliot left off, choosing the chorus precisely because of these difficulties. Each of their plays responds to a different crisis of political representation—the Second World War, the American Civil Rights movement, the Northern Irish Troubles—that makes the idea of a communal voice attractive, as a way of uniting a group of people in a moment of conflict, but also troubling, insofar as it threatens to erase differences amongst members of that group. Rather than trying to make this collectivization look easy, these postwar playwrights use the lyric chorus as a way of registering what is lost when one voice speaks for all.

The second chapter considers voice in radio drama. In mid-century verse plays written for the BBC, Walcott and Plath cultivate voices that sound like they come from lyric poems, taking advantage of the radio as an invisible medium. But, at the same time, they draw attention to the invisible bodies behind the dramatic voices. By creating voices that both invite and obstruct lyric reading, Plath and Walcott reveal the tension present in all lyric poetry: the tension between embodied, individual voice and the lyric speaker.

The topic of the next section is lyric's special attention to the material properties of language, which can be an obstacle or a tool for theater. In Chapter Three, I consider plays that use counted meter to cultivate an intentionally jarring effect, much like the alienation effect theorized by Bertolt Brecht. Brecht argues for the use of unnatural or stylized dramatic elements that alienate the audience in order to provoke them to turn a critical eye on their own lives and circumstances. We see exactly this in Auden's *The Age of Anxiety* (1947), Barnes's *The Antiphon* (1958), and Arden's *Live Like Pigs* (1958). In all of these plays, the use of counted meter produces an alienation effect, drawing the audience's attention to a specific crisis of communication.

Chapter Four covers the verse plays that go beyond Brechtian alienation, foregrounding the way that words look and sound at the expense of their meaning. In extreme cases, this resistance to communication puts the poetry at odds with theatrical presentation, insofar as it strains the audience's ability to attend to and understand what the characters are saying. I start with the Wooster Group's *Nayatt School* (1978), a reworking—and, ultimately, a dismantling—of Eliot's *The Cocktail Party*. I compare this paradigmatic example of postdramatic theater to an earlier example, William Carlos Williams's *Many Loves* (1941), and a later one, Laurens' *The Three Birds* (2000). In all three cases, attention to the materiality of language begins as a means by which to undercut the efficacy of realist theater, but ends up undercutting the communicative function of language itself.

I conclude with two chapters on time in verse drama. This is another domain in which verse drama anticipates avant-garde and postdramatic theater. As Warden observes, one of the defining characteristics of avant-garde theater is its challenge to Aristotelian linearity, and the received conventions by which Western theater represented time on the stage up until the twentieth century.[63] In Chapter Five, I demonstrate the continuity between the late modernist verse drama of Yeats and the postdramatic verse drama of Samuel Beckett. Both Yeats's *Purgatory* (1939) and Beckett's *Rockaby* (1981) manipulate time according to the conventions of lyric temporality.

The book ends where it began, with verse drama's anachronism. The last chapter considers plays in which the playwright, with the cooperation of the director and performers, intentionally cultivates a sense of anachronism. In the early twentieth century, verse dramatists like Maxwell Anderson embraced the prevailing stereotype of verse drama as something old-fashioned. In this sense, modern verse drama is similar to the "distressed genres" of the late seventeenth and early eighteenth centuries, as theorized by Susan Stewart. But, starting with Stein, and continuing through the plays of Harrison and Greig, verse dramatist leverage that anachronism as a means of shoring up a kind of prophetic authority. This is not the fusty historical verse drama of the early twentieth-century, but it draws on the idea that verse drama is somehow "out of time."

This is the kind of thing that is possible in modern verse drama: belatedness becomes prophecy, texts become bodies, poets become characters, and characters become poets. I do not mean to suggest that the tension between the lyric and the dramatic is the only source of inspiration behind modernist, avant-garde, postdramatic, or contemporary theater; the goal is merely to acknowledge a hitherto neglected force behind the experimentation in all of these movements. Verse drama, considered in this light, is no zombie—no haunted ruin—but a living tradition, characterized by a spirit of experimentation and discovery. Let's take a look.

PART I
VOICE

CHAPTER 1
THE CHORUS

The story of theater and lyric poetry begins at their shared point of origin: the ancient Greek chorus. In the *Poetics*, Aristotle claims that tragedy evolved from the dithyramb, a poem in honor of Dionysus, performed by a large choir and accompanied by an aulos.[1] Although dithyrambs featured some back-and-forth between the chorus and the chorus leader as well as narrative elements, they lacked the strong sense of plot of their tragic contemporaries. In the *Republic*, Plato's Socrates treats dithyrambs as poems delivered by the poet himself.[2] Friedrich Nietzsche takes the dithyramb to be the original lyric form. In his account of the evolution of the dithyramb in *The Birth of Tragedy*, we already see some of the hallmarks of the lyric ideal that would be codified much later. Imbuing the dithyrambic chorus with a sense of transcendence and universality, he calls it "a chorus of the transformed, who have forgotten their civic past and social rank, who have become timeless servants of their god and live outside all social spheres."[3] Around the same time, tragedy began to develop along a parallel track. By the fifth century, tragedy could be distinguished from the dithyramb by its addition of another character, separate from the chorus, in dialogue with the chorus, leading Nietzsche to take the tragic chorus as the progenitor of all drama—the "primary dramatic phenomenon," which involves "projecting oneself outside oneself and then acting as though one had really entered another body, another character."[4]

This shared ancestry might come as a surprise, given the modern tendency to define lyric and dramatic in contrast to one another. As Herington points out, "Probably the chief block to our full comprehension of the ancient view that *tragedy, and, indeed, all drama, is a species of poetry* is the chasm that has opened up between these two arts in modern times."[5] It is also surprising because the chorus seems so far removed from both poetry and drama in modern practice. Despite the canonical status of Aeschylus, Sophocles, and Euripides, the chorus no longer seems like an essential feature of a play. In fact, it often seems out of place or awkward in modern theater, perhaps because of a decline in participation in the civic and religious ceremonies in which groups of people speak in unison. The dithyramb is even further removed from our experience: the public performance of lyric poetry—at a reading or poetry slam, say—is rare enough; the group recitation of verse to commemorate an occasion has effectively disappeared in the West.

This squeamishness about collective speech is a modern hang-up, one which begins in the Elizabethan era, when the size of the chorus was reduced, as in *Henry V*. Like the "crooked figure" that can "attest in little place a million," a single actor stands in for a whole chorus.[6] But unlike the other limitations the audience must pardon, there is no logistical constraint preventing a larger chorus. Shakespeare's one-man chorus, then, is evidence of some misgiving about collective speech, especially when that chorus is so manifestly a propagandizing spokesman for the regime.

And indeed, the plural chorus too is inherently political, even when the play is not overtly so, for the plural chorus implies that it is possible to represent a group of people with one voice. In Athenian tragedy, for instance, the choruses are made up of the citizens: Aeschylus' *Agamemnon* has a chorus of Argive elders, Sophocles' *Oedipus the King* a chorus of Thebans, and so on. These collective voices are centered around the *polis* and often the political elite. And, given our pluralistic societies and wariness of the tyranny of the majority, it's hard to imagine using a single voice to represent a political community today. In such circumstances, a convention which claims to represent a collective becomes at best unrealistic and at worst suspect.

And so, after the seventeenth century, the chorus is all but abandoned on the English stage. It does not get revived until the Christian verse drama movement of the 1930s and '40s.[7] During this period, Eliot, Sayers, Charles Williams, and Fry wrote religious plays, many of them with choruses. Eliot's first three stage plays constitute a series of experiments with the chorus—experiments that presumably fail, given that he abandons the chorus after 1939. This failure results from the generic and political implications of the chorus. The genre problem, as diagnosed by Eliot, is that the chorus starts to sound more like lyric poetry than drama, becoming a mouthpiece for the poet-playwright. Politically, the chorus becomes newly suspect after the Second World War, when writers and audiences have new reasons not to trust a single voice that purports to speak for the whole.

Several playwrights chose to take up the chorus in Eliot's wake. In *The Just Vengeance* (1946), Sayers crafts a chorus that avoids, through its self-awareness, the pitfalls that beset Eliot. The members of her chorus acknowledge and meditate upon the politically fraught position of the chorus. Shange and Heaney stage their own variations on the self-aware chorus. It is the ambiguity of the choral voice—that it can be mistaken for the voice of a lyric speaker—that these writers use to create self-aware choruses capable of offering political commentary. Although they come from three different national traditions and speak to different historical moments, Sayers, Shange, and Heaney all respond to a crisis of voice and representation that makes the idea of a communal voice both attractive and fraught. Warden observes this desire for unity in British avant-garde performance of the time, which she attributes to the avant-garde's sense that resisting fascism "required a group mentality, off stage and on."[8] Along similar lines, the playwrights I discuss here—while not part of the avant-garde—all write for civic communities in moments of political crisis: England during the Second World War, African-American women in the Civil Rights and Black Arts Movements, and Northern Ireland during the Troubles. Their plays acknowledge the attractions of a unified collective identity, especially in times of conflict, but they also insist on what is lost or obscured by collectivity. Thus, they confirm W.R. Johnson's characterization of choral poetry: "What choral poets do is not so much to state the fact of good community as to imagine the possibility of good community, to persuade the choral audience that both their hopes of goodness and their fears of social and moral danger are genuine."[9]

T.S. Eliot's Experiments

Eliot's first three stage plays—*The Rock* (1934), *Murder in the Cathedral* (1935), and *The Family Reunion* (1939)—feature choruses, in contrast to his last three—*The Cocktail Party* (1949), *The Confidential Clerk* (1953), and *The Elder Statesman* (1958)—which forego the chorus entirely, despite the fact that these later plays are adaptations of various works of Attic drama.[10] A closer look at his first three plays reveals his struggle with the political implications and formal tensions the chorus brings to verse drama.

His first play, *The Rock*, is the most chorus-heavy. It was commissioned to raise money for new churches in London suburbs, and fittingly the subject is a church being built. The play alternates between scenes depicting the church's construction, scenes from church history, and choral interludes, which strongly resemble lyric poetry. This resemblance is due in part to the authority Eliot gives the chorus, which "speak[s] as the voice of the Church of God."[11] Its speeches sound liturgical or prophetic, as in the play's opening:

> The endless cycle of ideas and action,
> Endless invention, endless experiment,
> Brings knowledge of motion, but not of stillness;
> Knowledge of speech, but not of silence;
> Knowledge of words, and ignorance of the Word.
> All our knowledge brings us nearer to our ignorance,
> All our knowledge brings us nearer to death,
> But nearness to death no nearer to God.
> Where is the Life we have lost in living?
> Where is the wisdom we have lost in knowledge?
> Where is the knowledge we have lost in information?[12]

Eventually, passages like this found their way into Eliot's *Collected Poems* (as opposed to his collected plays) under the title "Choruses from 'The Rock'"—an indication of their proximity to lyric poetry.

Although the play fared well with audiences during its run at the Sadler's Wells Theatre in London in May 1934, scholars and critics almost unanimously disliked it. Most fault it for dramatic flaws: tedious dialogue, lack of action, flat characters, and predictability. Although Randy Malamud claims that the choral passages "unify an otherwise free-form production," most critics think they clash with the rest of the play.[13] David Ward sees "an uneasy association of modes in which a crude expressionism alternates with rather flaccid experiments in the choric mode."[14] It is true that the tone and diction of the chorus's verse—typified by its use of apostrophe and repetition, as in the passage quoted above—contrasts sharply with the colloquial prose of the workmen, who drop h's at the beginning of words and g's at the end of words, use nonstandard sentence constructions like "what's done." The diction, tone and content of these conversations is very different from the prophetic, elevated choral passages that seem to transcend any specific time and place. In its only performance, the contrast was underscored by the drastic changes in lighting between scenes. Eliot himself was quite critical of *The Rock* in "The Three Voices of Poetry." Looking back on the play, he laments that the only discernible voice in this text is "the second voice, that of myself addressing—indeed haranguing—an audience."[15] He explains: "This chorus of *The Rock* was not a dramatic voice; though many lines were distributed, the personages were unindividuated. Its members were speaking *for me*, not uttering words that really represented any supposed character of their own."[16] The problem, as Eliot sees it, is that the chorus functions as his mouthpiece.

The Chorus

For Eliot's third voice of poetry to work, it requires a striking coincidence: the third voice must be what the poet "would say in his own person" as well as "what he can say within the limits of one imaginary character addressing another imaginary character" at the same time.[17] Ideally, there is a kind of exchange: "the author imparts something of himself" but is also in the process "influenced by the characters he creates."[18] We see Eliot struggling, in all of his plays, to achieve this balance. In the choral plays in particular, he is testing the limits and affordances of the chorus—specifically, whether it is possible to craft a collective voice that combines the meditative insights of the first voice, the rhetorical effectiveness of the second, and the dramatic effectiveness of the third.

Following the failure of *The Rock*, Eliot strove for a chorus that better represented its members in his next play. Like *The Rock*, *Murder in the Cathedral* is an occasional piece, written for the first Canterbury Cathedral Festival in 1935, and later transferred to London's Mercury Theatre. The play stages the assassination of Thomas Becket, the Archbishop of Canterbury, in 1170, and it deals mostly with Thomas's meditations on his impending death, revealed through conversations with a chorus of poor women of Canterbury, other priests, a series of tempters, and a homily he delivers on martyrdom. The play ends with the priests and the chorus commenting hopefully on the aftereffects of the archbishop's death, culminating in the chorus's final prayer, which expresses a vision of a unified, peaceful Christian community.

Eliot himself asserts that this chorus marks "some advance in dramatic development" because he "made some effort" to identify with the poor women of Canterbury, instead of putting his own words in their mouths.[19] But this chorus still engages in lyric meditations or makes universal pronouncements like the ones in *The Rock*. There seems to me a clear difference between the clipped, frank lines of conversation in passages like this:

We do not wish anything to happen.
Seven years we have lived quietly,
Succeeding in avoiding notice,
Living and partly living.[20]

And the sprawling, prophetic lines of passages like this:

Ill the wind, ill the time, uncertain the profit, certain the danger.
O late late late, late is the time, late too late, and rotten the year;
Evil the wind, and bitter the sea, and grey the sky, grey grey grey.[21]

Staging the Lyric

Not only is there a visible and audible difference of line length here, but also poetic inversions like "ill the wind" and unidiomatic expressions like "no continuing city" that mark these lines as a different kind of speech. The repetition of the "O late late late" line forces the actors to slow down considerably, creating a change of pace to accompany the switch from dramatic to meditative speech. Such passages seem more like lyric poetry than drama. In fact, Eliot used a few lines he cut from *Murder in the Cathedral*, revised only slightly, to begin "Burnt Norton" in *The Four Quartets*.

Eliot declared *Murder in the Cathedral* a "dead end" in terms of vocal experimentation and set out to "find a rhythm close to contemporary speech" in his next play, a very loose adaptation of Aeschylus's *Eumenides*, titled *The Family Reunion*.[22] It depicts Harry, Lord Monchensey, returning to his family estate after a long absence. In the course of the play, Harry reveals to his family what has been weighing on his conscience—his belief that he murdered his wife—and learns from his Aunt Agatha that his father attempted to murder his mother when she was pregnant with him. With this cycle of violence coming to light, he resolves to renounce his title and leave his family, although it is unclear what form this renunciation of the world will take.

The chorus in this play is composed of Harry's aunts and uncles, who speak both together as the chorus and individually as named characters. Individually, these aunts and uncles do not seem to have much insight or eloquence. They are shallower than the play's main characters, Harry, Mary, and Agatha. Given their concern with gossip, competition, and maintaining appearances, it is hard to believe that these characters would admit: "We like to appear in the newspapers / So long as we are in the right column" or "We like to be thought well of by others / So that we may think well of ourselves."[23] In these moments, they seem to have a greater degree of self-knowledge and insight as members of the collective than they do on their own. Elsewhere, Eliot endows this chorus with the authority and tone of a prophet:

> And the past is about to happen, and the future was long since settled.
> And the wings of the future darken the past, the beak and claws have
>   desecrated
> History. Shamed
> The first cry in the bedroom, the noise in the nursery, mutilated
> The family album, rendered ludicrous
> The tenants' dinner, the family picnic on the moors.[24]

While the audience might believe that these characters have a sense of foreboding, it is hard to believe that they understand that "the future was long since settled," given that they spend most of the play fighting against fate. The contrast between the voice of the chorus and the voice of the individuals is evident when Violet follows up this passage by saying, "It is the obtuseness of Gerald and Charles and that doctor, that gets on my nerves," while Charles says, "If the matter were left in my hands, I think I could manage the situation."[25] This contrast is not necessarily a problem, if psychological realism were not one of Eliot's goals, but it does underscore the clash that occurs when the chorus moves between the first, second, and third voice of poetry. This play too Eliot deemed "defective."[26] Among other problems, Eliot faults these passages for being "too much like operatic arias": "so remote from the necessity of the action that they are hardly more than passages of poetry which might be spoken by anybody."[27]

Among scholars of ancient Greek tragedy, there is a similar debate about the extent to which the chorus ought to function as a character and speak directly to the events of the play. Following Aristotle's prescription that the chorus should be regarded as one of the characters, many of these scholars favor Sophocles, because his choruses are more relevant to the action than the ones in Aeschylus or Euripides. Richmond Lattimore, for example, denigrates Euripides for writing "some lovely lyrics" for his choruses that "have nothing to do with what is going on in the play."[28] And yet, Albert Weiner contends that every chorus, even in Sophocles, is anti-dramatic, interrupting the story with meditative passages that seem only tangentially related to the plot.[29] He classifies these interruptions as lyric, and speculates that their function was to give the audience a break from the tragic events unfolding in the plot of the play.

Whatever should be said about Sophocles, Weiner's assessment certainly applies to Eliot. Many—although not all—of Eliot's choral passages interrupt the action. Certainly, the action sometimes grinds to a halt as a result of the insistent repetition and long, sprawling lines like the ones quoted above. Even when the passage is thematically relevant, the meditations take on a more universal tone, as if the chorus is stepping out of character—even out of the play entirely—to reflect on the events from a different point of view. For many playwrights, as we will see, the inherent versatility of the chorus is a blessing, but for Eliot it is a curse, because he resents the incursion of the lyric mode—what he calls the first voice of poetry—into the dramatic plot.

Staging the Lyric

Dorothy L. Sayers's *The Just Vengeance*: The City as Body of Christ

Certainly, collective identity and political personation are topics of urgent conversation among Christians like Eliot. Pope Pius XII's 1943 encyclical, *Mystici Corporis Christi* [On the Mystical Body of Christ], takes up the doctrine of the Universal Church as the Body of Christ in the midst of the Second World War, "urged [. . .] by the circumstances of the present time."[30] The pope exhorts humanity to remember the promise of "divinely-given unity" at a moment when "nation rises up against nation, kingdom against kingdom, and discord is sown everywhere together with the seeds of envy and hatred," while carefully distinguishing this "divinely-given unity" from a collective identity based on nation or ethnicity.[31]

Like the pope, Sayers, an Anglican, is clearly attracted to the Body of Christ as an alternative to other, more politically fraught notions of collective identity circulating at the time, while remaining, like other postwar playwrights, keenly aware of the limitations and dangers of collectivity. Her 1945 play *The Just Vengeance* dramatizes the process of collectivization, tracking the struggle of the individual voice as it is absorbed by the voice of the community, ultimately accepting this kind of collectivity as a necessary evil. Despite the chorus's possible associations with authoritarian or fascist forms of personation, Sayers does not eschew it—she uses it precisely because of its political baggage. Her chorus draws our attention to what is paradoxical or problematic about collective voice, especially what is lost in the process of personation. This is made possible by the extra-diegetic position of the chorus, both part of the dramatic action and outside of it—the very thing that made it so vexing for Eliot.

The play is, according to Sayers, a miracle play "set against the background of contemporary crisis," that is, the war.[32] Sayers offers this summary in her introductory note:

> The whole action takes place in the moment of the death of an Airman shot down during the late war. In that moment, his spirit finds itself drawn into the fellowship of his native city of Lichfield; there, being shown in an image the meaning of the Atonement, he accepts the Cross, and passes, in that act of choice, from the image to the reality.[33]

Sayers's phrasing is telling: verbs like "finds" and "drawn into" suggests his passivity and surprise at what is taking place. And indeed, he is surprised to find himself in Lichfield, hesitant to join the company of citizens, and skeptical of the religious implications of affiliation with the city. What follows is a kind of trial to determine the fate of his soul, in which the city intercedes on his behalf so that he can join them in heaven. The first part of the play consists of his exchanges with the various citizens of Lichfield, and then the second part of the play presents a series of dramatizations of Bible stories, including a passion play. The play ends with the citizens of Lichfield triumphantly singing as they enter the heavenly City of Zion with the Christ figure, called the Persona Dei.[34]

Sayers was commissioned to write the play in 1944 for the 750th anniversary of the Lichfield Cathedral, as a celebration of and thanksgiving for the building's survival of German bombings.[35] In her introduction to the play, Sayers explains, "the verse, as well as the whole architecture, of *TJV*, is constructed for performance in a cathedral, rather than for reading in the study."[36] According to Sayers, the style of verse and the religious setting go hand in hand:

> The circumstances called for a stylized presentation, moving in what may be called large blocks of action rather than in the swift to-and-fro of dialogue; the emphasizing of important affirmations by repetitions; and a rhythm enabling the actor's voice to overcome those acoustical difficulties which, in a large ecclesiastical building, no arrangement of microphones can wholly eliminate.[37]

These features of stylization—the large blocks of text, the use of repetition, the use of counted meter—are elements more often seen in lyric poetry than in the realist drama of Sayers's day. It is intriguing that these elements are at home in—indeed demanded by—the ecclesiastical setting.

Given the ecclesiastical setting of the play, these references to "Lichfield" could have two possible meanings: to designate the city or the church. In fact, Sayers intends to invoke both the political community as well as the religious community. The chorus is both. Following Saint Augustine, we might call these two Lichfields the "City of God" and the "City of Man." In the beginning of the play, the two Lichfields are in tension with one another: there are members of the political community, like the Airman, who want no part in the church. But, as the community undergoes its transformation from the City of Man to the City of God, the two Lichfields are resolved into one eternal, heavenly city.

Sayers foregrounds the heterogeneity within Lichfield even before the play begins, in the list of *Dramatis Personae*. Here she lists the various members of the chorus individually, by name, as in the case of historical figures like George Fox and Samuel Johnson, or by other descriptor, like Informer, Inquisitor, Rich Man, Roman Soldier, Early Martyr, Protestant Martyr, Hunchback, Harlot, Widow, and Child—and that is just to name a few. As is evident from this sample, the group covers a vast swath of history, from the Roman conquest of Britain to the present day, as part of the celebration of 750 years of the city's history. The list includes men and women, and people of all ages and classes—all of them from Lichfield.

This long and specific list suggests not an undifferentiated crowd, but a collection of distinct individuals. In a letter to the costume designer Norah Lambourne, the director Frank Napier explains,

> [T]he Chorus is the most foxing part. They are to represent a panoramic view of the citizens of Lichfield through the ages [...] From my point of view, I believe that the way to get the effects will be like this. The Chorus are on stage throughout in different groupings and I think I can get good results by changing the groups to bring out different colours at different moments to accord with the mood of what is going on – In fact the idea is to use the Chorus as our paintbox... We can get a varigated [sic] effect by making them move around amongst each other to indicate the varied life of the City.[38]

His description suggests kaleidoscopic variety, a kind of patchwork composite. One can get a sense of this effect by looking at some of Lambourne's costume plates.

This idea of the members of the chorus as different colors in a paintbox anticipates the association of characters and colors in Shange's play. Auden calls for something similar for a chorus near the end of *On the Frontier* (1938); meant to "represent the typical readers of five English newspapers," the chorus members are to be dressed "according to their shades of political opinion," from conservative to communist, so that they are easy to distinguish visually.[39]

Sayers also distinguishes among the voices of individual characters through contrasting patterns of diction. The first character to stand out is George Fox, the founder of the Society of Friends. He stridently repeats the cry, "Woe to the bloody city of Lichfield!"—the same denunciation the historical Fox proclaimed in 1651.[40] Later, when Fox greets the newly arrived Airman, his seventeenth-century diction is obviously distinct from the Airman's more colloquial twentieth-century speech. Fox's antiquated words and constructions like "thou hadst a concernment" contrast sharply with the Airman's matter-of-fact lines like "Well, I am here. What am I supposed to do?"[41]

PLATE I   THE JUST VENGEANCE

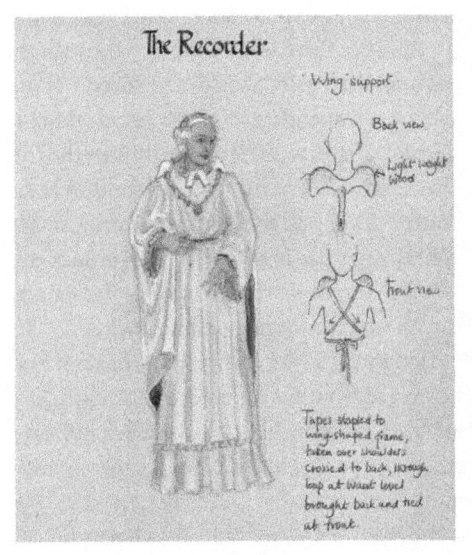

A. The Recorder

B. The Persona dei

C. The Lunatic, one of the characters who had suffered misery and oppression

Figure 1 Costume plates for *The Just Vengeance* (1946) by Norah Lambourne. Reproduced by permission of the Dorothy L. Sayers Society.

Staging the Lyric

Both of these individual voices are distinct from that of the chorus. As Fox denounces the city, the chorus enacts a kind of invocation of it, beginning in a whisper: "Lichfield! Lichfield! / Whisper the name of the city through the oblivion."[42] Their volume increases as they first "Speak" and then "Cry the name of the city!"[43] In this series of commands, the chorus is speaking to itself, summoning all of the Lichfield dead to assemble and constitute the City of God. Their auto-imperatives are reminiscent of the instructions the chorus gives itself in ancient Greek theater.[44] They are also imposing order on the assembly, calling for "coherence" and "articulat[ion] [...] in the confusion of syllables."[45] The city is not—or should not be—a chaotic crowd of strangers, but an orderly, unified community in which each person has a place.

The main plot of the play is the judgment of the Airman, who has just been shot down in aerial combat. The people from his hometown, Lichfield, have shown up to assist him, one of their own, in his interrogation, but he is skeptical of their help, at least at first. As part of his trial, the Airman is asked to recite the creed. He responds "mechanically," according to the stage directions, with the first line of the Apostle's Creed, and the chorus quickly "pick[s] him up and carr[ies] him along with it" in spite of himself.[46] When he realizes what is happening, he tries to disavow what he has just said. But the Recorder explains, "What is speaking in you is the voice of the city, / The Church and the household of Christ, your people and country / From which you derive."[47] When the Airman tries to give a more accurate account of his beliefs, the chorus once again "overrides" him with the next line of the creed. Something similar happens in the passion play in the second half, when he joins in with the chorus shouting "Crucify him!"[48] Once again he is surprised to hear his own voice joining in with the chorus, and he exclaims, "What on earth am I doing? / That is not in the least what I meant to say; / I can't think what came over me."[49] In both scenes, the Airman tries to resist absorption into the collective, revealing the tension between individual will and collective will even as the collective voice overrides what the individual intends to say.

The Airman ultimately surrenders himself to the collective body, at the very same moment that the Persona Dei is crucified in the passion play. Even as the Persona Dei utters Christ's final words from Luke's gospel, the Airman says,

> This is it. This is what we have always feared—
> The moment of surrender, the helpless moment
> When there is nothing to do but let go . . .
> "Into Thy hands"—into another's hand
> No matter whose; the enemy's hand, death's hand,

Which says, "You must," the moment not of choice
When we must choose to do the thing we must
And will to let our own will go. Let go.
It is no use now clinging to the controls,
Let some one else take over. Take then, take . . .
There, that is done . . . into Thy hand O God.[50]

This passage is the Airman's last line; from this moment on, he is part of the chorus. So, we have three different events occurring simultaneously: Christ's death on the cross, reenacted in the passion play-within-a-play, the Airman's death in combat, and the Airman's absorption into the City and the chorus. It seems that the two changes for the Airman are linked: he is born into the eternal city of Lichfield as his individual life on Earth comes to an end. Like his own death, which is a "moment not of choice," his entrance into the collective is not entirely voluntary. They both involve "let[ting] some one else take over," whether it be God or collective voice. This conflation of Christ's crucifixion, the Airman's death, and joining the chorus suggests that becoming part of the collective involves a loss of voice that leads to a loss of self, similar to death.

The conflation of Christ's crucifixion with the Airman's entrance into the church brings us back to *Mystici Corporis Christi*. Pope Pius claims that the Body of Christ was born the moment when Christ died on the cross—not when Christ gave Peter the keys to the Kingdom of Heaven, nor even when Christ sent his apostles the gift of the Holy Spirit at Pentecost. Sayers seems to confirm this teaching, suggesting in her own way that the transformation from City of Man to City of God is somehow, mystically, always bound up in Christ's death.

In addition to this loss of self, which the play dramatizes, Sayers also acknowledges the ways that communities, both political and religious, can go bad. After all, it is the chorus of Lichfield that demands Christ's crucifixion in the passion play-within-a-play.[51] Sayers thus implicates the chorus, at least to some extent, in Christ's death. As the Persona Dei is being nailed to the cross, the Chorus cries: "Bind on the back of God the sins of the City."[52] In the litany that follows, the chorus asks that Christ bear, and therefore atone for, sins like pollution, corruption, inhumane living conditions, income inequality, and lack of concern for one's neighbor. They highlight particular institutions, like the justice system:

Bind on the back of God the laws of the City;
Bind him for the priest; Bind Him for the assessor,
For the upright judge and the incorruptible jury.

Staging the Lyric

As well as:

> The school, the asylum, the spires of the Cathedral,
> The Courts of Justice, the police, the prison, the dock,
> The gallows, the stern and salutary institutions,
> The state and the standards, the shambles and sewers of the City.[53]

The implication of this prayer seems to be that Christ died not only for the sake of individuals but for the institutions themselves. Like individuals, these corporate bodies are capable of sin—what we might today call structural or institutional evils—and they are also capable of being redeemed.

The play ends with the Airman being welcomed into the City of Zion alongside his fellow citizens, suggesting that the whole play has been a kind of intervention on the part of his fellow citizens for the salvation of his soul. Ultimately, Sayers seems to be making the case that the community is not always right or just—that it too is in need of redemption—and yet, imperfect as it is, the community facilitates individual redemption through collective intercession.

Personation in Ntozake Shange's *for colored girls*

Three decades later, African-American playwright Ntozake Shange wrote *for colored girls who have considered suicide / when the rainbow is enuf*. Although the context and form of the play make it quite different from *The Just Vengeance*, the plays share a desire to explore the appeal of collective identity as well as its problems. Like Sayers writing in the wake of the war, Shange writes *for colored girls* at a moment when her community could benefit from a strong sense of group identity, and many critics, including Neal A. Lester and P. Jane Splawn, have heralded the play as a celebration of a unified community of African-American women.[54] But such a summation glosses over Shange's exploration of difficulties inherent in collectivization and individuation. Like *The Just Vengeance*, *for colored girls* evinces a certain amount of distrust of the way groups of people are represented by a collective voice. Whereas Sayers is writing in the wake of fascist regimes in Europe, Shange writes against the way that both white American culture and the male-dominated Black Arts Movement have represented Black women in a monolithic, reductive way. Shange's play asks its audience to see these women—long lumped together into a single, homogenous group—as individuals with unique voices and experiences, even as it celebrates what they have in common.

For colored girls presents a series of twenty poems recited by seven unnamed women, each identified by the color she wears. Each woman reflects on her own experiences as a Black woman living in the United States during the 1960s and '70s. The play began as a workshop exercise inspired by a white feminist poet, Judy Grahn. It was first performed in 1974 in bars and other alternative theatrical spaces in Berkeley, California. When it made it to Broadway in 1976, Shange herself played the "lady in orange." As in *The Just Vengeance*, the use of a spectrum of colors serves as a visual marker of the heterogeneous nature of this chorus. The word "colored" in the title thus signifies on two levels: as the term of choice in the 1970s for Black Americans, it denominates a group identity, but insofar as it refers to the different colors they wear, "colored" also serves as a marker of each character's distinct individual identity. Even though Shange differentiates the characters, they do come together to form a kind of chorus, singing a song or chanting lines of verse. But rather than call it a chorus, she calls the group voice "everyone," a name that strips down some of the literary pretensions that are sometimes

Figure 2 *for colored girls who have considered suicide when the rainbow is enuf* (1976). Pictured l-r: Rise Collins, Trazana Beverly, Paula Moss, Seret Scott, Aku Kadogo, Laurie Carlos, Janet League. Photograph by Martha Swope © New York Public Library for the Performing Arts.

associated with the word "chorus" and seems to emphasize the retained individuality of each one.

Shange coins the term "choreopoem" to describe this play. A choreopoem differs from typical verse drama insofar as it incorporates song and dance, and from a musical in that the spoken portions are verse poems rather than prose dialogue. In performance, the choreopoem integrates the physical art of dance with the verbal art of poetry, just like the ancient Greek choruses that followed established patterns of choreography in performance. Thematically, the choreopoem meditates on the relationship between the body and language. She highlights this connection in her note to the choreopoem: "With the acceptance of the ethnicity of my thighs & backside, came a clearer understanding of my voice as a woman & as a poet."[55] For Shange, then, there is a continuity between physical body and voice, even if they are not perfectly united.

Critics like Klaus Schwank have argued that the form of *for colored girls* is a reaction to the patriarchal masculinity of the Black Arts Movement, begun in New York City in the 1960s. Similarly, Cheryl Clarke makes much of Shange's decision to omit the Black Arts Movement from the list of influences she offers in her preface to the choreopoem, highlighting the importance of the West Coast women's independent press movement instead.[56] Shange has said elsewhere that she was "genuinely inspired" by the Black Arts Movement, but also recognized its limitations.[57] She seems to have in mind its patriarchal tendencies, as well as its strong sense of individualism. Rejecting the idea of the isolated genius working alone to create great art, Shange values art that establishes and celebrates a cohesive group identity for African Americans, especially women.

The choreopoem begins with the "lady in brown," who plays a role similar to the chorus leader in ancient Greek drama. Her opening speech could be read as a commentary on the work as a whole:

> dark phrases of womanhood
> of never having been a girl
> half-notes scattered
> without rhythm/no tune
> distraught laughter fallin
> over a black girl's shoulder
> it's funny/it's hysterical
> the melody-less-ness of her dance[58]

This description reveals that what follows will not be a coherent narrative, but rather a collection of fragmentary "dark phrases of womanhood" and "half-notes scattered / without rhythm/no tune." The audience is meant to take this unspecified "black girl" as an archetype, and this description as an expression of an experience that is typical for Black women living in the United States.

From there, the opening monologue moves into a ritual of self-constitution, similar to the opening of *The Just Vengeance*, in which the chorus calls on the citizens to assemble. *For colored girls* begins with a series of auto-imperatives commanding "somebody/anybody" to "sing a black girl's song."[59] The purpose of these actions is to "bring her out / to know herself / to know you."[60] The monologue ends with the repetition of the lines "let her be born / let her be born / & handled warmly."[61] The implication here is that singing the song of this archetypal "black girl" will facilitate a kind of birth or manifestation on the stage.[62] The identity of the "you" here may at first seem ambiguous, but it is a part of the ritual of self-constitution: the lady in brown is addressing herself, but not only herself. It is a moment of triangulated address, which allows the lyric poet to constitute her subjectivity and her poetic power.[63] Something like that seems to be happening here. In fact, so central is this self-constituting that John Timpane has said the play represents "the tortured moment of becoming itself, *the* moment of emergence and discovery."[64] Crucially, this "you" is plural—this self-constituting ritual establishes a collective identity.

If this opening sounds hopeful, it is also tinged with pessimism. Paradoxically, the melody of this song is "melody-less" and without rhythm or tune. The disjointed grammar of the line "without rhythm/no tune" reinforces the sense of incoherence. Instead of using parallelism, Shange juxtaposes fragments of two different constructions so that they clash with one another, and she inserts a slash to reinforce this clash visually. According to Timpane, "the proliferation of virgules" in the play "shows that alternatives are always present, always in conflict or tension."[65] Timpane also points out that there are no complete sentences until the seventh line of the monologue, reinforcing the overall sense of confusion and incoherence proposed by the lady in brown.

In fact, their performance is not just unintelligible, according to the lady in brown: it is unseen and unheard. She speculates:

this must be the spook house
another song with no singers

>   lyrics/no voices
>   & interrupted solos
>   unseen performances[66]

Given that the rest of the play does involve singers, lyrics, voices, etc., these lines must describe the condition the performer ought to aspire to: that is, they are trying to get as close as they can to a performance that is voiceless, interrupted, unseen, and disembodied, as a way of reflecting the experience of African-American women in daily life.

After this preface, six other women appear and introduce themselves, and then the lady in brown announces, "this is for colored girls who have considered suicide but moved to the ends of their own rainbows."[67] This declaration promises some hope, both with respect to the individual women who have "considered suicide" but moved beyond it, and with respect to the prospect of community, given that the characters are assembled together and will soon sing in unison. So far, it seems possible that they will succeed in their purpose, "to share our worlds witchu."[68]

But the prospect of a collective identity becomes more complicated when more voices are introduced. As Sarah Mahurin observes,

> Though the characters are, on the one hand, a collective entity simply by virtue of their simultaneous presence in one text and on one stage, there exists, at times, a strange sense of distance between them, one that is only exacerbated by the effect of having each woman identified with one particular color—there can be no visual overlap of red with blue, or orange with purple. And, unlike realist characters, whose speech acts are most always organically progressing dialogues, the colored girls perform discrete poems and thus speak almost exclusively in monologue, a form that neatly separates their lines into individual rather than communal performances.[69]

Unlike most critics, who think the play succeeds in creating a unified community through ritual incantation, Mahurin argues that the women are visually and verbally disconnected from one another. As she points out, their monologues do not betray any awareness of the others or what they have said.[70] Nevertheless, the women do dance together, even if they do not talk or listen to one another. Their unity is nonverbal, based on music and physical movement rather than words. Mahurin, for her part, calls this "communality of *body*"—it is physical rather than vocal collectivity.[71] In fact, this "everyone" refers to their physical bodies as a single entity—"our whole body," they call it.[72] It anticipates the "anti-individualist cobody" McSweeney strives for twenty-first-century verse plays.[73] The phrase "our whole body" suggests some process of collectivization is at work, in which one body represents the multiple bodies of its constituent members. But so far, our examples of collectivization in Eliot's and Sayers' plays have been vocal, not physical. Is it possible to collapse physical entities in this way?

Let me invoke Thomas Hobbes here, who theorizes political representation with respect to a theatrical phenomenon. In the *Leviathan*, Hobbes considers one of the foundational political questions in modern societies: how to reconcile individual people into a single "person," which he calls "the Sovereign." Hobbes explains the process by which a "feigned" or "artificial person" acts or speaks on behalf of another person, coining the term "personation" to designate this process:

> A multitude of men are made "one" person when they are by one man or one person represented, so that it be done with the consent of every one of that multitude in particular. For it is the "unity" of the representer, not the "unity" of the represented, that maketh the person "one." And it is the representer that beareth the person, and but one person; and "unity" cannot otherwise be understood in multitude.[74]

The chorus enacts a kind of personation not unlike this Hobbesian political personation. The chorus is a kind of "artificial person" through which the multitude of individual characters are united. But this "person" is not a single body, but rather a single voice. And yet, consider the image of the Sovereign depicted on the frontispiece to Hobbes's *Leviathan*.

It is a body made up of bodies. In this visual rendition of personation, the individual bodies of the personated are not collapsed into a single body, but remain distinct, even as they make up a corporate body. Perhaps this is the only way to render visually what is essentially a verbal phenomenon, the Sovereign *speaking for* the represented. Shange does something similar in her staging of *for colored girls*: the ladies aspire to a kind of unity of body and voice as they sing and dance together, but the individual bodies remain visually distinct, so that there is always the reminder that this is a collective made up of heterogeneous individuals. In this way, Shange asks the audience to see the ladies as individuals, even the chorus inspires solidarity and a sense of pride in their shared identity as African-American women.

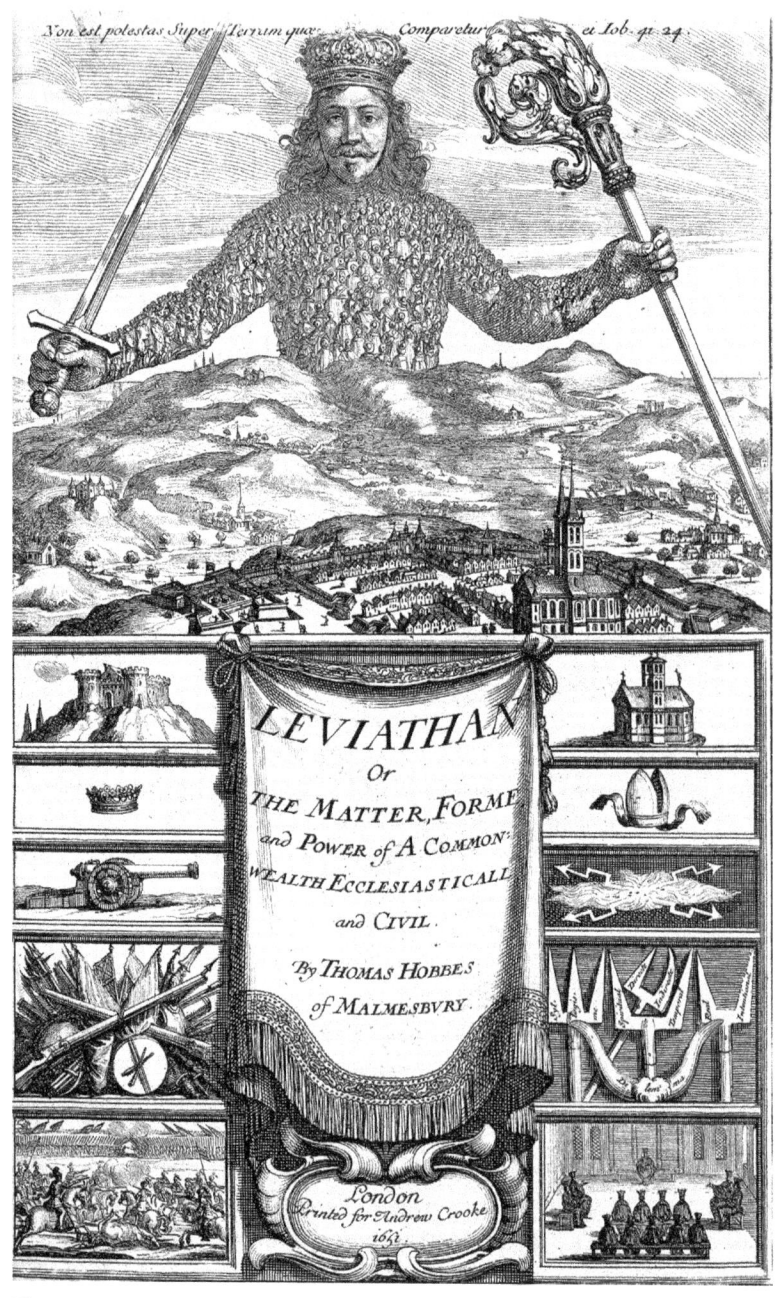

Figure 3 Frontispiece of *Leviathan* by Thomas Hobbes, engraving by Abraham Bosse (1651).

As the play goes on, there are more and more passages spoken by "everyone." This would seem to indicate a unification has taken place. But their collective speech is limited to fragments and echoes—repetitions of the same words and phrases ("music," "delicate," "oh sanctified"), started by one lady and then repeated by everyone.[75] At the end of this incantation, "all of the ladies fall out tired, but full of life and togetherness."[76] As Timpane reads it, their individual experiences "coalesce in a chant that unites the subjective and the intersubjective."[77] Note though that the climax of their unity comes when their speech is the most disjointed and impressionistic. Although these women can come together, their speech can never be organized into a unified, coherent speech act. And yet somehow, through her paradoxical staging of the chorus, Shange manages to represent their unrepresentability.

Seamus Heaney's *The Cure at Troy*: The Chorus as Implicated Mediator

Now I want to consider a third historical moment when the chorus facilitates the expression of the promises and perils of collective identity: the Troubles in Northern Ireland. Seamus Heaney wrote *The Cure at Troy* (1990)—an adaptation of Sophocles' *Philoctetes*—twenty years into the Troubles, a series of violent clashes between British security forces, Irish Republican paramilitaries, and Loyalist paramilitaries, which began with a civil rights march and subsequent riots in Derry in 1969 and ended, more or less, with the Good Friday Agreement in 1998. This was a crisis of personation, in Hobbesian terms: How does the Sovereign represent all of its constituents when there are factions at odds with one another? In this case, Protestants, loyal to the United Kingdom, were pitted against the Catholics, most of whom wanted to leave the United Kingdom and join the Republic of Ireland. The play was chosen to celebrate the tenth anniversary of Field Day, a theater company founded by Brian Friel and Stephen Rea in response to the conflict. Their goal was to create a "fifth province of the intellect where questions of culture and identity, art and politics could be explored."[78] Like Sayers and Shange, Heaney uses the chorus to expose rather than conceal differences and ruptures within the community. But Heaney's chorus is not the voice of the community, but the voice of the poet, both part of and estranged from the community. It acts as a kind of implicated mediator in the dramatic action, much like Heaney himself.

The plot in Heaney's version is essentially the same as Sophocles'. The only major departures occur in the choral passages Heaney inserts at the

Staging the Lyric

beginning and end. There, he makes explicit reference to the Troubles, with lines that mention hunger-strikers and police widows.[79] In these speeches, the chorus displays considerable self-awareness, both with respect to their motivations and the implications of their actions, or what I will call diegetic self-awareness, and with respect to their extra-diegetic awareness of themselves as part of a chorus in a theatrical performance.

In contrast to *Philoctetes*, Heaney's play opens with the chorus already on stage. As a result, it is the chorus, rather than Odysseus, who summarizes the background of the drama: that the Greek hero Odysseus and Neoptolemus, the son of Achilles, have come to Lemnos to retrieve Philoctetes, the expert archer the Greeks abandoned there years before. The chorus's preface primes the audience to be suspicious of Odysseus' account—of all of the characters, in fact:

> Every one of them
> Convinced he's in the right, all of them glad
> To repeat themselves and their every last mistake,
> No matter what.[80]

But rather than shift all of the blame onto the three principal characters, the chorus admits, in a moment of diegetic self-awareness, "I hate it, I always hated it, and I am / A part of it myself."[81] As in Sophocles' play, the chorus is composed of Greek men who have sailed from Troy with Odysseus and Neoptolemus. They too are part of the plot against Philoctetes. Yet they resent their inability to extricate themselves from this decade-long feud, fueled by "self-pity" and "self-regard", just as Heaney himself resented his own entanglement in the Troubles.[82]

The chorus moves from this diegetic observation into extra-diegetic reflection. The chorus claims to be "a part of you," that is, the audience.[83] They explain, "For my part is the chorus, and the chorus / Is more or less a borderline between / The you and the me and the it of it."[84] This is an instance of *parabasis*, a common convention in ancient Greek drama, a moment that usually occurred near the middle of the play, when the chorus leader would speak directly to the audience in the name of the poet. Here the chorus knows and acknowledges itself *as a chorus*. Its claim to the position between "you" and "it" makes sense in light of the tradition of thinking of the chorus as a kind of mediator or interpreter for the audience. So too, in the context of the play, it serves as a mediator between the characters, assisting Neoptolemus in his mission. But there are a few complications underlying this assertion: In what sense is the chorus between itself ("me") and the audience, or between itself and the action? And how can there be a border between three things anyway? This paradoxical border between three entities echoes the configuration of the Northern Irish conflict, with its three "sides": Republican paramilitaries, Loyalist paramilitaries, and British security forces.

Heaney's chorus takes its extra-diegetic theorizing one step further, linking the role of the dramatic chorus to that of poetry:

And that's the borderline that poetry
Operates on too, always in between
What you would like to happen and what will –
Whether you like it or not.[85]

In what sense does poetry, *qua* poetry, exist between what humans want to happen and what the gods will? Elsewhere Heaney has said that poetry "operates" on the border between the ideal ("What you would like to happen") and the actual ("what will – / Whether you like it or not").[86] In other words, it can partake of the real world, a world of conflict and violence, as well as of the transcendent or divine order. On the diegetic level, we find the chorus claiming a semi-divine status, mediating "Between / the gods' and human beings' sense of things."[87] Indeed, the chorus will later speak as the vessel of Hercules, mediating not simply between parties but between planes of reality, or between what the characters would like to happen, and the will of the gods, reconciling these two visions by helping the characters to accept the divine plan for their lives. By analogy, Heaney suggests that poetry can play a role in healing the divide between the ideal and the actual: by inspiring human beings to transcend their petty resentments and self-regard, and by helping them to accept their fate.

In fact, it is the chorus that enforces the will of the gods at the end of the play. In Sophocles' version, Hercules appears and forces Philoctetes to go with Odysseus and Neoptolemus, despite his refusal.[88] Heaney has the chorus play this role, speaking as Hercules. In the middle of the chorus's final speech, there is a clap of thunder and a volcanic eruption, and Philoctetes exclaims:

Hercules:
   I saw him in the fire.
Hercules
   Was shining in the air.
I heard the voice of Hercules in my head.[89]

Staging the Lyric

At this point, the chorus becomes "ritually clamant" and speaks "as Hercules."[90] The stage directions cast it as a kind of ventriloquism, a voice that Philoctetes hears "in his head" and that the audience has to imagine as they look at the same three actors who have played the chorus. In the speech that follows, the chorus instructs Philoctetes to go with Odysseus and Neoptolemus, affect the necessary rapprochement among the three characters.

Like Sophocles' play, which has been denigrated for its happy ending, Heaney's ending could strike audiences as naïve or cheap, especially in the context of twenty years of sectarian violence.[91] And yet, despite the apparent celebration of the mediating power of poetry, the play denies that poetry has the power to resolve such conflicts. In the climactic final scene, still speaking as Hercules, the chorus admits: "No poem or play or song / Can fully right a wrong / Inflicted and endured."[92] Such wrongs include the many horrors of the Troubles, which Heaney makes specific reference to here: innocent people in prisons, the death of the hunger strikers, the death of British police, and the grief of their families. These lines acknowledge poetry's—and also the poet's—inadequacy to heal or resolve human suffering.

Nevertheless, the play ends on a tentatively hopeful note. After the disclaimer above, the chorus goes on to say:

> History says, *Don't hope*
> *On this side of the grave.*
> But then, once in a lifetime
> The longed-for tidal wave
> Of justice can rise up,
> And hope and history rhyme.[93]

There is, then, a chance of a miraculous alignment of the ideal ("hope") and the actual ("history"). The word "rhyme" suggests not a perfect coincidence—that is, what happens is never exactly what was hoped for—but there is a similarity, a link, albeit with a subtle difference, as in rhyme. Heaney reinforces this idea with the use of actual rhyme. Most of Hercules' speech rhymes, but without a set pattern; so, the rhyme of "lifetime" and "rhyme" comes as a surprise, but does not feel like a departure from the style of the rest of the passage. This balance of optimism and reasonable doubt, paired with a satisfying but unexpected rhyme, makes this passage especially moving and memorable, and it is frequently quoted, beyond even the

Northern Irish context, by those who espouse tempered hope in other moments of conflict.

The chorus, speaking in its own name, gets one final speech, a much longer valediction than in Sophocles. In light of what they have seen, the chorus admits that "I leave / Half-ready to believe / That a crippled trust might walk / / And the half-true rhyme is love."[94] All of these qualifications—"half-ready," "half-true"—temper the play's hopeful message, but do not invalidate it. Heaney insists on the possibility of hope, in the Philoctetes story and in the Northern Irish conflict, but by admitting the limitations of the chorus and poetry as a mediator, he evades charges of sanguine naivete.

But what can poetry do in a situation like this, if it cannot right wrongs? Heaney seems to think that poetry, instead of enacting justice, inspires people to act justly by revealing unseen possibilities—by giving them a vision that transcends the mundane world of the actual. Compare Sophocles' Hercules, who comes down from on high to command Philoctetes to accompany Odysseus and Neoptolemus back to Troy after Philoctetes refuses. In Heaney's version, by contrast, the chorus-as-Hercules tells Philoctetes, "I have opened the closed road / Between the living and the dead / To make the right road clear to you."[95] He is not forcing him, as Sophocles' Hercules does, or tricking him, as Odysseus tries to do in both versions, but endowing him with a vision of the "right road." It is a moment of divine revelation. Likewise, poetry, as Heaney sees it, is a venue for revelation. It too can open the road between life and death—at least within the world of the poem—to impart some kind of insight or inspiration. It is this liminal position—between the mundane and the transcendent, the real world of what happens and the ideal world of hope—from which Heaney draws power. This is the position of the chorus, the position of poetry, and ultimately, the position of the poet.

Thus, in all three of the postwar plays, there is tentative hope: for redemption in *The Just Vengeance*, for understanding in *for colored girls*, for reconciliation in *The Cure at Troy*. The chorus then is more than the poet's mouthpiece; it voices the deepest yearnings in the souls of the people. And yet, these poets are painfully aware of the problems with this kind of collectivity. It can lead to exclusion, stereotyping, sectarianism, and totalitarianism. The chorus allows them to acknowledge these dangers and limitations. It is this deft and multivalent use of the chorus, drawing on the literary tradition and its political associations, that makes these plays successful, even if the communities they represent are themselves impossible.

CHAPTER 2
RADIO DRAMA

With a chorus, the difficulty is collapsing multiple individuals into a single voice; in this chapter, the problem is abstracting the body, given its physical particularities, into a disembodied voice. This voice is one of the essential features of lyric. Since Eliot's time, efforts to define the lyric have emphasized its unique mode of enunciation, what Northrop Frye calls the "radical of presentation." But instead of defining lyric speech as the poet talking to himself or nobody, as Eliot does, Frye characterizes lyric as an act of address in which the poet "turns his back on his listeners" and "pretends to be talking to himself or to someone else."[1] From Frye's account, Culler gleans what he considers the two essential features of lyric address, "indirection" and "voicing."[2] By "indirection" he means the various ways that the poet speaks to the reader by addressing someone or something else. As I mentioned in the last chapter, Culler takes "triangulated address" to be the "root-form of presentation" for all lyric poems.[3] "Voicing" (not to be confused with "voice") is Culler's word for the impression of a speaking subject that is created by the text of the poem. "We encounter lyrics in the form of written texts to which readers give voice," Culler insists, building on Paul de Man's claim that "the principle of intelligibility, in lyric poetry, depends on the phenomenalization of the poetic voice."[4] When Culler says that "readers give voice" to a lyric poem, he means that they supply the voice themselves by reading it aloud (or imagining it read), guided by the "effects of voicing"—the clues that contribute to the impression of a speaking subject.

It is easy enough to imagine how this notion of the lyric as a script for performance is compatible with a belief in the universality of lyric poetry. In the introduction to *Soul Says*, for example, Helen Vendler describes the lyric voice as "the voice of the soul itself"—not any particular soul, but an abstraction.[5] Such a voice, detached from any body or context, allows any reader to step in and become the "I." Although she acknowledges some exceptions, she contends that the "traditional lyric" strives for a "stripping-away of the details associated with a socially specific self."[6] The details that remain, in a poem like Langston Hughes's "Dream Variations," for example, are always "severely circumscribed," so that the poet can depict an abstract representation of personal experience across differences of time, place, or identity. In his reading of Shelley's "To a Skylark," Robert von Hallberg argues that the skylark can be a figure for "the grandest aspirations of poetry" only because it "cannot be seen, only heard."[7] Poetry, he avers, is a "sourceless power in the dark," a power "behind visible forms," and not just in Shelley's poem.[8] When the singer comes into the light—when the poet shows his face—the spell is broken.

Theodor Adorno theorizes the lyric very differently, and yet still endorses the ideal of lyric abstraction. Like Culler, Adorno understands voice as a textual phenomenon, a product of language, not to be confused with the voices that emanate from human bodies. For Adorno, "the highest lyric works are those in which the subject, with no remaining trace of mere matter, sounds forth in language until language itself acquires a voice."[9] In this passage, he aligns with de Man, Culler, and Vendler, all of whom invoke the same distinction: between the physical voice—associated with the particular, the contingent, and the embodied—and, the effects of voicing—a function of language. For all three, textual voicing allows the lyric poem to achieve a kind of universality beyond the contingency of the individual, even if, as for Adorno, such universality depends on individuation as a starting point.

Given the opposition between "mere matter" and "language itself" in approaches as diverse as Adorno's, Vendler's, and Culler's, where does this abstraction leave the body? Is there a place for the body, in all its physicality and particularity, after lyricization? These questions are raised implicitly by Confessional poets, who put pressure on the idea of a universal lyric by incorporating details from their personal lives. One effect of these highly individuated lyric voices is that they make readers aware of the disjunction between their own identity and the "I" they give voice when reading these poems. Postconfessional poets like Olena Kalytiak Davis ironize this Confessional impulse, even as they eschew the universal, abstract lyric. Davis's poem "The Lyric 'I' Drives to Pick up Her Children from School: A Poem in the Postconfessional Mode," is a self-conscious send-up of Confessional poetry as well as the critical obsession with the lyric speaker. The poem consists mostly of a list of actions, observations, and reflections attributed to an entity called "i." The use of lower case distinguishes the "i" of this poem from the lyric "I," Vendler's voice of the soul. Some of i's experiences are idiosyncratic—like "'i' feels the power of being a single mom in a red truck"—such that we both can and cannot imagine ourselves voicing them.[10] Others are quotidian, like the year, make, and model of a truck, or observations about the weather. Idiosyncrasies and particularities like this are, of course, everywhere in lyric poetry, and they usually do not put readers off. What makes Davis's poem different is that it foregrounds to the disjunction between personal experience and lyric utterance. The verbs are conjugated as if the sentences are in third person, suggesting that we treat the first-person singular pronoun as a name. This puts some distance between "i" of the poem—what Roland Greene would call the poem's "person-representation"—and the "I" that voices the poem.[11] Some of the i's experiences are common and relatable—running late to pick up a child for example—but even these seem to fall outside of the purview of the typical lyric utterance. Often the issue is not idiosyncrasy, but that they are women's experiences, like wearing a diaphragm. The joke then depends upon a perceived, if undermined, assumption: that there is an opposition between her experiences as a woman poet and the content of a typical poem. The gender dynamics of the default lyric voice come to a head at the end, when the speaker gives in to the temptation of second-person address:

"i" has fucked with the facts so "you" think she's robert lowell. (*but whoever saw a girl like robert lowell?*)

"i" doesn't care if "you", silent human auditor, present or absent, never heard of, could give a flying fuck about, robert lowell.[12]

However you read the complicated proliferation of pronouns here, the final line emerges as a parody of the lyric poet's preoccupation with address as well as the metapoetic games played by poets like John Ashbery. Taken together, these last two lines suggest that the preceding poem has been an illusion, an imitation of the Confessional style that nonetheless belies the real, experience of the "girl" behind the poem. That is, they register the disjunction between the "i" created by the effects of voicing, and the real person that lies behind or beyond the poem, utterly inaccessible. Confessional poetry, then, is still a form of abstraction from embodied experience, a way of "fucking with the facts" to turn a real "i" into a lyric "I," a game that a female poet—a "girl"—can't win.

Verse drama is well-suited for exploring the tensions between lyric abstraction and embodiment, given the space it occupies somewhere in between the printed poem and the embodied performance on stage. My primary examples in this chapter will come from radio plays in verse, because of the radio's unique status as a disembodied medium that still evokes the body. One of these poets, Plath, is known for writing in the

Confessional mode. But the parallels between Plath's expression of particular, embodied experience in *Three Women* (1962) and that of Walcott, in his radio play *Harry Dernier* (1952) over a decade earlier, suggests that this reaction to New Criticism's abstraction of the lyric precedes the Confessionals. In both Plath's and Walcott's case, the radio is the ideal venue for experiments with a lyric "i" that gives voice to individual experience. The radio voice resembles that of Shelley's skylark, unseen and therefore indeterminate in the growing darkness, something between animal and "blithe spirit."[13] Like Shelley—and Davis, for that matter—Plath and Walcott create voices that oscillate between embodied particularity and lyric transcendence, on a continuum that is for Adorno no continuum at all, but the constitutive dynamic of lyric itself.

We tend to think of the radio as a vehicle for news and information. With the rise of podcasts, there has been a revival of interest in the narrative and dramatic potential of aural media, harkening back to the heyday of the radio play in the 1940s and 1950s. But there is also an affinity between radio and lyric. Beginning with the first live poetry reading program in 1928 and reaching a modest height in the 1950s with programming like the BBC's *Third Programme*, CBS's *Radio Workshop*, and NBC's *Radio Guild*, there is a significant history, largely obscure today, of lyric poems and verse dramas performed on and written for radio. Poets like Langston Hughes, Dylan Thomas, Louis MacNeice, and Ted Hughes wrote pieces in verse to be performed on these shows. While poetry features rarely topped the list of most popular programming, they were prominent enough during the 1950s and 1960s that the BBC's weekly magazine, *The Listener*, had a regular poetry review column, alongside columns that reviewed drama and journalistic features.

In his 1959 book *The Art of Radio*, BBC producer Donald McWhinnie calls the association between stage drama and radio drama "superficial," arguing that the radio is more compatible with print media than performance.[14] This is because the radio, like a written text, signifies through words rather than through bodies on stage. At the same time, the voice we hear in a radio broadcast does retain a trace of a physical body, even if this body is not immediately present to the audience. I think of it as disembodied rather than unembodied.

In this respect, radio is like the lyric. The lyric offers a textual voice—what Culler calls "effects of voicing" and Greene calls a "person-representation"—and invites the reader to imagine the person behind the voice. As Leslie Wheeler puts it, writing about Edna St. Vincent Millay's work for radio: "Radio possesses an inherent likeness to the printed lyric poem—a medium similarly haunted by impossible presence," a presence akin to what Steven Connor calls the "vocalic body," a "projection of a new way of having or being a body, formed and sustained out of the autonomous operations of the voice."[15] Both the textual voicing of lyric poetry and the vocalic body of the radio are illusions, of a someone who is not really there. Like Millay before them, Walcott and Plath were fascinated by radio's impossible presence. For both of them, the radio serves as an inspiration and venue for their poetic experiments with lyric address.

Playing with the ambiguities permitted by the radio, Walcott's and Plath's plays participate in a wider trend within the world of experimental radio drama of the late 1950s and early 1960s. Hugh Chignell identifies a decisive turn toward more experimental writing for radio after the success of Samuel Beckett's *All that Fall* in 1957. Reflecting a long preoccupation with the absent or constricted body, Beckett's radio plays reveal the range of ways he experimented with the capacity of the human voice to produce the illusion of a physical body or coherent identity.[16] A play like *Embers*, for example, invites the listener to wonder whether a voice really does signify a physical presence, and, in turn, whether a silence in fact signifies an absence, as Henry tries to ignore the sounds and voices he can hear in order to conjure a hallucination of his father. This is one of several *Third Programme* productions of the late 1950s and 1960s, a period when, along with Beckett, playwrights like Harold Pinter, Giles Cooper, and Rhys Adrian began to test the limits of what radio afforded.

For Walcott and Plath too, the disembodied voice of radio offered ways to explore new configurations of the relationship between voice and body. And just as someone like Beckett seeks to dismantle and examine the conventions of theater, in their work for radio Walcott and Plath scrutinize the traditional workings of voice in lyric poetry. Plath, a woman, and Walcott, a Black man from a colonized country, were both figures on the margins of traditional Anglophone lyric poetry. Their experience with marginalization led them to explore the ways in which the lyric poem, far from being truly universal, typically presupposed a subject who is white, English, and male. Challenging the normative accounts of lyric address that persist from the Romantic era into lyric theory today, the radio poems of Plath and Walcott explore the relationship between the voice and the body, revealing that they are, in the end, inseparable from one another. In *Harry Dernier*, Walcott presents a critique of lyric indirection, as well as the ideal of lyric world-making. The titular character tries and fails to overcome his unfortunate circumstances by imitating great works of the Western literary canon. In these parodies of famous instances of lyric address, the play manifests the failure of the conventions of lyric address in the face of actual physical circumstance. If, as Culler argues, in lyric address we see a poet's attempt to reconstitute the world through language, then Walcott's deflation of lyric address amounts to a devaluation of the entire poetic tradition. Plath's challenge is aimed at the prevailing notions of the lyric voice. Blurring the line between poem and play, *Three Women* responds to what she sees as an idealization of the neutral, abstract, and universal voice of the lyric poem, restoring the bodies and experiences that have been written out of such poems, and pointing to the ways that, though it purports to be neutral, the lyric ideal is in fact predicated on a male speaker. But *Three Women* also contextualizes an ambiguity inherent in the word "voice" itself: the word can be used to designate a physical voice, like that of an actor, but it can also designate what Culler calls "effects of voicing." In pursuing her focused critique, then, Plath widens out to address a tension present in every lyric poem—the tension between the individual, particular, embodied "I" and the transcendent, universal, linguistic "I." In this way, radio plays like *Three Women* and *Harry Dernier* rethink the essential trope of lyric poetry: if the lyric poem is characterized by its meditation on voice, the radio poem is characterized by a narrower meditation on the tension between the textual effects of voicing and the embodied voice.

Parodying Lyric Address in Derek Walcott's *Harry Dernier*

In *Theory of the Lyric*, Culler puts forward indirect address as one of the defining features of the lyric, arguing that all lyric poems are, on some level, concerned with matters of address. Along similar lines, William Waters argues that lyric poetry "persistently revolves around, or thinks about, the contact that it is (or is not) making with the person to whom it is speaking."[17] Where in J.S. Mill's influential formulation poetry is overheard, Culler frames the lyric instead as a matter of "address to the reader by means of address to something or someone else."[18] Even in those cases in which the poem seems to be addressed to the reader or the listener, in his view the possibility of straightforward address is complicated by the poem's metapoetic commentary, a "blurred you," or the kind of acknowledgement of the artificiality or impossibility of address Culler finds at the end of Ashbery's "This Room": "Why do I tell you these things? / You are not even here."[19] In Culler's account, address renders the lyric an event of language. Insofar as it is "not determined by its apparent communicative purpose," it becomes an event in its own right.[20] This poetic act can have several functions. Earlier in the book, and in his essay "Apostrophe," Culler argues that "to apostrophize is to will a state of affairs," in the sense that, implying and thereby creating the subjectivity of the object, animal, or concept it addresses, apostrophe marks the height of poetic pretension. But to some extent this structure applies to all forms of lyric address, insofar as they allow the speaker to demonstrate poetic power by willing something to happen through language.

Walcott's *Harry Dernier* takes up the matter of address in a systematic way. One of Walcott's earliest works—rumored to have been written when he was 16—it was recorded in November 1951 for broadcast on the BBC's *Caribbean Voices* program, produced by Reggie Smith and featuring Errol Hill as the voice of Harry Dernier and Betty Linton as the voice of Lily the Lady.[21] Though Hill's performance was praised by the program director, Henry Swanzy, and by Dylan Thomas (in attendance at the recording), after listening to the playback in January 1952 Swanzy deemed it "utterly indigestible," and *Harry Dernier* was never broadcast.[22] Despite that, it remains a text inspired by the radio and dependent on that medium for its effect. It requires that the audience be able to hear, but not see, the speakers. In keeping with his surname, Dernier, the main character thinks he is the last man on earth, the lone survivor of some unspecified apocalypse, a state of isolation that seems to prompt the play's fundamental concern with communication.

Walcott wrote the play at the height of what Peter Kalliney has described as an era of heightened collaboration between metropolitan Modernists and late-colonial writers. After the Nationality Act of 1948 and the creation of the British Commonwealth of Nations in 1949, an unprecedented number of people from former colonies immigrated to the United Kingdom.[23] While, as Eric Falci observes, this migration of Commonwealth subjects constituted a key influence on British poetry of the period, Kalliney describes how the influence went both ways, establishing a fragile but significant symbiosis: metropolitan Modernists invited late-colonial intellectuals to "revive and reshape" British culture in a period of cultural stagnation after the wars, and late-colonial intellectuals like Walcott used these institutions and connections to find audiences for their literary output, as well as their critiques of empire.[24] The BBC Overseas Services provided an important context for this collaboration, on programs like *Caribbean Voices*, which employed writers and broadcasters from these regions living in London to select and perform pieces written by and for audiences in Britain's current or former colonies. Glyne A. Griffith notes that these institutions were "colonial in orientation," but "the program's content and form were, in many instances, antithetical to the very colonial enterprise that had brought the program into existence."[25]

As a radio play, *Harry Dernier* offers an example of such "antithetical" work, mounting a critique, however elliptical, of the British Empire. The prescribed sound effects evoke a tropical island, perhaps in the West Indies, and although the script does not provide any hints of Harry's ethnicity, it does present him as a man educated in, but currently isolated from, Western literature and culture. At one point Harry wonders aloud, "Is that New York / Signalling through human wires underground, the communications of / The utterly dead?", a speculation that implies his relationship with metropolitan centers like New York had at some time been mediated by the telephone or telegraph—more forms of disembodied communication technology.[26] But the people who once sent these signals have died, or so Harry implies. The centers of civilization and culture have been destroyed, leaving only the periphery, with Harry Dernier, the last known survivor, to bear the legacy of Western culture alone. In this way, Harry's situation parallels that of the Commonwealth writers like Walcott who, in Kalliney's account, were put in the position of carrying on the legacy of British culture when it seemed to be collapsing. But where, for Kalliney, the years from the end of the Second World War until around 1970 defined a period of productive competition and symbiotic collaboration, in Walcott's play we can see suspicion of this Commonwealth-wide cooperation as early as 1951.

Harry Dernier is structured as a series of failed attempts on the protagonist's part to consolidate his subject position according to famous models of address from the Western canon. In the course of the play, Harry addresses a series of would-be interlocutors: himself, a skull he finds, an imagined companion named Quant, his own echo, a woman called Lily the Lady, and, finally, God. In each of these attempted exchanges, the play evokes a famous instance of dramatic or poetic address, and in the failure of each attempt we can see Walcott's indictment of what amounts to an imperial presumption that the poet can "will a state of affairs."

The play begins with a familiar form of poetic address, the speaker speaking to himself. But rather than consolidating the speaker's subjectivity, as in Culler's account of Romantic apostrophe, this self-address diminishes it. He asks himself, "Who am I?" and later, "Who is Harry though?"[27] The question "Who am I?," a common spur for poetic meditation, frames the opening speech as a kind of generic instance of poetic address. From here, Walcott goes on to target canonical scenes of address from the literary tradition. Evoking *Hamlet*, for instance, when Harry notices a skull in the sand, he picks it up, saying, "Well ... let's have a look at you, skull."[28] Then, inspired by a pair of "earrings" the skull is wearing, he anthropomorphizes and even feminizes the skull, saying, "Wash your face now, girlie. / Smile now, smile, lady." This pretense of affection begins to fade as he considers her "withered Cleopatra's brain" and the "two hollow jokes your sockets / Are telling," and ultimately he calls the skull a "hag," and tosses it away in disgust.[29] Even as Harry retreats from direct address in the present tense into third person and past tense—"How bald she looked!"—he continues to imagine her as a person, but now wants to keep her at a safe distance. Direct address proves not to mollify his isolation but, in a way, to make it worse, his impulse toward intimacy provoking only revulsion.

Rehearsing the scene of Hamlet's address to "Poor Yorick," Harry's speech parallels it in both structure and thematic concern. Both Hamlet and Harry pick up a skull, address it, and then throw it down. Both apostrophize the dead in order to draw close to them, but, confronted with the revolting physical reality of death, they retreat. Harry's urging his skull to smile recalls Hamlet asking Yorick's skull, "Where be your gibes now, your gambols, your songs, your flashes of merriment, that were wont to set the table on a roar?"[30] And like Hamlet, whose "gorge rises" when he imagines Yorick's corpse, Harry is repulsed by the thought of the deceased woman's body.[31] But despite these close parallels, Harry's address remains a deflated version of Hamlet's soliloquy, with none of the verbal charm or emotional appeal. It is as if Walcott has taken this famous instance of dramatic address and stripped it down to the essential, harsh truth behind it: that address, no matter how poetic, must fail in any attempt to talk with the dead.

When this attempt at conversation fails, Harry invents an imaginary interlocutor named Quant.[32] This scene is presented as a kind of mock creation story. Whereas the biblical God declares, "Let us make man in our image" in Genesis 1:26, Harry begins by proposing, "Today I think I'll create a man." Like God, Harry then also refers to himself in the first-person plural, wondering to himself, "What shall we call him? / Let's see. Kirk ... Queen ... Quant."[33] With this list of random names, though, Harry presents a very different figure than the God of Genesis, who, in his omniscience, does not suffer from the momentary uncertainty Harry has about what to call his man. Although like God Harry imagines his creation as made in his own image, here that image is of someone "unshaven, pot bellied, bald." In these ways, then, Harry's invention of Quant is a paltry imitation of divine creation.

Later in the play, Harry confronts God himself. This is the first address to elicit a response. What he gets back, though, isn't from God but from a voice the stage directions call "The Echo":

> **Harry**   God, God, my God … GOD …
> **The Echo (*sounds distantly*)**   Od.
> **Harry**   MY GOD
> **The Echo**   I GOD
> **Harry**   Why hast thou forsaken …
> **The Echo**   Shaken. . . .

This exchange recalls George Herbert's poem "Heaven," in which another human speaker addresses God and hears answers from a divine echo. If apostrophe is the "pure embodiment of poetic pretension," as Culler claims, then a poem ventriloquizing God's response presents a kind of limit case of that pretension.[34] Indeed, in putting words in the mouth of the divine, Herbert structures the poem so that God's speech is reactive, even derivative. Drawing out this very implication, Harry cries:

> Ha! The alter echo. Have you no voice, Thunderer
> But mine? Nut cracker of the world, do you depend
> On me to keep your image wobbling?[35]

Inverting the doctrine that humanity is made in God's image, Harry asserts instead that God depends on him for his image and his voice. God is like a nutcracker, with a mouth that moves but does not speak unless ventriloquized by humankind.[36] Once again, then, Walcott's invocation of a canonical instance of address deflates the pretensions of the form. Where Herbert's speaker finds comfort in the echo's voice, Harry's echo seems to mock his cries. In this respect, Harry's echo is more like Yeats's in "Man and the Echo," where it selectively repeats the hopeless phrases "Lie down and die" and "Into the night."[37] Harry regrets his scornful ridicule and begs God to pardon him and relieve his loneliness. God, though, is only an echo, and the renewed address, like the first, can only fail.

At the end of the play, Harry tries to speak to God one more time. In this final, desperate prayer, Harry alternates between his own desperate pleas ("Burn your pride Harry") and prayers from other sources, like the *Agnus*

Dei and Augustine's *Confessions* (by way of Eliot's *The Waste Land*). The line from Eliot ("O God, thou pluckest out, I God thou pluckest") evokes the I/Thou dialectic that Johnson considers the fundamental feature of lyric.[38] It also enacts a grammatical inversion, highlighting the way that the distinction between these two positions—that of God and humanity—depends precariously on only a very slight grammatical difference. In some sense, it is only a matter of sentence structure. Yet, Harry also somehow sees this I/Thou dyad as what persists, regardless of circumstances:

> If I wrecked worlds, and knew all, even I die,
> Two things are left, things indestructibly,
> More than death, germ, and sky,
> You, God, and I. . . .[39]

These are the final lines of the play. Perhaps this is a version of the Christian doctrine that the relationship between God, as divine creator, and the human soul, as a creation made in his own image, will persist even beyond the destruction of the physical world of "earth, germ, and sky." But, in the context of the poem's densely allusive engagement with the literary canon, it could also be a comment on the way the poetic structure of address, in presuming the I/Thou relationship it seeks in the first place, creates its own event of language, somehow floating free from the physical world.

In thus repeatedly returning to the failures of poetic address, *Harry Dernier* evokes the Western poetic tradition only to deflate its pretensions and casts doubt on whether Commonwealth intellectuals like Harry Dernier, isolated on an island at the end of civilization, can renew Commonwealth culture by writing poetry of their own. Harry repeatedly attempts to "will a state of affairs" through poetic address and repeatedly fails. Implicated in those failures is the role poetry in particular has played in British colonialism. Intellectuals from the colonial periphery like Harry Dernier—or Walcott himself—know Shakespeare, Herbert, and Eliot in the first place only by virtue of the role English literature plays in colonial education.[40] And the scenes of address that in Harry's speech are legible as participating in a transnational, transhistorical tradition of poetry are themselves predicated on the British colonization of the West Indies—calling into question visions of the lyric as a universalized form, operating outside history. In this light, the appearance of an unbroken lineage of poets experimenting with lyric address thus depends on erasing how that lineage is rooted in colonial histories.

Staging the Lyric

Embodied Voicing in Sylvia Plath's *Three Women*

The other feature that Culler uses to characterize lyric address, as I have mentioned, is its effects of voicing. The poem creates the impression of a speaking subject, and the reader supplies the voice, thereby contributing to the illusion. This textual voicing is voice of a different kind, not the physical voice that emanates as sound from the body of a speaker when it is performed as part of a poetry reading or a verse play, but an impression created by words on the page.

Plath plays up the tension between these two different phenomenalities of voices in *Three Women*. Somewhere between a poem and a play, *Three Women* was commissioned by Douglas Cleverdon for the BBC *Third Programme* and broadcast on August 19, 1962.[41] The following issue of *The Listener* ran reviews of *Three Women* in both the drama and the poetry section, an indication of its generic indeterminacy. The review in the drama section avers, "the outstanding dramas of the week were neither of them plays."[42] Writing fifty years later, the *New York Times* theater critic Alexis Soloski found that it was "hard to recognize as a play" because it has "no character descriptions, no stage directions, and no dialogue."[43] A report generated by the BBC's Audience Research Department raised doubt about whether the radio was in fact a suitable medium for the work, suggesting that, "To be rewarding ... this poem needed to be seen in print and pondered upon." All these responses suggest that Plath's work struck its first audience as more of a poem than a play. Nevertheless, it has been staged a few times since its original broadcast: by Barry Kyle of the Royal Shakespeare Company at the Brooklyn Academy of Music in 1974, and by Robert Shaw at the Jermyn Street Theatre in London in January 2009.[44] Where Soloski saw the text as a poem, not a play, Shaw reports that "it never occurred to me to think of anything else except a play. It seemed very simple and straightforward to me."[45]

The play involves three characters: the Wife, the Secretary, and the Girl.[46] All three women are pregnant, but where the Wife gives birth to a son and brings him home, the Girl gives birth to a daughter and gives her up for adoption, and the Secretary has a miscarriage. In lieu of dramatizing or even narrating their stories, the play presents a series of intercut lyric monologues—more like a sequence of lyric poems than a play. *Three Women* begins with the Wife's reflection on her pregnancy:

> I am slow as the world. I am very patient,
> Turning through my time, the sun and stars

Regarding me with attention.
The moon's concern is more personal:
She passes and repasses, luminous as a nurse.
Is she sorry for what will happen? I do not think so.[47]

In anthropomorphizing the sun, moon, and stars, the passage attempts "to will a state of affairs," for Culler the essential move of lyric. These lines assert the ability of the sun and stars to regard with attention and of the moon to experience concern, sorrow, and astonishment. Even when the Wife poses questions, the lines do not seem to be addressed to any other characters or to the audience, but instead enact the kind of indirect address that we have come to expect from a lyric poem.

Such lyric passages are interspersed with a few moments that do adduce past experiences, but even here the tendency is toward lyric meditation more than narration *per se*. When she describes her miscarriage, for example, the Secretary evokes the moment of realization in the past tense, then quickly shifts to a series of blurred moments in the present tense, in which she is sitting at her desk, riding the train, and walking home. How do we locate the moment when she is speaking? At first it seems as if the present moment is sometime later in the same day as the miscarriage, but later in the poem it seems that quite a bit of time has elapsed. With present-tense questions like "Am I a pulse / that wanes and wanes, facing the cold angels? / Is this my lover then? This death, this death?", it seems she has stepped outside of the chronological, narrative timeline of her life altogether to reflect on this traumatic event, the repetition of "this," a reference to the miscarriage, suggesting that for her it has taken on a kind of eternal presence.[48]

Something similar happens at the climactic moment of the Wife's monologue. In the passage that, however elliptically, concerns her labor and delivery, questions ("What pains, what sorrows must I be mothering?") and exclamations ("O let me be!") outweigh narration or description. Yet her speech is too composed, too abstract, to be understood as a transcription of what she is saying or thinking. As with the Secretary's monologue, here the more dramatic or narrative mode remains deeply fused with the lyric.

This creates the impression that, despite the differences in the characters' stories, they are all part of a single lyric poem. Indeed, even in production, it is somewhat difficult to distinguish among the voices. Burns Singer observed in his review of the 1962 production, "The mothers were not sharply enough differentiated psychologically."[49] Expecting formal characteristics like tone, diction, and figurative language to serve as markers of identity, Singer assumes a certain homology between speech and voice, and thus conflates the textual voice with the physical one.

Plath's play works against such conflation, beginning with the provocative subtitle, "A Monologue for Three Voices." What does it mean for a monologue, which is by definition spoken by a single character, to be written for three voices? Are we to understand that these three voices belong to a single person? We could hear these as the voices of the same woman at three different moments in her life, just as between 1960 and 1962 Plath herself gave birth to a daughter, miscarried, and gave birth to a son. Certainly the illustration opposite the title page in the Turret Books edition points in this direction.

In it, the faces of three female figures overlap like a Venn diagram, the woman in the center sharing one eye with the woman on her right and the other with the woman on her left. Though they have different hairstyles, the overall impression is that we are seeing the same woman from different angles. Plath herself painted a similar self-portrait in 1951.

Although there is only one distinct figure in this painting, its cubist style, as well as its title, "Triple-Face Self Portrait," creates the impression of a single woman whose face has been refracted at three different angles. *Three Women* does something similar: the motifs and echoes that repeat in all

Figure 4 Linocut by Stanislaw Gliwa, from Turret Books edition of *Three Women* (1968).

Figure 5 Sylvia Plath, "Triple-Face Portrait" (1951). Courtesy of Lilly Library, Indiana University, Bloomington. © 2022 Estate of Sylvia Plath. Reproduced by permission of Faber and Faber Ltd.

three women's monologues suggest an analogous kind of prismatic reflection among the characters. In these ways, the play calls into question the assumptions we have learned to make about the correlation of voice and person.

This kind of ambiguity is uniquely suited to the radio. But it has antecedents in the Victorian dramatic monologue. In that form, Herbert Tucker argues, it is in the tension between lyric representations of the self and narrative representations that the character of the speaker is produced. Though Tucker frames his argument in relation to character, not voice, he explores an opposition very much like the one I have considered above: that between the decontextualized, generalizable soul of the Romantic poetic tradition and the historicized, particular character on which narrative and dramatic genres mainly rely. In Tucker's account, Tennyson's "St. Simeon Stylites," for instance, "stands for an exalted subjectivity ironically demystified by the historical contextualization that is the generic privilege of dramatic monologue and [...] one of its indispensable props in the construction of character."[50] Likewise, in Browning's "Johannes Agricola" and "Porphyria's

Staging the Lyric

Lover," character "emerges as an interference effect between opposed yet mutually informative discourses: between an historical, narrative, metonymic text and a symbolic, lyrical, metaphorical text that adjoins and jockeys with it for authority."[51]

As in the dramatic monologue, in the radio play, character is revealed as the site of a clash between different notions of the self. But where the former stages that clash as between the historical and the ahistorical, the latter manifests it in relation to embodied and disembodied subjects. Thus, whereas for Tucker in the dramatic monologue the narrative element introduces the "historical particularity that lyric genres exclude by design," in the radio verse drama the act of performance introduces the physical particularity that lyric forms exclude by design.[52] Such drama depends on voices speaking the lines—physical voices of the actors and, by extension, the characters—while at the same time many radio plays, like lyric poems, trope on voice itself, incorporating the kind of figurative language on which lyric poetry is largely premised, and making manifest the conventions of lyric voicing. On the radio, these two phenomenalizations of voice can be distinguished but never entirely disentangled, as the listener experiences textual voicing by means of physical performance.

At stake here is a more fundamental ambiguity in the word "voice" itself. Finding that in twentieth-century American poetry there is "no consensus" about what voice means, Leslie Wheeler stresses "the voice's multiplicity of meanings."[53] It is easy to confuse voice as linguistic phenomenon with voice as acoustic phenomenon, clearly manifesting the identity of the speaker and thus revealing the speaker's gender, class, ethnicity, or age—although, crucially, actors can also counterfeit such identity markers. In treating stylistic features like imagery or diction as if they were markers of a specific author's voice, literary critics end up conflating physical voice and textual voicing. Culler's designating the aspect of voice that is solely linguistic as the "effects of voicing" obviates the problematic essentialization and exclusion inherent in phrases like Adorno's "the voice of humankind" and Vendler's "the voice of the soul," circumventing questions of identity by focusing on the structure of address itself. But, as Tucker shows, there is a long tradition of works that, interpolating lyric voicing with individual specificity, themselves confuse textual voicing and the physical voice.

Considering the roots of this confusion, media theorist Alexandra Keller points to the "liminal status" voice occupies in relation to the body and the mind.[54] For Keller, the "crux of the voice problem" is the "head/body split."[55] The mind originates both the thoughts themselves and the words to formulate them, while the physical voice expressing the formulations depends on the body, which controls the pitch, timbre, and so on constituting that physical voice. Issuing jointly from the mind and the body, voice calls into question the division commonly assumed between them. Keller thus alerts us to how the confusion of physical voice and linguistic voicing reflects a fundamentally dualistic understanding of the relationship between the mind and the body.

Insofar as the aural nature of radio represents a challenge to this dualism, considering the medium helps illuminate what is at issue in the confusion of voice and voicing. Listening to the radio we hear a voice, but there is no visible body from which the voice issues. With the proliferation of headphones and earbuds, the experience of the radio voice can even approximate the experience of hearing a voice speaking inside one's head. And yet the presence of a physical voice does imply the existence of another body, somewhere else. As Allen S. Weiss puts it, "[t]hough the radiophonic voice is 'disembodied,' the body is never totally absent from the radio," even if that voice "is often radically disfigured, transformed, mutated."[56] In McWhinnie's terms, radio listeners "clothe the sounds [they hear] with flesh and blood."[57] Along similar lines, Derek Furr observes the tendency of listeners to use the word "flesh" to describe the particular character of poet's voice, when listening to them read their own work on the radio.[58] Repeatedly, then, we see how the disembodied voice always retains some trace of the body and, thus, as Keller suggests, "Radiophonically speaking, the disembodied voice emphasizes all the more the irresolvability of its nature in relation to the body that produces it, and of which it is an essential, if contingent, component."[59] Precisely because it is disembodied, that is, the radio voice provokes anxiety about the body itself.

In this light, consider Harry's anxieties about the female body and sexual reproduction, which he shares with Shakespeare's Hamlet.[60] Throughout his conversation with "Lily the Lady," he insists that he is merely imagining her, to which she responds, "I'm flesh and blood, like you. / Touch me, touch and see."[61] This is the first time in the play the listener is invited to imagine the presence of a person other than Harry. It is the conversation itself that produces her, rendering her, in Connor's terms, a vocalic body. When Harry says to himself, "You think you see a woman, Harry," it is the very act of dismissing his hallucination that gives rise to the audience's own hallucination. At this moment the voice becomes something like a body, through an act of speech.

Harry, though, rues this capacity of language to invoke bodies. He asks Lily, "Where did you get / Flesh to wrap you, the old carnal metaphor /

Staging the Lyric

Around the destructive argument of the bone, the bone?" His reference to her body as "the old carnal metaphor" seems an indictment, of its superficial appearance of vitality and even beauty covering up the cruel reality of "the bone," human mortality. Here, where the living body is defined as a mere metaphor—figurative, even fanciful—human mortality has the status of factual and irrefutable argument, as irreducible as bone. In the context of the play's overall meditation on poetic address, we can see in Harry's question a comment on the process by which poetic language, from metaphor to apostrophe, in producing its own dimension of reality obscures the facts of reality. Harry wonders aloud about where Lily's "flesh" came from, but in the context of the play, it came from his own words. He is the "breeder of sinners," to quote Hamlet.[62]

Whatever its source, Lily's flesh remains for Harry a source of anxiety. Responding to what he perceives as sexual advances, he tries to spurn her, summoning up a less threatening addressee in Quant, and redirecting his apostrophe to him:

> SHUT UP ... SHUT UP ...
> Quant, here, Quant. Morass and filth here, boy;
> Get me a clean-laundered country with the sea respectable
> In a bluegreen snood. Spread me a meadow where I can eat
> Without a feeling of dung.
> What are you but a scentless heap of moving earth,
> A miser's last hoard of eyes and pennies
> Of blood? Here's the sea's rim, woman,
> Go clean yourself, Salome.[63]

Dernier instructs Quant to create a world essentially devoid of bodies, one where Lily would have no place—a "clean-laundered country," dressed modestly with a "bluegreen snood." But if his resorting to apostrophe seems an attempt to constitute an alternative poetic reality of his own, almost immediately he turns back to again address Lily, rhetorically asking, "What are you but a scentless heap of moving earth, / A miser's last hoard of eyes and pennies / Of blood?" Formulated as an accusation of Lily, Harry's question doubles as self-indictment: he is the miser who has hoarded earth, eyes, and blood—fragmentary memories of the bodies of people he has known, assembled in his imagination to form an interlocutor. The process of imagining a body, as Harry describes it, anticipates McWhinnie's account of how a listener experiences the radio: "cloth[ing]" words with "flesh and blood." But for Harry, even if it is imagined, this physical body serves as an impediment to his attempt to will a state of affairs through speech.

Importantly, this embodied intrusion is gendered. Of Harry's several interlocutors, the only one who has a body—even an imagined one—is female, as if for Walcott the female body is particularly resistant to poetic world-making through lyric address. Plath takes this tension between the female body and lyric enunciation as her point of departure. For her, highlighting the tension between lyric voicing and embodied performance helps illuminate the way that what is framed as the universal voice of the lyric poem in fact issues forth from a subjectivity clearly gendered as male.

This helps us understand some of the responses to the first BBC production of *Three Women*. Reacting to the play's many lyric passages, contemporary audiences frequently remarked that Plath's text did not seem to fit the medium of radio, as in the BBC Report mentioned above, which, again, recounted the listeners' view that "this poem needed to be seen in print and pondered upon"—that it seemed more like a printed poem than a performance piece. This response reflects that the attempt to synthesize lyric voicing and dramatic character in *Three Women* is indeed perplexing, but we might see this as part of Plath's point, as a way of addressing the unacknowledged opposition between the lyric voice and the physical body. In this way, Plath highlights the way the tradition of the lyric poem compromises its capacity to accommodate a woman's voice: marking the lyric voice with individual, physical difference, the female body precludes the possibility of lyric voicing. Evoking anything specific to women's experience (like pregnancy, labor, or motherhood), the voice of a lyric speaker cannot be heard as the "voice of the soul"—at the very least the identification of reader with the lyric I is incomplete. It seems that the lyric I forfeits claims to universality in proportion to its self-identification as the voice of an individual, embodied subject.

The play explores this tension in passages that consider writing in relation to the pregnant female body. In one instance, the Secretary laments,

Is it so difficult
For the spirit to conceive a face, a mouth?
The letters proceed from these black keys, and these black keys proceed
From my alphabetical fingers, ordering parts,
Parts, bits, cogs, the shining multiples.[64]

Staging the Lyric

She describes gestation and writing (or typing) as automatic and unwilled processes. But where the typewriter easily facilitates her creation of words, her body has failed to facilitate the creation of human life. The functional part of her body is mechanized, her "alphabetical fingers" participating in the automatic workings of the typewriter, while the rest of her body is "found wanting." In such observations, we might hear the Secretary's fear that, interpolated into the world of the office, the typewriter, and writing (a man's world) she has become more of a machine (or a man) than a woman. In the context of the whole work, we can understand that fear in relation to Plath's attempt to spin out some of the implications of the dichotomy by which the body and women, on the one hand, are defined in opposition to the mind and men, on the other.

In all three monologues, this dichotomy is formulated by contrasting images of roundness and flatness. Throughout the play, women, especially pregnant women, are associated with roundness—with the moon, the earth, hills and mountains. Men, on the other hand, are flat. In her office full of male coworkers, the Secretary tells us,

> There was something about them like cardboard, and now I had caught it.
> That flat, flat, flatness from which ideas, destructions,
> Bulldozers, guillotines, white chambers of shrieks proceed,
> Endlessly proceed—and the cold angels, the abstractions.[65]

The Secretary is afraid that spending her days in the office has flattened her as well, rendering her incapable of bearing a child. The hospital too appears as another realm dominated by male flatness. Touring the delivery ward, looked down on by male doctors for being pregnant and unmarried, the Girl observes that they "hug their flatness like a kind of health," as if the fact that they cannot become pregnant were a comforting mark of superiority.[66] "It is these men I mind," the Secretary later says, "the jealous gods / That would have the whole world flat because they are," and she goes on to add,

> I can see the Father conversing with the Son.
> Such flatness cannot but be holy.
> "Let us make a heaven," they say.
> "Let us flatten and launder the grossness from these souls."[67]

Broadening the scope of her critique beyond the men she knows, the Secretary mockingly stages the conflation of the body (of whatever has dimension, roundness, or physicality) with sin, and of the soul (of whatever is abstract, disembodied, and flat) with holiness—a vision of the world by which the default mode of humanity is defined as masculine, a norm from which the woman represents a kind of deviation, even perhaps a corruption.

In the context of radio verse drama, such a critique of flatness might well inform the way we approach the problem of voice. That is, we might understand theories of the lyric that presume a disembodied, universalized lyric voice as perpetuating that flatness, especially if we consider that, where dramatic speech is performed and thus embodied, the linguistic voice, existing only on the page, is literally two-dimensional. While many accounts of lyric poetry assume the possibility of a voice that is not embodied, gendered, or particularized in any way, in presenting a series of lyric voices that are aggressively particularized, embodied, and female, Plath's play suggests that voices cannot be entirely abstracted from the bodies from which they originate. The plays do invite lyric reading, prompting the audience to give voice to the lines—even troping on voice, as lyric poems often do, by means of apostrophe and anthropomorphism. And yet, even as they invite lyric phenomenalization on a linguistic level, they prevent it on a dramatic level. The lines bid the reader to say "I," to voice the poem themselves, but the actor's physical voice usurps this voicing. Thus, Plath constructs a radio verse drama that invites lyric reading and blocks it at the same time.

Her critique of the disembodiment of lyric voice, then, operates both thematically and formally. Thematically, it works against the contention that gendered experience cannot be the purview of lyric speech, and formally its handling of dramatic voice disrupts the phenomenalization of lyric voice. Describing the work of Caryl Churchill, who herself wrote radio plays for the BBC, Elin Diamond wrote that "There is no 'writing the body,' but rather a foregrounding of the apparatus that makes the writing impossible."[68] About *Three Women*, we might say that it does not write the female body into lyric poetry but, rather, highlights the way in which notions of lyric voice exclude such writing.

Like *Harry Dernier*, *Three Women* stages the lyric so as to make manifest its characteristic failures. Like the verse plays that experiment with the chorus, these radio plays use the disjunction between voice and character as the point of departure for experimentation. Along the way, they map out new ways of understanding the relationship between voices and bodies. The radio plays dramatize the way that certain normative models of lyric enunciation, even as they try to eschew embodiment, particularity, and the

Staging the Lyric

physical world itself, are in fact predicated on an Anglo-American male subject. Outsiders to this lyric tradition, Walcott and Plath raise fundamental questions about the lyric's capacity for world-making and subject creation, and at the same time they introduce new possibilities for lyric poetry on the radio.

PART II
WORDS

CHAPTER 3
COUNTED METER

Despite the experiments with voice discussed in Chapters One and Two, verse drama has retained a reputation as an inherently conservative form throughout the twentieth century and into the twenty-first. Playwrights have been quick to adopt the moniker "poetic drama" as a way of distancing their work from the baggage of the term "verse drama." And meter itself seems to be the problem. In 1981, for instance, Anthony Easthope described iambic pentameter as the voice of "solid institutional continuity."[1] Three decades later, playwright Richard O'Brien lamented the widespread impression that verse drama is "an unshakeably hegemonic and conservative medium" and wondered what could be done to challenge this association.[2]

This wasn't the case before the Second World War. Scholars like Morra and Warden have been at pains to correct the record—at least with respect to Eliot—by uncovering his avant-garde *bona fides*, in his early work with Rupert Doone's Group Theatre. In *State of the Nation: British Theatre since 1945*, Michael Billington observes that verse drama was primarily associated with Marxism, at least in England, up until the beginning of the Second World War, thanks to plays like Auden's *The Dance of Death*.[3] Moving beyond Left-leaning collectives like the Group Theatre, Morra argues that Yeats, Terence Gray, Laurence Binyon, John Drinkwater, and Lascelles Abercrombie were united in their own kind of revolt against nineteenth-century theater, even if this revolutionary spirit is more obvious in production than in the scripts.[4] In 1912, Binyon declared that it is in verse, and not in prose, that we see real rebellion against the status quo: "Prose accepts, poetry rebels," he avers.[5] At least some of early-twentieth-century verse dramatists thought of their plays as part of the avant-garde, then, in the aesthetic and political senses. On the other side of the Atlantic, verse drama was associated with the Provincetown Players, whose collaborative amateur theatricals constituted "the most influential American theatre group of the early twentieth century" and one of the "central cultural phenomena in New York's Greenwich Village," according to theater historian Brenda Murphy.[6] But by the early 1950s, the Unity Theatre, a workers' theater group, was parodying Eliot and Fry with plays like "Cocktails in Camberwell" and "The Proletariat Observed."[7] What changed?

Staging the Lyric

Morra attributes it "in no small part" to its religious associations.[8] Verse drama's most prominent revival took place in the context of the Canterbury Cathedral Festival; this is where writers like Sayers, Fry, and Charles Williams got their start, and this was where Eliot achieved his first commercial and critical success with *Murder in the Cathedral*. In spite of the diversity of themes and political affiliations among these playwrights themselves, Morra observes, "all verse drama seemed to become associated with Christian themes and consequently with the moralizing tendency of a self-righteous few."[9] Even so, Billington argues that "although they were leagues apart stylistically," the Christian verse drama movement and Leftist groups like Joan Littlewood's Theatre Workshop shared "more in common than one might suppose," including a suspicion of the naturalism that dominated mainstream theater at the time.[10] By the late 1950s, however, a new kind of realist theater came on the scene, with the formation of the English Stage Company and its 1956 production of Osborne's *Look Back in Anger* at the Royal Court Theatre, and with it, according to Morra, came a growing sense of the opposition between verse drama and the new national theater.

But there is another force at work here, solidifying verse drama's association with the past. The affiliation with the church and opposition to the national theater are both uniquely English hang-ups, so why does the stereotype of verse drama's conservativism transcend national borders? Part of the answer lies in the free verse revolution in lyric poetry. Beginning in France in the late 1880s and spreading to English-language poets after the turn of the century, poets and critics began to argue that poetry did not have to—in fact, should not—be written in meter. As Pound declares, "To break the pentameter, that was the first heave."[11] For many Modernist poets, vitality of expression began to replace meter as the distinguishing feature of poetry. Timothy Steele calls this "revolt" against counted meter "perhaps the most striking feature" of Modernist poetry and free verse its "most significant legacy."[12] In *Missing Measures*, Steele traces the way that the Modernist reaction against Victorian style, on the grounds that it was "vague and overly decorative," "fustian," and "mannerish," led to a rejection of meter of any kind.[13]

If meter is suspect in poetry, then it is doubly so in theater. Bertolt Brecht, who was himself a poet as well as a dramatist, rejected strict counted meter, preferring what he called "irregular rhythms" to the "the oily smoothness of the usual five-foot iambic metre."[14] And yet, Brecht admits that gest, the stylized acting method he taught, can still be "achieved" in a "regular rhythmical framework" through rhetorical devices like anaphora and circumlocution—

both of which draw the audience's attention to the formulation of words rather than their meaning.[15] He observes that actors delivered with "greater force" lines from the older Schlegel-Tieck translation of Shakespeare than those from the more contemporary translation by Hans Rothe. The "almost unreadable, stumbling verses" of the Romantic-era translation forced the actors to deliver them in a heightened, self-conscious way, thus achieving the alienation effect Brecht wanted for his productions. Brecht preferred to write in irregular rhythm, which he distinguishes from "formless" verse, a combination of lines that differ in meter and length.[16]

Elizabethan drama—with its frequent combination of iambic pentameter and prose in Elizabethan drama, which serves as a frequent reminder to audiences that characters are speaking in verse—seems to have been a source of inspiration for Brecht. According to Walter Benjamin, Brecht said that the idea of epic theater "first came into his head" at a rehearsal for a 1930 production of his adaptation of Christopher Marlowe's *Edward II* in 1930.[17] The purpose of epic theater, Brecht explains, is to expose rather than to entertain, to appeal to reason rather than mere emotion. In his 1948 treatise "A Short Organum for the Theatre," he argues, "We need a type of theatre which not only releases the feelings, insights and impulses possible within the particular historical field of human relations in which the action takes place, but employs and encourages those thoughts and feelings which help transform the field itself."[18] To foster the proper critical attitude, Brecht prefers performances that "leave the spectator's intellect free and highly mobile" rather than those that hypnotize or anesthetize the audience.[19] For Brecht, absorption into the plot of the play and identification with the characters are passive processes inimical to reflection and evaluation. In order to free the spectator's intellect, Brecht recommends creating an affective distance between the audience and what they see on stage, which he calls "the alienation effect." By way of definition, he explains, "a representation that alienates is one which allows us to recognize its subject, but at the same time makes it unfamiliar."[20] Thus, Brecht welcomes "unnaturalness" in theater, as the means by which a play produces the alienation effect.

Thanks to the free verse revolution—which cast counted meter as stilted, anachronistic, and lacking vitality—writers came to conceive of meter as something awkward, distracting, and incompatible with natural expression. In the theater, it became a way of signaling a departure from realism. In this chapter, I will trace the hidden history of counted meter in English-language plays of the Modernist era, connecting the dots between the Leftist verse drama of the pre-war period and the postdramatic theater of the late 1960s

Staging the Lyric

and beyond. While Eliot was working to make meter "unconscious" or "transparent" in plays like *The Cocktail Party*, writers like Yeats, Auden, and Barnes moved in the opposite direction, drawing the audience's attention to it.[21] In their hands, counted meter becomes a technique of alienation on the stage. Each finds their own way of making meter strange and off-putting. Starting with Yeats, counted meter is heightened and stylized as part of a ritual, with greater intensity of expression than is possible in the naturalist drama or melodrama of his day. The use of meter then becomes increasingly alienating in the hands of writers like Auden and Barnes, while simultaneously serving as an index of social alienation in their plays. This potential for alienation makes these plays attractive to the new generation of experimental theater groups like New York City's Living Theatre, which staged verse plays by Auden, Stein, William Carlos Williams, and Kenneth Rexroth during the 1950s. By the late 1950s, Arden was using counted meter, often juxtaposed with prose and song, according to Brecht's principles for epic theater. His methods are very much a continuation of what we see in Auden and Barnes. In all of these ways, and in all of these contexts—New York, Boston, Dublin, London, Stockholm—verse drama continued to play an important role in experimental theater of the mid-century, even as counted meter was being denigrated as old fashioned in both mainstream theater and the poetry world at the time.

Mixing Prose and Verse, from Shakespeare to Yeats

In his early plays, Yeats's prosody is fairly traditional; yet, in these plays we find the seeds of a stylized technique which would reach full flower in the performances of the postwar theatrical avant-garde. *On Baile's Strand* (1904) follows the Elizabethan practice of assigning verse to noble characters and prose to commoners—the practice which earned verse drama its anti-democratic reputation.[22] Certainly it motivated, at least in part, some of the earliest rejections of verse drama during the eighteenth century, as I mentioned in the introduction. *On Baile's Strand*, a tragedy based on an Ulster cycle myth, "The Death of Aoife's Only Son," embraces the Elizabethan approach.[23] The exchanges between the nobles in the play—Conchubar, Cuchulain, and Cuchulain's son—are in blank verse, while the conversations between the Fool and the Blind Man, the peasants whose comic plot intersects with Cuchulain's tragic story, are in prose.[24] The characters acknowledge these class-inflected speech differences. Cuchulain, for example, does not recognize his son when they first meet, but notes that he "speak[s] highly."[25] When asked to identify himself, the young man declares, "I will give no other proof than the hawk gives / That it's no sparrow" and invites them to "look upon me, kings. / I, too, am of that ancient seed, and carry / The signs about this body and in these bones."[26] Offering only appearance and speech, the young man convinces the others that he is of noble birth.

When Cuchulain converses with the Blind Man and the Fool, he switches to prose, like Prince Hal with Falstaff. But, at the end of the play, as Cuchulain realizes that he has killed his son, he switches back to verse in the middle of a prose conversation. It takes him a few lines to make the transition from prose to verse, as he casts about for someone to blame:

'Twas they that did it, the pale windy people.
Where? Where? Where? My sword against the thunder!
And though they love to blow a smoking coal
'Till it's all flame, the wars they blow aflame
Are full of glory, and heart-uplifting pride,
And not like this. The wars they love awaken
Old fingers and the sleepy strings of harps.
Who did it then? Are you afraid? Speak out![27]

His verse gets off to a rough start, with lines that are difficult to scan, especially the second one: "Where? Where? Where? My sword against the thunder!" Eventually, though, he settles into fairly regular iambics. The Blind Man, pulling the Fool away from the spectacle of Cuchulain's deranged grief, gets the last word: "There will be nobody in the houses. Come this way; come quickly! The ovens will be full! We will put our hands into the ovens."[28] These lines of prose undercut the tragic seriousness of Cuchulain's anguish with the peasants' comic, quotidian practicality, and cement the association of commoner's prose with comedy, as well as the opposite association of noble verse with tragedy.

Later in his career, Yeats' use of meter is stranger—and estranging. Take, for example, the first of his Noh plays, *At the Hawk's Well*, performed in 1916.[29] Yeats considered the Japanese Noh play to be an inherently aristocratic form, as he explains in his introduction to Ezra Pound's *Certain Noble Plays of Japan* (1916), a volume that includes Pound's retellings of four different Noh plays, based on fragmentary manuscripts composed by Ernest Fenollosa. There are no longer any commoners among the dramatis personae,

Staging the Lyric

nor do any prose passages punctuate the verse. Inspired by medieval Japanese theater, Yeats calls for a minimalist set ("any bare space before a wall against which stands a patterned screen") and masks (with a face "noble half-Greek half-Asiatic"). The movements of the actors are likewise stylized, like that of a marionette.[30] The point of all this, according to Yeats, is to restore to dramatic performance the power it has lost in modern theater. In the introduction to *Certain Noble Plays of Japan*, he laments the effect of modern commercial staging on dramatic speech and movement:

> For nearly three centuries invention has been making the human voice and the movements of the body seem always less expressive. I have long been puzzled why passages, that are moving when read out or spoken during rehearsal, seem muffled or dulled during performance. I have simplified scenery, having "The Hour Glass" for instance played now before green curtains, now among those admirable ivory-coloured screens invented by Gordon Craig. With every simplification the voice has recovered something of its importance and yet when verse has approached in temper to let us say "Kubla Khan," or "The Ode to the West Wind," the most typical modern verse, I have still felt as if the sound came to me from behind a veil. The stage-opening, the powerful light and shade, the number of feet between myself and the players have destroyed intimacy.[31]

To restore this intimacy—and thereby recover the expressive power of Romantic lyric—he eliminates the curtain, stage lighting, and the performance hall itself, preferring to stage the play in smaller, domestic spaces for a coterie audience.

In keeping with the stylized set and costumes, Yeats calls for the verse to be performed in a stylized manner. He thinks the delivery ought to approach that of song: "as if mere speech had taken fire, when he appears to have passed into song almost imperceptibly."[32] The play begins with the First Musician intoning:

> I call to the eye of the mind
> A well long choked up and dry
> And boughs long stripped by the wind,
> And I call to the mind's eye
> Pallor of an ivory face,
> It's lofty dissolute air,

A man climbing up to a place
The salt sea wind has swept bare.[33]

This is no longer the smooth blank verse of *On Baile's Strand*. In performance, especially under the direction of Robert McNamara, the actor playing the First Musician intones these lines of iambic trimeter in a high, strident, monotone chant, as if to signal the beginning of a religious ritual.[34] The rhymes draw the audience's attention to the sound of the words, as well as the line breaks.

In this way, the stylized use of verse is part of a systematic effort—along with the masks, the minimalist set, the Noh-inspired dance of the hawk—to make theater strange. Yeats intends the audience to ponder the actors' words and gestures, without recourse to the conventions by which they are accustomed to interpreting theater. Carrie Preston has observed that the use of Noh allows Yeats to circumvent the two extremes of the popular theater of his day, "the animated, stylized gestures of popular melodramas" as well as the "naturalistic acting in realist plays."[35] Verse is an integral part of this project, as it cannot be subsumed by melodramatic or natural speech. Yeats's goal, ultimately, is to facilitate a kind of contemplation: he wants the play to "enable us to pass for a few moments into a deep of the mind that had hitherto been too subtle for our habitation."[36]

W.H. Auden's "Curious Prosodic Fauna" in *The Age of Anxiety*

Auden likewise employs verse in an anti-naturalist way, to the point of awkwardness and confusion. The most striking case is his dramatic poem *The Age of Anxiety*, published in 1947. One of several long dramatic poems written just after the war, it has been declared "unstageable." And yet, it was performed by the Living Theatre in 1954, adapted as a symphony by Leonard Bernstein in 1949, and as a ballet by Jerome Robbins in 1950. There is, however, a resistance to performance intentionally embedded in the play. The alienating nature of the verse is part of an effort to highlight the failures of communication and the isolation from community so prevalent in the years after the war.

The play is not about anxiety, as Edward Mendelson observes, but rather the "almost instinctive wish for a shared community we can imagine but never achieve."[37] The poem identifies two obstacles to real community: the solipsism of its would-be members and the artificiality of their interactions.

Staging the Lyric

Both problems are underscored by the frequent modulation of verse forms: the use of different verse forms for different characters reinforces the sense of separation that divides them, and the frequent changes remind the audience that their conversations are contrived. The parade of heterogeneous verse forms highlights the disjunction between the visual and the aural dimensions of poetry and makes the audience conscious of the text as text, in stark contrast to his contemporaries' attempts to write dialogue that is natural and unobtrusive. But in the context of this poem, the stylized dialogue helps Auden make the point that all attempts at communication in this new era are as contrived and, ultimately, false as the ones in this dramatic poem.

Set during the Second World War, *The Age of Anxiety* takes place on the evening of All Souls' Day. It begins in a bar, with four strangers: Quant, Malin, Rosetta, and Emble. The narrator explains that a bar offers "an unprejudiced space in which nothing particular ever happens, and a choice of physiological aids to the imagination" to the regular "lonelies" and "failures" as well as everyone else who has been "reduced to the anxious status of a shady character or a displaced person" by the war.[38] These people are not in a position to make genuine connections with others. Their words and actions are all directed inward, toward the private world of their imagination. This isolation is a reaction to "the universal disorder of the world outside."[39] In light of this preamble, the interactions that follow take on a kind of universality; the plot becomes an allegory for what happens to everyone in times of war.

For the most part, the narrator speaks in prose and the characters speak—and sometimes think—in verse, usually the four-beat alliterative line of Anglo-Saxon poetry.[40] Anthony Hecht calls the verse "complex and highly mannered," likening it to the Middle English poetry of William Langland.[41] Mendelson argues that "the anachronistic strangeness of its meter [...] calls attention to its artifice and self-consciousness."[42] The association of anachronism with artificiality emerges most immediately from the Modernist reaction against counted meter. Modernist poets like Pound and Eliot conflate the Victorian use of verse with the falseness of sentiment they perceive in Victorian poetry. Auden draws on this association, using deliberately contrived verse forms to suggest the artificiality of the characters' interactions. Auden reinforces the self-conscious contrivance by dividing and combining the four-beat alliterative line to create a variety of metrical and stanzaic patterns—by Mendelson's count, at least fifty. Some are borrowed from medieval Welsh poetry, while others, Mendelson surmises, were "invented for the occasion." The constant variation is part of what has provoked unfavorable responses. Richard Hoggart says it "much batters the reader," while Alan Ross, in the *Times Literary Supplement*, characterizes the poem as "a display of versatility rather than the result of any deep-seated conviction."[43] Both are reacting against what they perceive as an arbitrary selection of verse forms. This too is intentional on Auden's part. He wants the reader, or audience, to be aware of the constructedness of the text. As Auden says elsewhere, his "dream reader" is one who "keeps a look-out for curious prosodic fauna like bacchics and choriambs."[44] He wants his audience to be paying attention to the way the words sound and look, not just what they mean.

An example of Auden's deft manipulation of alliterative verse is the radio headlines that interrupt the characters' thoughts in the prologue. On the page, there is a pronounced visual break when the radio headlines break in with its shorter, italicized lines:

Now the news. Night raids on
Five cities. Fires started.
Pressure applied by pincer movement
In threatening thrust. Third Division
Enlarges beachhead. Lucky charm
Saves sniper. Sabotage hinted
In steel-mill stoppage.[45]

These headlines follow the established accentual pattern: there are still two half-lines (hemistichs) separated by a caesura, each hemistich has two accented syllables (lifts), and the accented syllables in the first hemistich usually alliterate with each other as well as the first lift of the second hemistich. But Auden makes the lines shorter by eliminating almost all of the unaccented syllables (dips), that are not counted in this kind of accentual verse. The meter has not changed, but the rhythm has: straightforward, declarative sentences, offset from the line and enjambed across the line break, give these headlines a choppier rhythm than the characters' thought-monologues. The mid-line punctuation of two or three words phrases like "Fools foe" and "Play Poker" creates a kind of staccato effect reminiscent of the newsreel bulletin.[46]

The effect of this radio broadcast is to break the ice among the four strangers. The "dialogue" that follows is not really a conversation, but a series of long proclamations, much like the thought-monologues that dominated the first half of the prologue. For this reason, Roberts says, "the characters speak in alternation, but do not communicate."[47] Eventually, Quant describes the group they have formed as follows:

> Four reformers who have founded—why not?—
> The Gung-Ho Group, the Ganymede Club
> For homesick young angels, the Arctic League
> Of Tropical Fish, the Tomboy Fund
> For Blushing Brides and the Bide-a-wees
> Of Sans-Souci, assembled again
> For a Think-Fest: Our theme tonight is
>
> *HOMO ABYSSUS OCCIDENTALIS*
>
> or
>
> *A CURIOUS CASE OF COLD FEET*
>
> or
>
> *SEVEN SELFISH SUPPERLESS AGES*[48]

This send-up of radio programming, with nods to imaginary donors and over-the-top subtitles, casts their makeshift community in an ironic light. He calls them "reformers," but their cause is no more serious than an "Arctic League of Tropical Fish." Likening their gathering to this list of fanciful, even oxymoronic, organizations calls into question the community they have forged. The sardonic moniker "Think-fest," which sounds like something out of Aristophanes, reveals what follows in Part Two as a parody rather than an actual conversation between members of a shared community.

In Part Three, "The Seven Stages," an alcohol-fueled dream sequence in which the characters seek a "state of prehistoric happiness," they seem to be making progress toward real human connection. But then the dream ends, and they wake up to find the bar is closing. The implication, it seems, is that they achieve real community only in a dream or hallucination. The narrator observes, "As everyone knows, many people reveal in a state of semi-intoxication capacities which are quite beyond them when they are sober."[49] But even in the midst of this collective dream-state, there are reminders of its falseness. One is the frequent modulation of line length and stanza form.

Counted Meter

These differences are especially obvious in print, where each character's speech has a unique shape on the page. For example, Quant speaks in four-line stanzas, with alternating lines of four accents and two accents. Rosetta's stanzas also have four-line stanza, but they are of equal length (three beats), and so create a very different shape on the page. Malin delivers a series of three-line stanzas of three-beat lines, while Emble's lines alternate between the four- and three-beat lines, sort of like ballad meter. And this is only the beginning of the variations in this section. In some passages, the lines are very short, as if Auden has inserted a line break between the two two-beat hemistichs of the typical accentual, as in this stanza, spoken by Quant:

> They sit, translating
> A vision into
> The vulgar lingo
> Of armed cities.[50]

Elsewhere, they are much longer, like these lines from one of Emble's later speeches:

> To the south one sees the sawtooth range
>   Our nickel and copper come from,
> And beyond it the Barrens used for Army
>   Manoeuvres; while to the north
> A brown blur of buildings marks
>   Some sacred or secular town.[51]

He is still using the same pattern of alternating four-beat lines and three-beat lines, but the lines themselves are longer, with more unaccented syllables. The effect of all this variation on the page is striking. Each character's speech has its own shape, making every change in voice obvious. This visual distinction between the voices of characters serves as a continual reminder of their differences, even as they move toward the same rhythm at the end of this section. Depending on the delivery of these lines, the verse forms (especially the number of lines in each stanza) might not be so salient in a performance, since all of the characters' lines maintain some semblance of accentual meter. But then again, this inconsistency of visual and aural impression makes sense in light of the theme of the poem: the characters seem, according to one sense, to be unified in their conversations, but are, according to another sense, speaking in fundamentally different ways.

Staging the Lyric

The formal variation also draws the audience's attention to the artificiality of the characters' language. Jacobs explains that the "dizzying" proliferation of forms and genres is a part of his exploration of the "manifold varieties of artifice."[52] By constantly changing the line length and stanza shape while keeping the alliteration constant, Auden has us counting accents and lines, often paying more attention to the sound than the sense. It is impossible to forget, as one might in later Eliot plays, that the characters are speaking in verse. We are never completely absorbed, because we always have at least one eye on (or ear to) the meter.

In the Living Theatre production of *The Age of Anxiety*, Julian Beck and Judith Malina played up the awkward discontinuities and difficulty of the meter to create a very anti-realist production. Jackson MacLow contributed the score, written in the twelve-tone chromatic scale, giving equal emphasis to all twelve notes and using tone rows to avoid repeating musical phrases. The result is a heightened sense of formality, an awkwardness incompatible with realism. Looking back on the production, Malina praises the score for its blend of "the rigors of the mathematical and the sensual pleasure of the pure flow of words and meters."[53] A young Ashbery attended one of the shows, and years later cited it as an influence on his own experiments with verse drama.[54] Thus, what could be deadly in performance—Auden's use of anachronistic prosody—became one of the means by which Beck and Malina breathed new life into the theater.

The "Dear Estrangement" of Blank Verse in Djuna Barnes's *The Antiphon*

In contrast to Auden's dizzying array of metrical forms, some of them rather obscure, Barnes reclaims the most common metrical form in English-language theater, blank verse, and complicates it by using antiquated diction, dense sentence constructions, and complex metaphor. This technique, a pastiche of Jacobean drama, renders the meter more noticeable and alienating. The effect is so powerful, in fact, as to give *The Antiphon* a reputation as the most difficult work by a notoriously difficult writer.

The difficulty of performing the text, and understanding the text in performance, has led many critics to speculate about whether or not the play was intended to be a closet drama. As Daniela Caselli explains, critics are "united in recognizing" its "resistance to theater."[55] It would seem to be an example of what Puchner calls Modernist "anti-theatricality." Meryl Altman insists that Barnes "understood the difference" between closet drama and "real drama" and "conceived *The Antiphon* in the hope that actors would someday realize it."[56] Barnes herself equivocates on this issue: in response to a scathing review, Barnes says, "I was aware the style is not 'popular', I also know quite well that it is not written as the 'well made drama' is written, I did not intend it to be 'staged'—that is, unless someone wanted to stage it." Later in the same piece, she admits, "It could be a closet drama. It depends."[57] Nick Salvato argues that the play must be a closet drama, given Barnes's thoroughgoing rejection of spectacle in modern society—an argument Alex Goody complicates, arguing that the play is not opposed to performance but simply seeks to make its audience uncomfortable with the display.

The critical controversy notwithstanding, the play has been produced a few times, often in translation. For its first full production, it was translated into Swedish by Dag Hammarskjold and performed by the Royal Swedish Theatre in Stockholm in 1961. In addition to this full production, there was also a "disastrous tryout"—Robert Giroux's phrase—at the Poet's Theater in Cambridge, Massachusetts: a bare-bones reading of the play with no sets or costumes organized by Eliot in 1956. Since then, it has been performed in San Francisco in 1984, a second time in the Netherlands in 1989, in Paris in 1990, and in Frankfurt in 1992.[58]

The play is set in 1939, at the beginning of the Second World War.[59] It takes place in the "Great Hall of Burley," the ruins of a fictional English estate. Middle-aged Miranda returns after many years with "Jack Blow"—her younger brother Jeremy in disguise—to meet her mother Augusta, her uncle Jonathan, and brothers Dudley and Elisha. As the bleak family reunion unfolds, we learn about the past traumas inflicted by their deceased father (and allowed by their mother), including his arrangement of Miranda's rape, and we see ongoing conflict between living family members, including verbal and physical violence inflicted by Dudley and Elisha on their mother and sister. There is also sparring between Augusta and Miranda, and the play ends with their deaths.

The play is full of self-conscious archaisms, including words like "escutcheon," "scumber," and "bruit." Barnes also makes use of seventeenth-century verb forms—like "stroken" instead of stroked—and revives now-obsolete usage from the seventeenth century, as when she uses the word "common" as a verb that means to profane the sacred. Critics are divided as to whether the play is better classified as Elizabethan or Jacobean. The more favorable responses tend to stress the similarities to Shakespeare, while the less favorable responses stress the similarities to the Jacobean revenge

Staging the Lyric

tragedies.[60] On the level of the plot, the play resembles Thomas Kyd's *The Spanish Tragedy* (1587), Thomas Middleton's *The Revenger's Tragedy* (1606), and John Webster's *The Duchess of Malfi* (1614) more closely than it does *Hamlet* or even *Titus Andronicus*. Barnes includes several elements from these revenge tragedies, including the death of the would-be avenger, Miranda, as well as the puppet show, a deflated instance of the play-within-a-play trope, which exposes Augusta's complicity in her daughter's rape.[61] Caselli argues that the play "counterfeit[s]" the revenge tragedy in order to emphasize the "travesty and adulteration that any revenge implies."[62] In this context, revenge becomes conflated with travesty, as both are ways of revisiting a past trauma. The purpose of the reunion in the play is not to heal or even understand past trauma but merely to recall, repeat, and insist upon the wound. So too with the play itself, Caselli argues. Barnes's parody of Jacobean revenge tragedy is, then, a kind of double-travesty, of a personal past and a literary past, that allows for a meditation on the nature of revenge itself.

The pastiche of Jacobean drama is evident in Barnes's word choice and syntax. Mimicking some of the more difficult passages in Webster's plays, Barnes gives her characters long, sprawling sentences that span several lines. Take, for example, Miranda's account of her own birth:

> Then began the trick—
> The balking embryo, that mischief's parcel,
> That legless flight, that gizzard brain,
> That sitting hummock crouching in the head,
> Computing its slow minting inch—that orphan,
> Purblind, faceless, jellied in its course,
> Rolling in a palm-full of the belly's Thames,
> A dockless hawser 'round about its neck,
> Praying without hands—lolled on its thumb,
> And time commenced.[63]

In this long sentence, Miranda piles image upon image in a series of end-stopped lines—a relentless list. And yet, the rhythm never coalesces into smooth iambic pentameter, thanks to trochaic substitutions, feminine endings, and even a few four-beat lines. The passage also serves as a good example of the way Barnes parodies the use of metaphor in Jacobean drama. Especially toward the end of the play, passages jam-packed with mixed metaphors disorient the audience and obscure the meaning.

This style baffled and delighted contemporary reviewers. Even the most favorable reviews remark on the difficulty Barnes's language poses for performance. In his review in the *New York Times*, Dudley Fitts concedes that "Miss Barnes has no ear for the stage" but revels in the pleasure of "the intricate, rich, almost viciously brilliant discourse, modeled more or less on the murkier post-Elizabethans."[64] Along similar lines, Marie Ponsot, in a review of the play for *Poetry*, praises it thus: "Though it might be hard to play, it is a joy and an excitement to read."[65] For both Fitts and Ponsot, the very thing that makes the play enjoyable to read—Barnes's virtuoso performance of Jacobean verse—would make it difficult to understand in performance. George P. Elliott's take in *The Hudson Review* is less laudatory: "To begin with, it sounds gorgeous, grandiloquent, in a pastiche Jacobean fashion, but page after page of grandiloquence, seldom relieved and then not for long, confusing, turgid, opaque—cumulatively this is mortal."[66] The *Times Literary Supplement* review also comments on this difficulty:

> Not even Bertold Brecht has gone to such lengths to alienate his audience . . . And it is not only her potential audience that Miss Barnes has alienated but producers and actors as well. Her chief weapon in the process of alienation is not her plot or her setting, but something more fundamental, her language. Archaic often, intense always, concise, mannered, conceited, even a philologist would find difficulty in understanding her diction at first reading and it is quite inconceivable that any actor could convey her gist to an audience that had not spent many hours in studying the text.[67]

Barnes's mannered style is off-putting even to experienced actors and producers: it is hard to say as well as to understand. But there is a fundamental agreement here among all the reviewers: this is a play that rewards study, like a lyric poem, even as it resists understanding. The effect is intentional. Her use of blank verse serves as the foundation of her systematic effort to alienate her audience, through the action of the play as well as its style. She selects a meter that usually strikes audiences as natural, or at least unremarkable, and turns it into something dense, stilted, even aggressive. In *The Antiphon*, the deliberately difficult diction and syntax render the metrical pattern obvious, line after line. Her verse is "opaque," to quote Elliott's review, the opposite of the transparency of *The Cocktail Party*. It never recedes into the background, but rather remains the point of focus throughout the play.

Staging the Lyric

In this way, her style creates a gulf between the audience and the diegetic world of the play. This method is quintessentially Brechtian, a variation on what he calls the alienation effect. We can never be completely absorbed into the action as long as we are struggling to understand what the characters are saying. Goody argues, "Barnes uses the verse form of *The Antiphon* to estrange her audience from the familiarity of popular cultural violence and the acknowledged strategies of poetic theatre."[68]

Barnes reinforces this distance between play and audience with frequent metatheatrical references. As Goody points out, the word "play" appears, in some form, nineteen times within the play. For this reason, Altman calls it "a piece about theater as well as a piece of theater."[69] The opening stage directions describe "flags, gonfalons, bonnets, ribbons and all manner of stage costumes" hanging over the balustrade of the ruined Burley Hall and Miranda "wearing an elegant but rusty costume, obviously of the theatre."[70] The play is rife with references to the physical artifacts of theater—costumes, properties, and curtains—as well as references to specific theatrical spaces like the Odeon and conventions like the soliloquy. Jack describes Miranda as "a member of the Odeon—/ A dresser to the opera—and say, for tragedy, / Swept the Comedie Francaise."[71] He picks up on this again later, describing her as a "tragedienne" who has "left the tragic gesture to the stage" and gone "forth alone to meet disaster."[72] Augusta accuses Dudley and Elisha of playing the fool, while Dudley and Elisha cast Miranda in that role.[73] In the end, Miranda claims she has become "One of a strolling company of players" who has been "wardrobe mistress" in addition to "tiring many parts."[74] At one point, Jack even suggests that they are performing a play without an audience, as if anticipating the play's reception as closet drama. He tells Miranda:

> The scene is set but seems the actor gone.
> No tither, weeper, wait or *cicerone*;
> No beadle, bailiff, barrister, no clerk
> In shorter no audience at all:
> My hands will have to be your clamor, lady.[75]

In performance, his denial of the presence of an audience reminds the audience they are an audience, thus preventing their immersion in the play. Indeed all of these references to acting and theater allow for Barnes's commentary on the nature of theater itself, as Goody and Altman have observed.[76] *The Antiphon* belongs to a mini-tradition of metatheatrical verse drama, which spans the twentieth century from Edna St. Vincent Millay's *Aria da Capo* (1918) to David Hirson's *La Bête* (1991), and includes Williams's *Many Loves*, which was performed for the first time in 1958, and will discussed in Chapter Four.

Barnes uses the antiphon as a figure for this distance between the audience and the play. The play's title—which in Greek means *sound* or *singing opposite*—is a reference to the choral odes of classical Greek drama. There is a potential for irony embedded in the word itself, as the prefix "anti" can mean both across *from* and *against*. In Christian liturgy, *antiphon* has come to refer to alternating chant or two parties singing or speaking face-to-face. Usually, a cantor or the choir sings the verses of a given psalm, while the rest of the choir or the congregation repeats the key refrain. This refrain often encapsulates the essence of the passage, or offers an interpretive key that unlocks its meaning. Barnes puns on these possible resonances of the term, with the references to characters facing—or not facing—each other. There are several reports of characters meeting one another face-to-face or back-to-back. The face-to-face, "antiphonal" meetings usually involve antagonism and aggression. Miranda's birth, the first meeting between Augusta and Miranda, is presented this way: Miranda recounts, "Yet in her hour, become by me, twice headed, / The one head on the other stared, and wept."[77] Jack, by contrast, describes his first meeting with Miranda as having taken place "back to back—a kind of paradox."[78] This back-to-back meeting seems to be a mark of the relative lack of tension in their relationship.

The play ends with another antiphonal confrontation of mother and daughter. Miranda tells Augusta:

> Rebuke me less, for we are face to face
> With the fadged up ends of discontent:
> But tie and hold us in that dear estrangement
> That we may like before we too much lose us.
> As the goldsmith hammers out his savage metal,
> So is the infant hammered to the dance.
> But if not wrapped in metric, hugged in discipline,
> Rehearsed in familiarity reproved;
> Grappled in the mortise of the ritual,
> And turning on the spirit of the play—
> Then equilibrium will be the fall,
> Abide it.[79]

Staging the Lyric

Ponsot describes this final scene as a climactic meeting in which "mother and daughter face each other in a final attempt to communicate."[80] In light of the circumstances, Miranda believes the only course for their relationship is a precarious estrangement, a relationship that involves opposition as well as paradoxical intimacy. It is a painful configuration, likened to the savagely punitive but also transformative art of metalwork. The disorienting chain of mixed and convoluted metaphors all point to the way that mother and daughter have been shaped and constituted by this mutual antagonism. Given that Augusta kills Miranda and then dies herself by the end of this conversation, this attempt to "hold us in that dear estrangement" seems to have collapsed. Thus, the antiphon becomes a representation for the failure to communicate, even as it locks the two parties in an antagonistic form of intimacy.

It is, then, a play about antiphony, about these face-to-face oppositions that involve both intimacy and estrangement. Returning to the idea of the antiphon as the essence of the psalm, there is a similar sense in this play that the antiphon is the controlling figure of the play. Toward the end of the play, Miranda cues up this way of reading the play:

> Where the martyr'd wild fowl fly the portal
> High in the honey of cathedral walls,
> There is the purchase, governance and mercy.
> Where careful sorrow and observed compline
> Sweat their gums and mastics to the hive
> Of whatsoever stall the head's heaved in—
> There is the amber. As the high plucked banks
> Of the viola rend out the unplucked strings below—
> There is the antiphon.
> I've seen loves so eat each other's mouth
> Till that the common clamour, co-intwined,
> Wrung out the hidden singing in the tongue
> Its chaste economy—there is the adoration.
> So the day, day fit for dying in
> Is the plucked accord.[81]

In this passage, she offers what could be an explanation of the title. The repetition of "there is" suggests a series of straightforward equivalences, but, once again, Barnes presents an entangled series of opaque metaphors: the antiphon is "the purchase, governance and mercy," "the amber," "the adoration," and "the plucked accord." What these mixed metaphors have in common is a relation (between the birds and the cathedral, things caught in amber together, between the bank and strings of a violin, and between lovers) that seems to offer something good (freedom, honey, music, love) but causes pain (being martyred, heaved, rent, wrung). All of these metaphors are instances of "dear estrangement," which involves intimacy and dependence but also antagonism and violence. In passages like this, the antiphon takes on a more universal resonance, suggesting that it represents not just the Hobbs family, but a wider social phenomenon in which "loves" become so "co-intwined" that they destroy one another, as Augusta and Miranda do at the end of the play. The implication is that all such "dear estrangements" involve an ambivalent mixture of antagonism and dependence, pathological but impossible to escape.

In addition to serving as the figure for the opposition between characters, the antiphon also serves as a figure for the relationship between the play and its audience, a kind of intimate, face-to-face estrangement. Barnes's mysterious, evocative description of the relationship between mother and daughter seems to apply equally aptly to the play's form: "wrapped in metric, hugged in discipline" and "grappled in the mortise of the ritual." The play's meter, along with its deliberately antiquated style, plays a major role in the alienation between the audience and the play. It is what "tie[s] and hold[s] us in that dear estrangement," line after line.

John Arden's Brechtian Ballads: *Soldier, Soldier* and *Live Like Pigs*

Modernist playwrights thus move from the use of counted meter as a marker of class division to its use as an index of divisions that cut through interpersonal relationships. It even becomes the means by which someone like Barnes can estrange the audience from the characters and the play in manner akin to Brechtian alienation. While neither Barnes nor Auden acknowledged Brecht as an influence, Arden, a member of the "first generation of post-Brechtian writers" claims his influence in no uncertain terms, and theorizes his use of verse as a Brechtian technique.[82]

In a 1961 interview, Arden claimed he had "always been interested in different experiments with verse and prose."[83] His first stage play, *All Fall Down* (1955), a student production which remains unpublished, combines spoken verse with prose and music. His most experimental uses of verse happen in the plays of the late 1950s and early 1960s. Arden acknowledges that the mixture of poetry and prose causes "obvious difficulties"—yet these are difficulties he wants to cultivate.[84] Unlike Eliot, who sticks with iambic pentameter in his later plays, so as to disguise the use of verse altogether, Arden makes it impossible to ignore the verse by juxtaposing it with prose and song. He also works to amplify the unnaturalness of the lines themselves via staging techniques, to render them "nakedly verse."[85]

In *Soldier, Soldier* (1957) and *Live Like Pigs* (1958), Arden associates spoken and sung verse with "outsider" characters, whose incursion into modern society disrupts the community and institutions around them, just as their verse lines interrupt the prose of the play. These figures are, to a certain extent, the descendants of Shakespeare's Falstaff or Yeats's Fool and Blind Man: often rural or working class, crossing spatial and social boundaries. But instead of entering the world of tragic nobility, they disrupt the lives of characters who are just barely above them, usually the lower middle class, with upward aspirations. These disruptive misfits who speak in verse resist institutional attempts to circumscribe or assimilate them. In this way, Arden reverses our expectations and associations: despite our association of meter with orderliness, Arden makes verse the technique of *disorder*, disrupting the (typically more organic and unruly) prose. In both plays, Arden's use of verse enacts on a formal level and reveals on a thematic level the tension between order and disorder, between familiarity and alienation.

In *Soldier, Soldier*, Arden mixes spoken and sung verse to create a sense of contrast and conflict between the verse-speaking soldier of the play's title and the rest of society. The play's subtitle, "A Comic Song for Television," suggests at the outset its musical quality. The plot of the play is based on the ballad "Soldier, Won't You Marry Me?", in which a girl repeatedly asks a soldier to marry her, but each time he turns her down, citing his lack of hat, coat, shoes. Once she has procured all of these items for him, he reveals that he still cannot marry her because he has a wife and children already. The play follows a similar trajectory, with a few salient differences: Mary, the girl targeted by the soldier, has already married, and the soldier swindles not only Mary, but her in-laws and their friends. This expansion of the scope of the soldier's trickery makes him not just a problem for one individual, but a problem for the wider community.

In his prefatory note, Arden correlates the use of verse with disruption. He admits that using verse in contemporary theater—and much more so on television—can be "embarrassing," perhaps in part because it seems out of place, an artifact from another time, in a medium in which prose has always dominated.[86] It is even more embarrassing, according to Arden, when that medium is as "intimate" as television, which typically means that the audience is divided into small groups of people watching in their private homes. For Arden, it might still be appropriate in large, formal gatherings, where a certain level of stiltedness can be tolerated, but it feels excessive when directed toward a small, intimate audience—a surprising claim, given the typical model of lyric reading: an individual reading a printed poem.

Nevertheless, Arden integrates verse into his plays purposefully and capitalizes on this potential awkwardness. Cultivating a sense of anachronism is an especially Brechtian technique. In "A Short Organum for the Theatre," Brecht articulates the alienation process in historical terms, as a kind of temporal dislocation: "if we play works dealing with our own time as though they were historical, then perhaps the circumstances under which he himself acts will strike him as equally odd; and this is where the critical attitude begins."[87] Arden capitalizes on the alienating potential of such temporal confusion in both *Soldier, Soldier* and *Live Like Pigs* by juxtaposing characters that seem to come from different time periods.

In an interview, Arden reveals that he intended *Soldier, Soldier* to "look realistic" but "sound deliberately artificial."[88] The contrast between natural sight and unnatural sound thus creates an even more alienating effect than a completely unnatural *mise-en-scène*. Arden also claims the play has a "sense of a little ballady sort of verse form."[89] His interest in the ballad evinces the influence of the folk music revival, which reached its peak in the late 1950s, when Arden was writing these plays.[90] Marxist revivalists such as A.L. Lloyd and Ewan MacColl drew upon the socially critical strain present in the British ballad tradition since the seventeenth century. Lloyd and MacColl sought to distinguish folk music from popular music, in spite of the long interaction and large overlap between the two genres, because of the association of popular music with consumerism. Michael Brocken argues that the second folk revival, much like its turn-of-the-century antecedent, contrived an "idealised past history" in its attempts to use music from the past to justify contemporary scholarly and political projects.[91] Both revivals omitted or falsified aspects of the tradition. Yet, as Brocken points out, this recalcitrant, unruly folk tradition continued to resist such attempts to bowdlerize, purify, or otherwise idealize the past.

Given his political sympathies, it makes sense that Arden would be interested in drawing on this folk music revival. But in what sense does *Soldier, Soldier* have a "ballady" form? Porter defines a ballad as a "short popular song that may contain a narrative element" or "combines narrative, dramatic dialogue and lyrical passages in stanzaic form sung to a rounded tune, and often includes a recurrent refrain."[92] *Soldier, Soldier* isn't a song, but it does tell a story that combines narrative, dialogue, and lyrical passages. Some, but not all, of the soldier's lines are in ballad meter (alternating lines of iambic tetrameter and trimeter). But the key similarity is Arden's use of refrain. The recurrent interjection of lines and tunes from the ballad "Soldier, Soldier"—and, to a lesser extent, the ballad "The Reformed Rake"—mimics the structure of the typical ballad, in which a lyrical refrain intercuts the narrative verse.

The character who makes most of these interruptions is the soldier himself. Hodgson calls him the "representative of disorder and anarchy" in the play.[93] His entrance in the opening scene causes all the talking in the bar to stop, and his first lines, which are shouted in verse, contrast starkly with the murmured conversations between the voices in the bar. His manner and habits offend and worry the conservative, religious Scuffhams. A vague sense of foreignness and anachronism accompany this disruptive behavior. The stage directions attribute to him a "hard lowland Scots" accent and stereotypical Scottish Highland dress, "tartan trews" and a "blue Balmoral bonnet," creating the impression of generalized, exotic Scottishness.[94] He reveals that he is a member of the "Caledonian Fusiliers," an archaic-sounding name for a Scottish regiment, reminiscent of the Royal Scots Fusiliers or the Royal Highland Fusiliers. Although he is not as blatantly anachronistic as the Sawneys in *Live Like Pigs*, his formal, antiquated diction, especially in the opening scene, suggests a sense of archaism about him.

Mary is the character next most likely to speak or sing verse, and she too is a misfit in the community. Mary, originally played by Arden's Irish wife Margaretta D'Arcy, lives with her in-laws, the Scuffhams, who are suspicious, even contemptuous, of her Irishness and Catholicism and later scandalized by her singing "Down Derry Down." As in the case of the soldier, Arden correlates her tendency to use verse with her inability to fit in with her new family and community. She first appears alone in her bedroom, isolated from the rest of the family, singing "Soldier, Won't You Marry Me?" to herself. When she later sings "Down Derry Down" with the Soldier, her father-in-law storms in, "black with anger" and later "trembling with rage," and admonishes her.[95] Her mother-in-law and her mother-in-law's friend Mrs. Parker declare her singing and her flirtation with the soldier a source of scandal and shame on the family. Arden's choice of an Irish song, and "a very old tune" at that, adds to the sense that Mary, like the soldier, is vaguely Celtic, as well as anachronistic—certainly out of place in the middle-class, Protestant world of the Scuffhams and the Parkers.

As the soldier ingratiates himself with some members of the community and scandalizes others, his influence over them leads them to begin speaking in verse. In the opening scene in the bar, the soldier draws in Mr. Parker, who eventually begins responding in verse. Similarly, although Mary begins in "rather unfriendly" prose, she switches to verse as she warms to him.[96] The Scuffhams and Mrs. Parker interpret her use of verse, specifically her singing, as a sign that she is being seduced by the soldier. In addition to seducing Mary, the soldier encourages licentious behavior in most of the people he meets, including Mr. Parker, who picks up dancing and drinking. As with Mary, the Scuffhams interpret these vices as evidence of the soldier's dangerous influence.

The Scuffhams seem to fear the soldier's insidious effect on their daughter-in-law and friend not only because he encourages immoral behavior, but also because he disrupts the borders between cultures and classes. Over and over again the Scuffhams lament (and Mrs. Parker gleefully reminds them) that their daughter-in-law is being seduced *by a soldier*. It is not that they do not want her to get remarried, but that they do not want her to marry someone of his class. When Mr. Parker tries to smooth things over between Mary and her in-laws, he protests, "They're none so bad, you know, aren't soldiers."[97] It is as if his profession makes their potential relationship a kind of miscegenation, with the implication that Mary's marriage to their son was already a case that bordered on impropriety. In the town more generally, there is a lot of talk about his rank: he encourages them to call him a "serjeant," but the stage directions tell the audience that he is a private. Their willingness to trust him seems predicated on his rank, which functions as a marker of class. To an audience with the Elizabethan hierarchy of prose and verse in mind, the awkwardness of the mixture of verse and prose mirrors the anxiety regarding mixture of classes and nationalities. Like the ballads that they sing, figures like the soldier and those susceptible to his influence cross geographical and moral borders in troublesome ways.

Such disruptive misfits populate many Arden plays, but the phenomenon reaches its peak in *Live Like Pigs*. This play, set in council housing in 1950s Yorkshire, stages a conflict between the itinerant, anarchic Sawneys and their more-respectable neighbors, the Jacksons. It is a study of "differing ways of life brought sharply into conflict," according to Arden himself.[98] The contrast between verse and prose mirrors the contrast between the Sawneys, associated with the ballad tradition, and the Jacksons, associated with mainstream, middle-class values, like upward mobility. Arden claims two sources of inspiration for the plot: an article he read in the *Barnsley Chronicle*, his hometown paper, about a "violent little episode" that caused him to "hoot with amazement at the capacity of seemingly mild and decent folk to set themselves off like fireworks when other people refuse to live 'on right lines,'" and a performance of Brendan Behan's *Quare Fellow* in which he found the "succession of short sharp scenes" a striking way of developing a sense of "two inimical blocs" of people. In the case of Behan's play, he is most struck by the formal technique—the rhythm of the scenes—that allows Behan to suggest two opposed and irreconcilable ways of life.

Live Like Pigs was written for London's Royal Court Theatre and performed on September 30, 1958. Mary Burke observes that it "drew criticism from various sectors of the political spectrum: the conservative *Barnsley Chronicle* considered it a bad reflection on the town, the left-leaning Royal Court circle saw it as an attack on the Welfare State, and a communist theatre-goer publicly berated the playwright for satirizing the working class."[99] This confusion of responses highlights the ambiguity of the play's message, present in the very title of the play. The title, according to Burke, comes from George Smith, a philanthropist and reformer, who said that "[Gypsies] live like pigs and die like dogs."[100] Burke explains the irony of the title:

> The title appears at first glance to confirm sedentary prejudices concerning the nomadic lifestyle. Ultimately, however, the manner in which events culminate in *Live Like Pigs* indicates that the bestial humans referred to are not the Sawneys, but their aspirational neighbours. In effect, the implication that the restless might have more to fear from the sedentary than *vice versa* upends the message of conventional plays centred on the threat of the anarchic to the propertied [...]

The title leaves ambiguous who the "pigs" are, and, further, whose lifestyle is disrupting whose.

Just as it is unclear whether the itinerant lifestyle is interrupting the sedentary lifestyle or vice versa, it is unclear whether verse is interrupting prose or vice versa. The play is mostly in prose, but it features two different types of verse song: songs within scenes and ballads between scenes. In the original production of *Live Like Pigs*, Lloyd wrote the tunes for and performed the between-scene ballads. Arden deliberately sets the ballads between scenes apart from the scenes that precede and follow them. Making these between-scene ballads even more unusual, they are not ascribed to any particular character. Arden's calls for the first ballad to "cut very violently into the hushed hum-and-shuffle that normally comes between the lowering of the house-lights and the rise of the curtain."[101] He recommends that the delivery be "dragging and harsh," an instance of "speaking-against-the-music" a la Brecht. This alienating performance prevents the audience from passively enjoying these songs.

The alternating structure of *Live Like Pigs* recalls the alienating dramatic structure Brecht advocates in "A Short Organum for the Theatre": "the episodes must not succeed one another indistinguishably but must give us a chance to interpose our judgment."[102] In order to give the audience the chance to consider each episode on its own, "the parts of the story have to be carefully set off one against another by giving each its own structure as a play within the play" and "knotted together in such a way that the knots are easily noticed." Such is the case in *Live Like Pigs*, which is divided into seventeen short scenes, a remarkable number in a script with fewer than a hundred pages.

Moreover, they infuse the adjacent scenes with the social significance necessary to function as gests. For example, the first ballad imbues the first scene with wider significance:

> O England was a free country
> So free beyond a doubt
> That if you had no food to eat
> You were free to go without.
>
> But if you want your freedom kept
> You need to fight and strive
> Or else they'll come and catch you, Jack,
> And bind you up alive.
>
> So rob their houses, tumble their girls,
> Break their windows and all,
> And scrawl your dirty words across
> The whitewashed prison wall.[103]

By creating a parallel between the Sawneys and an older tradition of violent dissidence, the ballad suggests that the action that follows illustrates a more general phenomenon.

Staging the Lyric

In his preface to the play, Arden reveals that alternating rhythm of ballad and scene was inspired by his experience with a musical performance at a public house in his neighborhood:

> An Irish labourer, one night as we walked past the pub, was chanting an interminable traditional song—he paused at intervals between stanzas; a roar of bar-room conversation flooded instantly into the gap. Then the song would continue and the spoken clamour die down . . . It was clearly impromptu and not a regular 'music-pub performance'; but the singer did seem in some strange way to be *conducting* an entire symphony of music and multitudinous chatter through the command of his single voice.[104]

It is as if the ballad tradition, with its associations with culturally marginalized and lower-class dissidence, underpins the play's entire structure.

Like the ballads intercutting the scenes, the Sawneys are associated with the past and with a marginalized group, and their manner of speaking seems old, even premodern. Like the soldier in Arden's previous play, they are vaguely Irish. In the original production, famous Irish actress Anna Manahan played Big Rachel and D'Arcy played Rosie, both using their native Irish accents. The Sawneys also resemble the Travellers, itinerant people found throughout the British Isles, although they deny this affiliation. In fact, the family patriarch Sailor looks down on Blackmouth for being "a Romany."[105] Nevertheless, they prefer an itinerant lifestyle incompatible with modern British society. Arden likens them to the "sturdy beggars of the sixteenth century": the "apparent chaos of their lives becomes an ordered pattern when seen in terms of a wild empty countryside," but now there is "no room for nomads."[106] During the sixteenth century, several acts were passed to regulate begging, criminalize vagrancy, and restrict the aid offered by monasteries to "sturdy beggars," an archaic legal term that designates beggars who are physically able to work, as opposed to "impotent beggars" who could not. Part of the reason he invokes this historical moment is to contribute to the sense of anachronism—the idea that the Sawneys are from the sixteenth century even though they live in the twentieth century—but another effect it has is to invoke the play's immediate political context, in the early days of the British welfare state, which began operating in 1949. It is a response in particular to the Housing Scheme, which intended to provide homes for families like the Sawneys and the Jacksons. While the Liberal reforms that created the welfare state certainly differ from the sixteenth-century reforms, they have in common a desire to eliminate begging and vagrancy, and in both cases, figures like these sturdy beggars threaten the new systems being put in place.

In his characterization of the Sawneys, Arden plays with the seeming opposition between order and disorder: what seems like disorder can actually be "an ordered pattern" in a different context. Similarly, verse is "an ordered pattern" that makes sense in poetry and drama before the twentieth century, but now verse often feels out of place in the contemporary mainstream: for many readers, it no longer seems natural and organic, but unnatural and difficult. The Sawney way of life, which has its own kind of order in a different world, is incompatible with the world of their working-class neighbors and the Housing Scheme's attempt to domesticate them. The parallel between their behavior and the ballad tradition is fitting: they resist institutional and cultural assimilation. Taking the conflict one step further than in *Soldier, Soldier*, Arden implies that such recalcitrant difference can lead to chaos and violence, like the riot the Sawneys eventually inspire.

The ballad tradition in particular introduces an element of populism and protest that calls into question society's status quo. It allows Arden to critique the tenets of liberalism (particularly the idea that different kinds of people can coexist if they do not infringe on each other's rights), capitalism (especially upward mobility), socialism (the welfare state), and modernity itself, with its exaltation of reason and rationality. Part of the reason Arden looks to the past for the source of verse's alienation effect is the intervening influence of modernism, which casts verse itself as anachronistic and unnatural. For his part, Arden sees the Modernist alienation of verse as a source of dramatic potential: these three plays explore new methods for making verse more alienating and less absorbing on the stage. This Brechtian alienation creates the critical distance necessary to present his diagnosis of contemporary society.

This series of case studies reveals a hidden continuity between Modernist verse drama and the Brechtian plays of the 1950s. As these examples from Yeats, Auden, and Barnes show, Brechtian alienation techniques like the ones used by Arden have their roots in the Modernists' experiments with counted meter. The experimental impulse, therefore, did not disappear from post-war verse drama; rather it was channeled through Modernist verse plays that resist theatrical realism—and conventional realist performance—without retreating from performance entirely. In fact, the contiguity of late Modernist verse drama and the Brechtian plays that came afterward is especially clear in avant-garde productions of these plays, like the Living Theatre performance of *The Age of Anxiety*. That several of these plays have been declared unstageable indicates the strength of the association between counted meter and printed poetry, but as we have seen in this chapter, and as we will see in the next, poetic elements are not inimical to performance, but rather inimical to dramatic conventions coming out of nineteenth century realism.

CHAPTER 4
LANGUAGE AS MATERIAL

Despite the feelings of alienation they identify and produce, the Brechtian dramas in the previous chapter are ultimately hopeful, at least in this sense: they all maintain the belief that characters, and poets, can communicate through language. They use stylized language because it allows them to get at some aspect of reality more effectively than realism can, given its ossified conventions and concessions to commercial audiences. But after Brecht, this hope dissolves. In postdramatic verse drama, attention to the material dimensions of language becomes attention to language *as mere material*, and faith in the power of this material to deliver semantic content dwindles. These two trends are linked. Auden, for all his self-conscious manipulation of forms, believed with Kierkegaard that his age's obsessive awareness of medium was "almost bound to end in madness."[1] In the second half of the twentieth century, we see this prediction come true.

An attention to the materiality of language comes out of the lyric tradition long before the late twentieth century. All poems, by virtue of the fact that they are written in verse, give some attention to the way that the words look and sound. The material dimension can be further accentuated with the use of rhyme, alliteration, consonance, repetition, as well as counted meter and other forms of rhythmic patterning. All of these patterns draw our attention to the very syllables and phonemes that make up words, as well as the aural effects they create. There are formal techniques that foreground the visual: eye rhyme, syllabic verse, concrete poetry, even the acrostic. Lyric theorists from Frye to Culler have identified this attention to the material properties of language as one of the essential features that distinguishes the lyric from other genres. In *Anatomy of Criticism*, Frye coins two terms to designate the aural and visual dimensions of language, "babble" and "doodle," respectively.[2] These techniques can be used to reinforce the semantic content of a poem—think of George Herbert's "Easter Wings" or Guillaume Apollinaire's "Il pleut"—but this is not always the case. Some formal features seem arbitrary or extraneous to the poem's meaning. In some cases, a lyric poem might even foreground the materiality of language at the expense of semantic content. As Culler observes, "rhythm, repetition, and sound patterning" are treated as

Staging the Lyric

"independent elements that need not be subordinated to meaning and whose significance may even lie in a resistance to semantic recuperation."[3] Von Hallberg considers this tension between sound and sense to be the defining feature of the lyric; in fact, he argues that a poem's "appeal to the mind's eyes and the body's ears is meant to arrest analysis" such that the "mission of criticism pulls against poetry itself."[4]

When trying to explain to my students this lyric interest in the non-semantic elements of language, I use the metaphor of a lens: in most kinds of writing, the material elements of language constitute the glass that you look through to see the content, something you may not even notice. Lyric poetry fogs up the glass, so that the reader pays attention, maybe for the first time, to something other than the meaning or message of the text. Sometimes this fogging of the glass disrupts the act of communication. As Mutlu Konuk Blasing claims in *Lyric Poetry: The Pain and the Pleasure of Words*, lyric poetry is "above everything else [...] keeps in view the linguistic code and the otherness of the material medium of language to all the humans do with it."[5] In other words, the lyric draws our attention to difference between what we say and how we say it; it exposes those properties of language that are extraneous to or even in opposition to communication.

While this emphasis on the materiality of language may be the *sine qua non* of lyric poetry, there is some theatrical precedent for this kind of attention to babble and doodle, even among plays written in prose. George Bernard Shaw, for example, was famous for the attention he devoted to the details of *mise-en-page* in the print publication of his plays, stipulating the typeface, margins, spacing, and hyphenation practices, even the specific type of paper and ink. W.B. Worthen attributes this attention to detail to Shaw's desire "to stage the value of modern drama as print literature" as well as "articulate a sense of the play as writing and performance."[6] But whereas Shaw's goal, according to Worthen, is to render each play "complete in its reading," the plays I will discuss here heighten the conflict between page and performance, such that neither is complete in itself.[7] The playwright's decision to render a play in lines of verse already demonstrates an attention to the appearance and sound of words. And the use of counted meter is an especially self-conscious way of foregrounding language in its material dimensions, as I discussed in Chapter Three. In this chapter, my concern is for the way that modern and contemporary verse dramatists stage the tension—inherited from lyric poetry—that can sometimes arise between the material properties of language and its semantic content. Instead of making language the invisible vehicle for meaning, these verse dramatists foreground the material dimensions of language at the expense of the semantic content—they intentionally fog up the lens.

There are at least two sources of conflict intrinsic to verse drama that these plays draw out and exaggerate. The first emerges from the mode of enunciation—stage performance in opposition to lyric address: a play is embodied—live actors deliver lines on stage in the presence of a live audience. The lyric, despite retaining the mark of aurality inherited from its supposed roots in oral performance, has long since been pinned to the page. In a live performance, the audience loses access to the doodle—they cannot see and study the text. Recall the BBC listeners who wished they could see the text of Plath's radio play. Their response suggests that attention to the materiality of language is easier to tolerate in print than in performance. It would seem, then, that the mode of enunciation is at odds with attention at least to doodle—and maybe even to babble. It is easy enough to incorporate rhyme or alliteration into a theatrical performance—musicals do it all the time—without obscuring meaning. And yet, throughout the twentieth century, we see audiences, critics, and even scholars decrying these techniques as distracting. Attention appears to be a kind of zero-sum good, where attention to linguistic patterns diminishes the audience's capacity to pay attention to what the words mean.

The opposition between performance and the lyric impulse to foreground the materiality of language is most pronounced in plays that foreground doodle, so much so that the decision to attend to the materiality of language can sometimes seem like a decision to ignore performance entirely. As a result, many experiments with this aspect of the lyric are written as closet dramas, or are denigrated as such. A good example from a play that has been staged is Arden and D'Arcy's *Friday's Hiding*, written in 1965, which features stage directions in verse. It is hard to imagine how a director would make this element of the script part of a stage performance. In their 1966 production of the play, the Lyceum Theatre Edinburgh chose to ignore the versification entirely and stage it as a kind of mime play, with minimal dialogue. The result is somehow at once a play without words (on the stage) and a verse drama (on the page).

Another challenge is the expectations conditioned by realist theater. With Ibsen's repudiation of verse drama in 1883, not only meter but all forms of verbal patterning came to be seen as inimical to realism. The thought is that human beings do not tend to give any thought to the material properties of language in the normal course of everyday conversation. If the dialogue is to strike the audience as realistic, characters in a play must not either. Bean, in her history of Poets' Theater in the United States, casts realism as a tyrant and Poets' Theater as but one form of rebellion against it. Prose drama is not immune to these charges: Harold Pinter's *A Slight Ache*, for example, has been described as "too patterned to be realistic."[8] Verbal patterning may be tolerated in musical theater—not because these audiences are less easily distracted or have a greater capacity for attending to the formal elements of spoken language, but because there is not the same expectation of realism in this context.

Eliot perceived this conflict between linguistic patterning and modern realism and sought to resolve it. Over the course of his career as a dramatist, Eliot came to believe that a play, in order to succeed dramatically, should make its language as transparent as possible. Rather than foregrounding language, he sought to make it the invisible conduit of meaning—not that he thought form didn't matter, but rather that "the chief effect" of formal elements like style and rhythm should be "unconscious."[9] This movement toward transparent verse is evident in the trajectory of his dramatic writing: from plays like *Murder in the Cathedral* that mix free verse, prose, and counted meter to plays like *A Cocktail Party*, written entirely in blank verse.

And yet, there are plenty of examples of playwrights who seek to fog up the glass rather than make it perfectly clear. Playwrights like Williams and Laurens, as well as theater companies like the Wooster Group, intentionally draw the audience's attention to the material properties of language—not in spite of the risk of obstructing communication but because of it. This obstruction is part of the point. Both *Many Loves* and *The Three Birds* thematize the failure to communicate, and use an attention to the aural and visual properties of words to enact such failure in the conversations between characters even as the works comment on it as a broader social phenomenon. In all of the plays I will consider here, attention to the materiality of language begins as means by which to undercut the efficacy of realist theater, but ends up undercutting the communicative function of language itself.

The Wooster Group's Destructive Examination of T.S. Eliot's Verse Drama

Since the late 1970s, the Wooster Group has been one of the most famous experimental theater workshops in the United States. *Nayatt School* rounds out a trilogy of plays called *Three Places in Rhode Island*, all loosely based on events from Wooster Group member Spalding Gray's life. These three

Language As Material

autobiographical plays—*Sakonnet Point, Rumstick Road*, and *Nayatt School*—were performed together from 1979 to 1982. *Nayatt School* is not a verse play, but it takes one, *The Cocktail Party*, as its inspiration.[10] It isn't an adaptation of Eliot's play, but it does stage several scenes, and it takes from it a thematic interest in the curative properties (or lack thereof) of medicine and religion.[11] As in all Wooster Group shows, the point of evoking another text is "encountering material" not representing character or place, as Andrew Quick observes.[12] Michael Vanden Heuvel argues that their use of *The Cocktail Party* at first implies a faith in "the cathartic possibilities of drama, religious faith, and medicine" but "[i]nstead of naturalizing these discourses, as in realist drama, The Group exposes them to the scrutiny of the spectator and reveals their rough and corrosive edges."[13] Wooster Group director Elizabeth LeCompte has acknowledged her own tendency to "circle around ideas, rotate the viewpoint," and that is exactly what we see them doing to the text of Eliot's play in *Nayatt School*: it is exposed, dissected, inspected, analyzed, rotated, and examined from another angle.[14] The goal is to put pressure on "the technologies of meaning production that exist both in the theater and also in popular culture (including the various technologies of communication—sound, video, televisual, as well as pictorial, cinematic and choreographic modes of expression)."[15] In the case of *Nayatt School*, verse drama—and maybe even poetry itself, by the end—comes under scrutiny.[16]

The show begins with Gray seated at an elevated table at the front of the stage with a record player in front of him. He introduces *The Cocktail Party* via a meandering, autobiographical monologue, addressed directly to the audience. The monologue varied from night to night, sometimes covering Eliot's biography or the play's production history, at other times the circumstances of Gray's own discovery of the play. In a recording of a show on June 4, 1979, for example, he can be heard disclosing the cost of the record, no longer in production, as well as the fact that the copy he has is an overdue loan from the library. He tells the audience that he has been listening to this play over and over, and the more he listens to it "the more it begins to break down." In some performances, he leaves it at that, implying that repeated listening has damaged the physical record itself. But in the June 4, 1979 show, he specifies that he means that it breaks down "as far as the meaning goes" too.

Using a record player, he plays some samples from the play for the audience, occasionally offering explanation or commentary. Near the end of a speech by Sir Henry Harcourt-Reilly, performed by Alec Guinness, Gray stops the record, saying, "I just want to mark that—it's one of my favorite lines." The passage comes from Act 1 of *The Cocktail Party*: "But, stretched on the table, / You are a piece of furniture in a repair shop / For those who surround you, the masked actors."[17] Sir Henry is describing the experience of undergoing surgery, an instance of the broader phenomenon at issue: the unsettling feeling of being turned into an object via the examination of others. Gray moves the needle to play the lines again, but instead of replaying the sound as before, he uses an eraser to slow the record down, distorting the words and rendering them unintelligible. The audience hears the words again—this time as sound, not as significant speech. In the June 4, 1979 recording, you can hear the audience laugh when he does this; they register the contradiction between Gray's professed affection for this particular line and his desire to obscure its meaning. It is a way of accelerating the breakdown of meaning that Gray just mentioned.

In the next scene, the metatheatrical monologue gives way to something like a performance of Eliot's play. He sits at the same table as before this time with another actor, Joan Jonas, who reads the role of Celia Coplestone opposite his Sir Henry. What follows is a kind of readers' theater version of a scene from Act II of *The Cocktail Party*. But instead of the expressive performance we might expect, given Gray's professed love of particular lines, his delivery is flat and emotionless. Vanden Heuvel claims that Gray's delivery "deprives the language of much of its power, reducing Eliot's carefully wrought verse to stilted, childish reading on the one hand, and frenetic gibberish on the other."[18] Moreover, during the last few minutes of their reading, there is loud, upbeat music playing in the background, such that some of the words are drowned out.

After this scene, the show moves away from Eliot's play to three "demented doctor" scenes, as Wooster Group member Kate Valk later called them. In the first, a dentist prepares to treat a patient's toothache; next, a doctor prepares to perform a breast exam on a female patient; and finally, a research in a medical lab reports the dangerous proliferation of chicken heart cells, an experiment gone wrong.[19] Although Gray plays the doctor in each of these vignettes, it is not obvious that any of them is supposed to be Sir Henry. They are, however, clearly inspired by Eliot's meditation on physical, mental, and spiritual health, but much less sanguine than Eliot about the possibility of healing. All three end on a troubling note, with the disturbing implications of the doctor's words left hanging in the air. The breast exam recalls the experience Sir Henry registers in Act I of *The Cocktail Party*: the unsettling feeling of objectification that comes about when one is subjected to intense

Language As Material

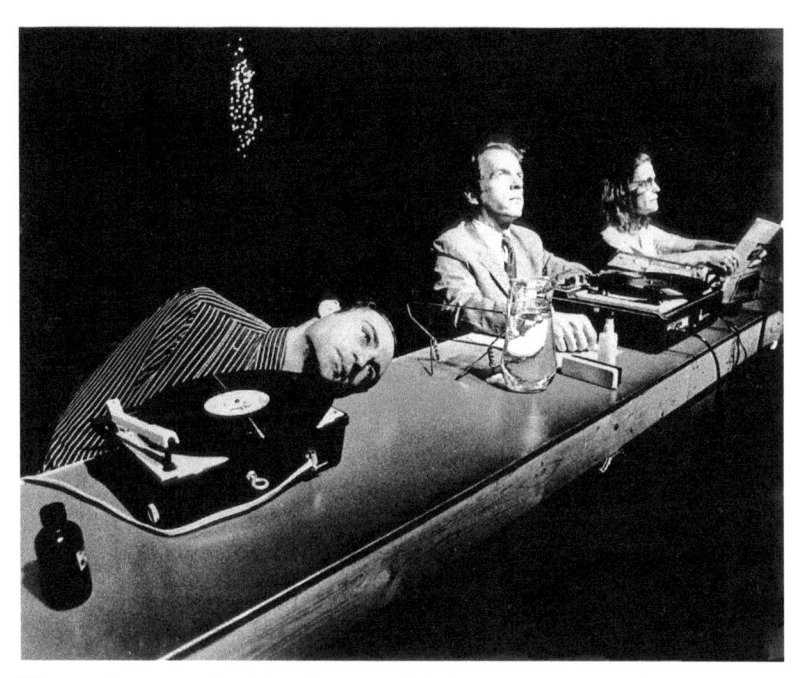

Figure 6 *Nayatt School* (1978). Pictured (l-r): Ron Vawter, Spalding Gray, Joan Jonas. © Bob Van Dantzig.

examination. The Wooster Group subjects Eliot's play to something analogous: breaking the play down and giving each component intense attention. In fact, "examination" is the term they use to refer to each part of the performance. In his opening monologue, Gray isolates a particular line and slows it down for the ostensible purpose of study, an act that distorts the sound of the line and obfuscates its meaning. The doctor's office vignettes that constitute a third examination isolate a single theme from the play—the ethics of treating mental health—and turn it into a distinct object of scrutiny in three autonomous playlets. This close scrutiny of the play distorts and obscures its meaning. It is part of a larger project of the Rhode Island trilogy, which, according to David Savran, "challenges the 'neutrality' of the scientific method to reveal that the phenomena under investigation will always be transformed in the process of presentation."[20]

Nayatt School ends with Gray, as well as Libby Howes and Ron Vawter, back at the table at the front of the stage, crouching over the record players, all three partially or completely naked, and attempting to destroy the records.

Figure 7 *Nayatt School* (1978). Pictured (l-r): Erik Moskowitz, Ursula Easton, Ron Vawter, Tena Cohen, Spalding Gray. © Nancy Campbell.

One way to read this scene is as a descent into chaos, after the tightly choreographed, even stilted scene before it, in which Gray and the rest of the cast act opposite child actors playing Lavinia, Alex, Julia, and Peter.[21] But this final tableau looks more like an attack—with the added intimation of sexual violence, thanks to Vawter's and Howes' simulated masturbation—than the gradual, unintended decline Gray implies in his opening monologue. In fact, the violent destruction of these records recalls the violent death of Celia, disclosed in Act III of *The Cocktail Party*, the scene the group performs just before this. Savran says *Nayatt School* "pulls *The Cocktail Party* apart and offers it as a sacrifice, much like Celia Coplestone herself."[22] Notably, Vawter, Howes, and Gray each attack a different record, on three separate players. One of these is *The Cocktail Party*, presumably, but the other two are less obvious. Perhaps they are the same records Gray plays at the beginning: Eliot's *Four Quartets* and Alec Guinness's *A Personal Choice*, a compilation of poems by Guinness's favorite writers, from Shakespeare to Ogden Nash. If so, the target of this desecration could be said to be poetry itself, or poetry of a particular kind, as many of the poems on *A Personal Choice*, like Eliot's late works, skew conservative as well as Christian. In any case, this ending realizes, in a shockingly concrete way, the dream of the postwar theatrical avant-garde, as articulated by Antonin Artaud in *The Theatre and its Double* (1938): of performance liberated from the literary text, of a theater that is purely physical. Artaud advocates a "theater of cruelty," his term for a performance that affects the audience viscerally rather than diverts, as realism does.[23] He calls for an end to "the subjugation of the theater to the text" and a recovery of a "unique language half-way between gesture and thought."[24] For this reason, Artaudian theater is often classified as antitextual. *Nayatt School* is antitextual in a literal sense, insofar as it launches a physical attack on a physical text. But the Wooster Group does not eliminate the written word in favor of total spectacle. Instead, they do the opposite, staging a verse play in iambic pentameter, arguably the most literary form theater takes, and tearing it apart. To be destroyed, language must first be rendered as material—in this case, a physical object, a record. Thus, *Nayatt School* properly belongs to Lehmann's category of postdramatic theater, in which "perpetual conflict between text and scene" becomes a "consciously intended principle of staging."[25] Even Artaud, however, does not oppose language as such; he advocates the use of language as "expression in space," which uses the "material side" of poetic language to act on the bodies of the audience, or, as he puts it, "fascinate and ensnare the organs" like an incantation.[26]

Insidetalk and Outsidetalk in Joanna Laurens's *The Three Birds*

Nayatt School is overtly postdramatic in its renunciation of expressive and immersive performance. But this so-called postdramatic impulse to isolate language itself as an object of intense study extends to plays that are less obviously experimental, both before and after this moment in theater history. Like Christopher Innes, I think the theater created in the 1970s by avant-garde performance groups like the Wooster Group "mark[s] the limitations of purely physical theater," such that what follows is less obviously experimental, at least along the Artaudian lines, but retains an interest in using antitextual techniques to stage a literary text. In 2000, a 21-year-old student named Joanna Laurens, with little experience in the theater, sent her first play, a verse adaptation of the myth of Philomela and Procne, to a few experimental theaters around London. She did this in spite of almost unanimous feedback that the play was too "poetic" or "wordy" for the stage. The Gate was willing to take a chance on it, and in October of 2000, they staged Laurens's first play, *The Three Birds*. The play was a hit, garnering favorable reviews and several awards.

Staging the Lyric

Laurens has since claimed that she knew so little about the theater world that she did not realize how unusual her play was. And yet, the eccentricities are obvious: the use of free verse in alternation with prose passages, frequent anachronism, neologisms peppered throughout, and untranslated words from obscure languages like Jersey Norman and Proto Indo-European. Reflecting on the experience four years later, she revealed that her goal, however inchoate at the time, was to test the theater's tolerance for something "non-natural":

> We all know what naturalism in theatre means. Well, most of us do. It conjures up images of a front room; carpet neatly tacked down along the front of the stage, a bowl of fruit, apples and pears on the table, artificial snow falling outside windows, realistic dialogue . . . But what is non-naturalism? How can we describe something that is a negative, defined by the fact that it's not something else? The fact is, non-naturalism is a false category, a category hiding lots of other forms, which we fail to see because we don't have the words for them yet.[27]

Her term "non-naturalism" I take to mean any kind of performance that works against the conventions and assumptions of theatrical realism. Laurens's own approach is not just a matter of content or setting, as the stereotypes she invokes might suggest. The non-naturalism of *The Three Birds* is evident primarily in the language—in the use of free verse, dialogue written in dead or obscure languages, idiosyncratic words and figures, and other stylistic elements that draw our attention to the words themselves, rather than their meaning.

The classical source material is a good fit for a play that thematizes communicative failure. The myth itself revolves around an act of silencing: Tereus' removal of Philomela's tongue. The play's subtitle, "After Sophocles," suggests that it is as much an adaptation of his lost play *Tereus*—the 57 lines that have survived—as it is of the more famous version of the story in Ovid's *Metamorphoses*. Based on her introductory note in the print version of the play, it seems that Laurens preferred to think of herself as adapting Sophocles because of her sense that the play itself had been "gagged by time."[28] Building on the symbolic potential of the circumstances, Laurens writes her own play that meditates on the disjunction between speech and communication.

The plot is basically the same as in Ovid. In Ovid's version, the story ends with the three principal characters transformed into birds: Tereus becomes a hoopoe, Procne a swallow, and Philomela a nightingale. Laurens downplays this act of divine intervention, leaving only an oblique reference in the epilogue, spoken by Philomela and Procne's father, Pandion:

> Three birds flew away when I got here,
>   pulled to air like jetwindow rain.
>   A questioning crested hoopoe.
>   A nightingale at mourning.
>   A sparrow.[29]

Besides toning down the supernatural elements in Ovid's version, she also significantly changes Tereus' personality and motivations. Her Tereus is in love with Philomela from the very start, before Pandion offers Procne as a bride. Laurens gives Tereus a moving, if hyperbolic, soliloquy in praise of Philomela in the opening scene:

> It's the small things of her that catch me.
> The shape of her ears
> the loose threads on her dress
> the curve her knife leaves in the butter
> (her buttercurves are unique)
> but mostly I love the sound of her name.[30]

Tereus declares his love for her again, before raping her at the end of Act One. Afterward, Philomela mocks him by repeating his fumbling confession of love. Although Laurens does not shy away from portraying the act as a rape, she does make Tereus more sympathetic than he is in Ovid. Moreover, after the death of Itys, he is not a wrathful king from whom Philomela and Procne flee in terror, but a mournful father, hopeless and full of regret. It is as if Laurens' portrayal of Tereus is calculated to make the audience uncomfortable: he is at once lover and rapist, victim and perpetrator.

The play is marked by its unique patterns of diction. We have already seen a couple of examples of her tendency to coin new compound words, like "jetwindow" and "buttercurves." Many of these compound words, which resemble Anglo-Saxon kennings, are intuitive enough: "backthoughts" or "sadsmilings," for example. Others are more difficult to interpret, such as "redrich," a noun the chorus uses to describe the quality of a voice; "flowerfaces," a verb that describes the effect the birth of Itys has on Procne, presumably softening her previously hardened face; or "flagsmile," the word Procne uses to describe the false façade of a happy marriage she and Tereus must present at a public festival for the benefit of their subjects. These idiosyncratic kennings crop up even in stage directions; one calls for the actor playing Tereus to "strugglepause" before moving on with his soliloquy.[31] These are not utilitarian coinages meant to economize words or clarify meaning—why invent a new word like "bonebolts" when an existing word like "joints" will do? Alliterative kennings like "bonebolts" and "redrich" seem to have been devised for their sound, not just their sense. Even with a word like "flagsmile," which has no precise equivalent, Laurens is working with the figurative associations that go beyond the literal meaning: the flag is an (anachronistic) metonym for patriotism, but she also seems to be evoking, sonically and semantically, the phrase "fake smile." It makes sense, but it requires some thought on the part of the audience—something we hardly have time to do as we try to follow the conversation between Procne and Tereus. A review of the 2006 production at Yale noted, "This confusing script, which involves an extensive mixture of imagery, though wholly colorful, often overshadows the performance itself."[32] Note, once again, the implicit rivalry between text and performance. Elsewhere Laurens creates new words by combining existing verbs with new prefixes or suffixes, as in "dispeak" (meaning "take back"). With these neologisms and kennings, Laurens experiments with communicative possibilities of English: How far can she take her modifications of existing language without rendering the dialogue incomprehensible?

Their conversations are also interspersed with Jersey Norman. Pandion calls his daughters "chiéthes", a term of endearment, and Philomela calls her father "péthe." These are easy enough to figure out in context, but others, like "fouaithe" or "cricots," pose greater difficulty. In these cases, the audience has little more than sound to go on. I suspect Laurens chose Jersey Norman at least in part because it was a regional language that fell out of use in the last two hundred years with the standardization of French and the globalization of English. In fact, all of the foreign languages in the play—Proto-Indo-European, Anglo-Saxon, Welsh, and Irish—have been subsumed into, or in some cases actively suppressed by, modern national languages. Her choice of Jersey Norman raises the possibility that the English used in the rest of the play represents a kind of language of the realm or of commerce that Philomela's family has learned in order to communicate with people from other places—a language they know but are less comfortable speaking.

Moreover, Philomela and Procne share their own unique patterns of diction. Theor conversations are especially dense with neologisms, as well as unidiomatic expressions and idiosyncratic grammar. They rarely conjugate their verbs according to standard English when they are speaking to each other. And they use unidiomatic expressions, such as "feeding face" and "having laughter."[33] The effect of these constructions is to imply a kind of private language between the two sisters. Acknowledging this private language, Procne tells Philomela, "You speak my inside out. / You talk the quiet thing inside."[34] Philomela is apparently the only person who can put Procne's internal thoughts and feelings into speech. But the "quiet thing inside" can only be externalized by means of these idiosyncratic and, to our ears, awkward constructions—an indication of the strain. The audience can just barely make sense of what they are saying to one another, and even then, it requires some knowledge of Jersey Norman or access to Laurens's footnotes. From our perspective, it seems as if Philomela and Procne are struggling against the limits of the English language in order to make their thoughts and feelings intelligible, and we are just barely privy to them.

Philomela and Procne talk about this private language as a kind of stand-in for—perhaps a representation of—an inexpressible internal reality. Hence the name Procne gives it: "insidetalk." Their shared language resembles another kind of "insidetalk," the lyric, at least according to the Romantics. Recall Wordsworth's definition of poetry in his "Preface" to the *Lyrical Ballads*:

> Poetry is the spontaneous overflow of powerful feelings; it takes its origin from emotion recollected in tranquillity: the emotion is contemplated till by a species of reaction the tranquillity gradually disappears, and an emotion, kindred to that which was before the subject of contemplation, is gradually reproduced, and does itself actually exist in the mind.[35]

While Philomela and Procne are not self-consciously creating poems in a moment of tranquility, Procne's idea that their shared language gives an external form to their internal emotional state resembles the Romantics' expressivist model of the lyric.

The similarities between their "insidetalk" and the expressivist lyric emerge most clearly in a scene after Procne's wedding. Waiting for Tereus, she looks up at the night sky in the hopes that it will inspire her:

> Where is my moon?
> When small I be,
> look I up there

and see he.
Now the Gods' roof is silent
to askings.
It speaks me no givebacks.
It slips me no dothats,
but stands like a coatrack
to hang my insidetalk on.
Where is my moon?[36]

This moonless sky offers her no advice—no "givebacks" or "dothats." It is merely an inert receptacle for her "insidetalk," which is of no use to her in Thrace. It is at this moment that she realizes that she must hang up this old way of speaking, like a coat she no longer wears, and try to speak a language her husband can understand. It is telling that Laurens stages this meditation in a scene that resembles stereotypical lyric address: the speaker, turned away from the other character on stage (Tereus) and from the audience, gazes up at that most poetical of interlocutors, the moon, and finds only an empty, dark sky. Procne's attempt to create an interlocutor through lyric address—the impulse to "will a state of affairs" that Culler sees behind every act of apostrophe—fails. There is no moon. And the sky is silent in response to her "askings." After this moment of lyric privacy, she must turn to Tereus and, re-entering the dramatic action, attempt to converse with him.

We see her speaking in two different modes in this scene: lyrically, via "insidetalk" addressed to no one in particular, riddled with idiosyncratic words and phrases, and dramatically, in more-or-less standard English. In her conversations with Tereus, she moderates her use of incorrect grammar and idiosyncratic expressions. Tereus later observes, "You talk clearer alone," that is, when she is not with Philomela.[37] He prefers her new way of talking to the sisters' "togetherspeak," which he calls "babble" that "murders doves / leaves them broken on the floor."[38] In response, Procne tries to put her longing for her sister into words, begging him:

Please, Tereus.
I can't say it out of me.
Wordnailings kill it,
pin it like a butterfly in collection.[39]

Here Procne sounds like Eliot's Prufrock, when he accuses the women at the party of fixing him "in a formulated phrase" like an insect "pinned and wriggling on the wall." It both contexts, language is figured as a kind of bind that constrains the speaker. After a failed attempt to express her feelings, she laments, "See, there it dies, riddled with wordholes."[40] An image more violent than the last, it suggests that words are like bullets, leaving holes in the "insidetalk" she wants to make intelligible to Tereus.

Philomela has similar difficulties communicating with other characters in the play. When they are alone together on their journey from Athens to the Thrace, Tereus approaches Philomela with a confession: "You are a fly / drinking at my eye / and I love you."[41] Philomela repeats his words—or, rather, she replicates the sounds, breaking down the words into syllables and phonemes in order to make sense of them. She delivers these lines, according to the stage directions, "As though learning a foreign language—hesitant and querying with intonation—not understanding the meaning." Tereus tries two more formulations: "I'll view. // an all of you" and "an I-you."[42] While we may not know exactly what he means, we get the gist—that he is expressing his sexual desire in an abstract way. But Philomela doesn't. Her halting repetitions of the words as she tries to make sense of them draw our attention to the sound, defamiliarizing otherwise familiar words so that we hear them as a non-native speaker might.

After the rape, her speech changes drastically.[43] Suddenly able to understand and speak clearly, Philomela accuses and mocks him, repeating his declaration of love over and over and laughing bitterly. As she repeats his words, the chorus begins to whisper the phrase "The king's child was good" in five different languages at once, enacting a kind of reverse Tower of Babel. There is a proliferation of tongues, but instead of one parent language being divided into its various descendants, this proliferation of languages moves backwards in time, to the languages from the past that have been absorbed or replaced by English. The emphasis is on the rhythm of the words, rather than their meaning—without the stage directions, the audience might not even know what the chorus is saying. She uses the five different versions of the refrain like so many instruments, creating a complicated sonic texture as the rhythms work in concert with one another. The competing rhythms never coalesce into a singular, regular pattern, but continue to phase in and out, unnerving the audience as well as Tereus.

Driven mad by her repetitive mockery and the relentless cacophony of the chorus and desperate to make it stop, Laurens's Tereus cuts out Philomela's tongue. Thus, Laurens gives him a very different motivation from other versions of the story, where Tereus is thinking and acting strategically to prevent Philomela from exposing his crime. In the moments after he cuts out her tongue, she continues to mouth her mocking words, but she can no longer make any sound. Surprised, she then "look[s] at the empty air where her words should be."[44] Here Laurens treats words as a physical phenomenon, as if they were material objects capable of taking up space.

In the scenes that follow, Laurens, somewhat surprisingly, continues to include lines for Philomela in the script. When we see Philomela again in Act Two, after a short time has passed, she delivers a silent monologue. Reading the print version of the play, one can tell that the speech is identical to the one she delivered aloud after the rape. But in performance, there is no guarantee that the audience will be able to understand the speech by reading her lips. Even an experienced lip reader would not be able to catch every word, especially if the actor mouths these words "quickly" and "furiously," as Laurens prescribes.[45] Although the stage directions say she is "desperately trying to communicate," there is no one on stage to communicate with. So, it seems more like a compulsive ritual she has been reenacting since her traumatic experience in Act One.

Philomela must depend on images and gestures to convey meaning. Before the silent speech quoted above, for example, Philomela has a long pantomime sequence in which the audience can discern her boredom, sadness, and rage based on her actions and gestures. She yawns, she sobs, she throws a wineglass. Later on, when Tereus approaches her, she communicates with him through gesture. Surprisingly, they are able to communicate and understand one another better in this scene than previously, in part because he deigns to adopt her idiosyncratic and ungrammatical patterns of speech, but also thanks to her effective use of pantomime. However, he does misread some of her gestures. She mimes killing herself, for example, which he immediately interprets as a suggestion that he kill her rather than keep her imprisoned. Is this what she meant? The audience can't be sure. Later, when the sisters are reunited, Procne is able to understand her gestures, at least enough to figure out what happened. When Philomela averts her gaze, Procne concludes that Philomela is ashamed, and reassures her. But there are no other clues to indicate that this is the right interpretation of Philomela's feelings; certainly she did not seem ashamed when she was accusing Tereus at the end of Act One. Later, based on the urgency of Philomela's gestures, Procne responds, "Yes softsister, I hear you."[46] But it is hard for the audience to share in Procne's hermeneutic confidence.

The tapestry is another instance of nonverbal communication used as a substitute for the spoken word. As Philomela weaves the tapestry, the chorus describes it thus:

He said writing is offbreaking bits of yourself
so she bleeds her torn story in the sun.
Red on white broadsheet she weaves with upcut freman
the vulgar vowels and clustered consonants
of her unsung requiem.

Her needle stutters tofro as she
punctures the sighing drapery collapsed
in her arms to give with each pierce
to contrapuntal string cords.[47]

In the first stanza, her tapestry is likened to a text written in red on white paper. Then it becomes a piece of music, a requiem. The second stanza continues this aural imagery. Her needle "stutters"—a word that sounds like "shuttles" but invokes instead the sound of a voice speaking. The loom becomes a musical instrument with strings that can be struck to make sounds. Unlike spoken language, which repeatedly fails in the play, the tapestry succeeds in conveying her message. The chorus takes one look at it, and asks immediately, "He did this?"—as if the meaning of the image was instantaneously accessible and required no time to interpret. In the next scene, Procne "reads" the image like a comic strip in sixteen frames, summarizing each scene aloud as she goes, her comprehension perfect and instantaneous. But then the audience wonders, how exactly would Philomela depict internal emotions like loneliness or desire? This is to say nothing of the amount of detail that a tapestry like this would require. It is a kind of fantasy of perfect communication, in which no detail is lost or misinterpreted, in stark contrast with the characters' vexed attempts to communicate with one another in spoken language.

This play too is antitextual, in its way. As in *Nayatt School*, there is a proliferation of words, and a foregrounding of those words in their material dimensions, but they are emptied of their power. What Philomela says after Tereus cuts her tongue out, however insistent she is, ultimately does not matter. The audience cannot see or hear it. All we know is what her movements and expressions seem to say, and these are filtered through the interpretive paradigms imputed by Tereus, Procne, and the chorus. Thus, Laurens hints at the pitfalls of spoken and nonverbal communication. The play is not merely antitextual, then, for it also shows us the limits of a purely physical theater, even as it undercuts the supremacy of verbal communication.

Staging the Lyric

Modernist Antecedents: Gertrude Stein's Byron *A Play* and William Carlos Williams's *Many Loves*

Perhaps more surprising than Laurens's play are the Modernist plays that anticipate the Wooster Group's postdramatic use of verse drama. But what Claire Warden argues about British theater in the second half of the twentieth century—that its most important experiments were "preceded and anticipated" by an earlier theatrical avant-garde—is true on both sides of the Atlantic.[48] One difference between Britain and the United States is that late-twentieth-century American playwrights tend to take their cues from Modernist poets as much, if not more, than they do from the theater world. Stein, for example, found that attention to language in its material dimensions was well-matched to the theater—in fact, it made for better theater. In her essay "Plays," she asserts, "Plays in prose do not read so well. The words in prose are livelier when they are not in a play. I am not saying anything about why, it is just a fact."[49] She also claims that the theater makes for better poetry, or at least that "[p]oetry connected with a play was livelier poetry than poetry unconnected with a play." Taken together, these declarations point to what is for Stein an essential compatibility. Recalling her experience attending Sarah Bernhardt's plays as a teenager, Stein explains,

> I knew a little french of course but really it did not matter, it was all so foreign and her voice being so varied and it all being so french I could rest in it untroubled. And I did.
> It was better than opera because it went on. It was better than the theatre because you did not have to get acquainted. The manners and customs of the french theatre created a thing in itself, and it existed in and for itself as the poetical plays had that I used so much to read, there were so many characters just as there were in those plays and you did not have to know them they were so foreign, and the foreign scenery and actuality replaced the poetry and the voices replaced the portraits. It was for me a very simple direct and moving picture.[50]

The very incomprehensibility of the language is what makes it enjoyable for her; she prefers the experience of a play as "a thing in itself": sound and spectacle to be taken in, rather than signs to be interpreted. For Stein, then, communication is a kind of distraction: one has to "get acquainted" with the characters and the story in order to understand what is happening and what it means. When this imperative is obviated by the use of a foreign language, she is freed up to enjoy the language as sound, the action as spectacle.

In her own writing for theater, Stein tries to recreate this experience by defamiliarizing English words through grammatical games and syntactic contortions. A good example of this is *Byron A Play* (1933). Like much of Stein's work for the theater, it has no plot, and its character names are not that of human persons but divisions of a playscript (Act I, Scene I, and so on). Whether or not it is a play in the theatrical sense, it is certainly a text *at play*—full of puns, especially on the word "play" itself. Even the title becomes part of the game, as in the following lines voiced by "Act 1":

> Byron a play
> Byron at play
> Byron they play
> Byron may play
> A play so they say[51]

These lines run through several possible permutations of the word "play," as well as the word "Byron," raising the possibility that it too might be a noun, a verb, a character, an actor—or, elsewhere in the play, an adverbial prepositional phrase ("by run"). Sequences like this anticipate—and likely inspire—Joyelle McSweeney's algorithmic word play in *The Commandrine* (2004) and *Dead Youth* (2013). These grammar games draw our attention to the parts of speech and to the way the sentence is constructed. To the extent they communicate anything, it is the question "What is a play or Byron."[52] Later on, "Scene 1" declares:

> I wish now to say what the relation is of a play
> > To words
> > Or not to words[53]

James Schaefer identifies the many puns embedded in these lines: we are invited to read "to" not only as a preposition, as the grammar of the sentence implies, but also—thanks to the allusion to *Hamlet*—as part of an infinitive, such that "words" becomes a verb.[54] Stein, of course, never tells us what the "relation" between "a play" and "words" is, but rather casts doubt on the entire enterprise of using words to make a play, at least in the traditional sense. Her approach is to play with words, rather than play the words—to treat them as ends in themselves, rather than a means to a communicative end. Like

Staging the Lyric

Marinetti's *parole in libertà*, Stein's plays call into question the suitability of language for the communicative ends to which it is traditionally put.

There are hints of this kind of verse drama—attentive to language as image and sound, skeptical of its communicative power—in Williams's too. His play *Many Loves* makes a useful case study insofar as it straddles the historical divide between Modernist literature and postdramatic theater: it was written in 1941, by one of the most famous American Modernist poets, and staged for the first time in 1958 by the experimental performance group the Living Theatre. The whole play is framed as a kind of experiment by its subtitle, "Trial Horse No. 1." The term "trial horse" comes from boxing, and it refers to an experienced but less-skilled opponent that a champion can practice with, as preparation for a future fight. In *Many Loves*, the "trial horse" is a certain kind of theater—stylized, experimental—being staged as a series of performances within the play. It takes the form of a series of "playlets," as Williams calls them, scenes that are being rehearsed by an experimental theater company, led by playwright and director Hubert. Each one stages a different vignette, with an entirely different cast of characters, a nod to the structure of Noël Coward's *Tonight at 8:30*.[55] But unlike Coward's plays, Williams's prose playlets are linked by a metatheatrical frame story, rendered in verse, that reveals the tension between the Hubert, the director, and his frustrated patron and would-be lover Peter, who wants the performance to conform to conventional theatrical norms. Hubert says he rejects "the firearms and other claptrap" of the mainstream theater of his day, and seeks new forms that achieve "something else, in the words themselves, / tragic without vulgarity" or "coarseness."[56] His own approach he describes as a kind of "trial and error" that allows him to "restudy / the means" to find a new way "to present love, / dramatically."[57]

Williams pursues similar ends, except that in *his* play, verse drama is the trial horse. He uses metatheatrical interludes in verse—the conversations among Peter, Hubert, and Hubert's fiancé Alise—to mount a "counter-plot" to the prose playlets.[58] Bay-Cheng argues that the counter-plot "attacks the sentimentality of realist drama as a façade for sexual power and exploitation."[59] The play itself stages several realist dramas: both in the prose playlets and the metatheatrical frame story in verse. We see Hubert trying to mount a similar attack on sentimentality in the miniature love stories he is rehearsing. But by the end of *Many Loves*, Williams exposes even Hubert as a hypocrite. The fact that Hubert must hide his relationship with Alise from Peter to ensure backing for the production suggests that both love and theater are compromised by crass financial considerations. But the ending, in which

Hubert and Alise are bullied by Peter to get married on the spot, is not a happy one. Alise realizes that Hubert will not run away with her because he still harbors some kind of love for, or dependence on, Peter. Their marriage is already a sham, and the minister, when he arrives, declares the whole scene "preposterous." Peter's love for Hubert is undercut too; the rest of the cast and crew laugh as he tries one last time to warn Alise away from Hubert.

Bay-Chang's use of the word "attack" is apt. Hubert thinks of himself as launching an attack on theater—and love too, claiming that the best way to represent love today is "by spitting in it."[60] By framing the entire play according to a concept from boxing, Williams intimates aggression under the surface. Bay-Cheng locates this aggression in the verse itself, describing Williams's verse as "an antagonistic, even combative test of his audience." The audience, then, is the target of this experimental training, the opponent this trial horse is squaring off against; the purpose of training with this kind of trial horse is to unravel the bad habits of interpretation (and bad taste) that developed from the training they received from realist plays. Bay-Cheng thinks the play "mocks the audience's perceived need for plot, cogent character, and naturalistic dialogue" by making Peter the representative of this approach to the theater, "thereby suggesting," Bay-Cheng speculates, "that such expectations reveal perverse desire."[61]

The metatheatrical frame is part of this attack, insofar as it contributes to the uneasy feeling the audience experiences all along. The play opens on the cast and crew preparing for a theatrical performance. Williams's stage directions call attention to the way that this metatheatrical frame story punctures the illusion of theater, explaining, "It is as if the spectator had come into the theater as might a friend of some member of the company, and what confronts him is an illusion of the theater more profound than an audience is ever allowed to see."[62] This is similar to what happens in *Nayatt School*, both in Gray's opening monologue, as the audience is filing in, and a few scenes later, when the cast sets up for Act III of *The Cocktail Party* in full view of the audience. This opening scene, at once exposé and illusion, makes theatrical space feel "darkening, menaced" as the actors continue their preparations without acknowledging the audience. This vague sense of menace lingers even after the scripted dialogue begins.

The play was staged for the first time many years later, in 1959, when Julian Beck and Judith Malina produced it for the Living Theatre, with Malina playing Alise.[63] Their production leans into the staginess of Williams's text, playing up the metatheatrical elements so as to erode further the border between the real world and the world of the play. For instance, the actors went down to sit with the audience between scenes, as if the playlets really were just rehearsals for a future performance. This decision may have been informed by Brecht's influential 1948 production of *Antigone*, in which the actors sat on benches on stage when they were not playing their parts. Brecht explains, "[t]he reason why the actors sit openly on the stage and only adopt attitudes proper to their parts once they enter the (very brilliantly lit) acting area is that the audience must not be able to think that it has been transported to the scene of the story, but must be invited to take part in the delivery."[64] Thus, it contributes to a systematic effort to "literarize" the theater. Literarization, according to Brecht, involves "punctuating 'representation' with 'formulation,'" thereby rendering the drama an object of study, like a work of literature, rather than immersive experience.[65] One way to cultivate this effect, Brecht says, is for the actor to "make visible preparations" for whatever he is about to do, so that the audience is conscious of each act as part of a performance.[66] The use of discrete playlets, the metatheatrical elements, the argument between Peter and Hubert about what theater ought to be, the use of verse itself—all of this works to "literarize" *Many Loves*.

Beck and Malina's production also made the play's unconventional beginning even more bewildering. They began with an open curtain, as Williams prescribes, and introduced into the preparation scene a blown fuse and blackout just before the show's start time. Consequently, the audience was made to sit in darkness as Hubert and an electrician work to figure out the problem with the lights and fix it so that rehearsals may proceed. On the European tour in 1961–62, this trick "caused a sensation."[67] Terrell W. Marrs observes that the effect is that "the audience was not entirely sure when the play started": is it when the lights come back on? Is it when Hubert and Peter switch from prose to verse? Is it when the first playlet begins?[68] This makes the audience conscious of the play *as a play*, instead of becoming immersed in the action and dialogue.

The verse too draws attention to itself as verse, especially in contrast with the prose, which is established as the baseline at the beginning of the play. The switch happens abruptly in the first scene: Hubert is in the middle of a passionate defense, in prose, of his emerging new style when he suddenly drops into verse, seemingly in the middle of a line. This first line—fraction of a line, really—looks like the second half of a shared verse line:

Hubert Yes, it can—believe me! And it *must* be all that, to come alive at all! There's nothing virginal, nothing completely novel left for us other than complexities.

>   But some one
> must first have seen the complex
> simple, simple as water flowing ...
> that was ice, and made it flow, so
> that it appears an easy matter: to
> give the word a metaphorical twist by
> the position it assumes, the elevation
> it induces—without pictorial effects—
> by the force of its meaning; a similarity
> to daily speech, the miracle being it
> sounds so, but by the awakening experienced
> is proven otherwise, charged to raise the
> spirit to a full enjoyment.[69]

Why switch to verse now, in the middle of Hubert's speech? Eleanor Berry's account of "sight-stanzas" in Williams's poetry is instructive here. She identifies "frequent and arbitrary strong enjambment," as early as "Canthara" (1917) and throughout *Spring and All* (1923), as a technique by which Williams tests his ability to set words as visual image against their expressive effect.[70] Berry explains:

> To arrange a text in sight-stanzas is to lay a grid across it that cuts the flow of language arbitrarily into visually equal segments; the interruptions made by the metrical divisions obtrude and have (will have until divisions of this kind are so accustomed as to go unnoticed) the effect of defamiliarizing individual words and the manner of their syntactical relations.[71]

The sight-stanza allows Williams to play image and rhythm against one another. This interplay of visible division and audible flow keeps the audience's attention on the visual and aural properties of language. The purpose of this defamiliarization, Berry says, is to "de-automatize the process of reading."[72] It also renders the poem "perceptible as a verbal object":

> More than simply an arrangement in lines whose length is not contingent upon the width of a line of type, a stanzaic format asserts that the text in question is to be read as a poem, that is, as a work of verbal art, a composition in the medium of language, in other words, that its language is to be looked at for itself, not looked through to get

at a meaning. A stanzaic format amounts to an invitation from the writer to give attention to the particulars of the language of the text, to regard them as intentional rather than contingent.[73]

This may be what Huber means when he praises poetry's ability to "give the word a metaphorical twist by / the position it assumes."

In *Many Loves*, the switch from prose to verse—which happens again each time a playlet ends and we return our attention to the three main characters—functions similarly. In performance, the audience cannot tell that Hubert, Alice, and Peter are speaking in lines of roughly the same visible length—and Williams's verse never quite lands on an audible pattern of accents or syllables. So, instead of playing with enjambment and line breaks to set image and sound against one another as he does on the page, Williams sets prose and verse against each other.

Hubert's first speech in verse, the lines quoted above, sets up a similar dynamic of division and flow. Hubert invokes ice as his metaphor for verse: writing good dramatic verse is like making ice flow. The ideal verse dramatist is one who can see the simple in the complex, can discern the liquid potential of the solid and realize that potential. In other words, take a form and "[make] it flow."[74] Notice that Hubert specifies water that had been ice; it is important to him that it once had a solid form. We see this interplay if we look at this passage on the page: the sentence itself does not flow, but appears to the eye as if it starts and stops, thanks to the syncopation of punctuation and line endings, particularly in the lines that end in "so" and "to." Hubert wants to write dialogue that flows like "daily speech" but affects the audience as poetry would, inducing "elevation," "awakening," and "enjoyment." "Elevation" and "enjoyment"—and even "awakening," although to a lesser extent—do not occur at the level of rationality; they are process that take place above and below reason, so to speak, at spiritual and physical level.

This paradoxical rendering of the real through the formalized—water flowing through ice—is what Williams himself strives for in his lyric poetry. Thomas Kilroy argues that *Many Loves* "strain[s] towards a theatrical version" of Williams's poetry, with words that "seize upon the particular, giving it such a vivid particularity that it becomes, by virtue of impression, general and extensive in application and even, at certain moments, universal."[75] He achieves this "realism of a peculiarly exaggerated kind" by combining language that is realistic in its frankness and spontaneity, as in the mainstream realist theater of his day, but, at the same time, forcing the audience's attention to the words themselves, as a lyric poet might, in a setting that is "at an extreme remove from the ordinary ground and tilth of common speech." Kilroy classifies this as a Brechtian move. Like Brecht—and Beckett too—Williams strives to get right up against the line between language's representational and non-representation effects, or, to put it another way, between language as mimesis and language as gesture. For Brecht, this kind of stylization ought to be grounded always in the natural. As Brecht explains, stylization must not "destroy naturalness" but rather "heighten it."[76] Kilroy sees Williams's efforts in this direction as part of a more general attempt, in the first half of the twentieth century, "To remain scrupulously faithful to the way people actually speak and yet devise forms of drama which would liberate the imagination from the more leaden features of naturalism."[77]

It seems to have worked. Or, at the very least, we can say that the Living Theatre production of *Many Loves* was a success, and on these terms, according to Beck.[78] Here is Beck in a letter to Williams, describing the first performance:

> The form of the play stood up wonderfully: all of the calculated effects seemed to come off with a genuine aplomb. The actors enjoyed acting it (always a sign of a good play), and the response was truly exciting. The language rang so clean that it seemed as if the play was written in an altogether new tongue. One listened for every word; and yet there was the constant feeling that what was being said was a factual duplication of everyday speech.

Williams's play, then, achieves what Hubert hoped for, language that sounds like "daily speech, the miracle being it / sounds so."[79]

Heidi Bean considers *Many Loves*, along with the other verse plays they staged in 1950s, to be crucial to the Living Theatre's development, despite the obvious differences between this play and the work the group would go on to do. Bean argues that these early experiments with verse "led directly to experiments in antitextual theatre."[80] Christopher Innes makes a similar argument about the continuity between the Living Theatre's "text-based, even highly literary" first phase and its later phases, which he classifies as "physical theater" insofar as the "core meaning" is "carried by the mise-en-scene."[81] The play itself cues up the conflict between drama as text and drama in performance. Hubert tells Peter: "It won't do. Let some idiot—in / the usual arty fashion—make / a book of it. But don't seek to produce it."[82] In

Staging the Lyric

Peter's mind, Hubert's work makes sense as closet drama, but not as theater. To succeed in the theater, a play must follow conventions, must make sense to the audience. Recall that the playlets in question are not even in verse. Peter is even more dismissive of the idea of a verse play; it too is incompatible with modern commercial theater. From Williams's perspective—and Beck's and Malina's too, presumably—the opposition between verse and the theater is conventional, arising from norms the audience has been conditioned to expect by mainstream theater in prose. Thus, verse becomes an attractive option for the Living Theatre, and the Off-Broadway movement that followed in its wake, who wanted to shake up conventional theater with new content as well as new forms.

But there is a crucial difference between this play, especially as staged by the Living Theatre, and Brecht's epic theater. Ultimately, Brecht, and the English-language playwrights like Auden and Arden who follow him, holds out hope, in theater and in language. The plays in this chapter are much less sanguine about the possibility of reform; in fact, they evince very little hope in communication itself. As Bill Blake observes, antitextual theater "is about prying away at the social instability of insight and exposing problems of miscommunication, not treating these problems as correctable."[83] For Lehmann, Brecht's epic theater is not a precursor to postdramatic theater, but "a renewal and completion" of traditional Aristotelian dramaturgy.[84] Rather, it is in the lyrical drama of Maeterlinck, the static theater of Claudel, and the landscape plays of Stein that he finds precedent for postdramatic attempts to undercut Aristotelian notions of plot, character, and time. Counterintuitively then, what could be considered a highly textual—perhaps even the most "literary"—form of theater, verse drama, sets up for the antitextual and postdramatic movements of the second half of the twentieth century. But over and over, we see antitextual performance groups like the Living Theatre and the Wooster Group reaching back to Modernist poets like Williams and Eliot for verse drama to stage (and sometimes tear apart). This is because verse drama, by its very essence, enacts a kind of autonomization of language, whether explicit, as it is in Stein's plays, or implicit, as it is in Williams's. This autonomization—a ceding of autonomy to the words themselves, no longer under the complete control of playwright or character—is a quintessentially postmodern impulse, and Lehmann takes it to be the *sine qua non* of postdramatic theater. But it is just as much a feature of lyric poetry, especially after Modernism, insofar as the poet gives himself or herself over to the coincidences and contingencies of the language in which they write, following the patterns of sound and sight as they arise. In the next section, we will see an analogous dynamic, but with respect to time: verse drama, by incorporating lyric notions of temporality, ends up contributing to postdramatic efforts to undercut the conventions by which time is represented and understood in the Western theatrical tradition since Aristotle.

PART III
TIME

CHAPTER 5
TEMPORALITY

Before I turn to plays that use lyric techniques to manipulate the audience's experience of time, I want to look at how poets do this kind of thing. In "I Catch Sight of the Now," Jorie Graham meditates on the human experience of time in the present. Even the present moment, which feels more real to us than past or future, reveals itself, in the course of the poem, to be an illusion—compelling and necessary, but illusory nonetheless. At the start, the "I" notices an:

> unforgettable though then hardly noticed green
> tiled ledge
> just up to my right in the glistening shower stall, [...][1]

The ledge is something she "always" sees, but on "this day," the light passing through the window, refracted through the water droplets formed by condensation, draws her attention to it for the first time. As she becomes newly conscious of her surroundings, she reflects on the singularity of the present moment:

> it's just day, just this day, another day, filled with the only
> of this minute, this split minute, in which if I
> reach now I can feel
> the years, the fissure in them,
> these fractions here inside the
> instant

For an instant, time appears to her as substance, as a thing that can be felt, filled, or split. Each minute is an object, made up of the accretion of past minutes and years, like a sedimentary rock. Graham reinforces this substantiation of time on a grammatical level, turning the adjective "only" into a concrete noun—something she also does to the adverbs "now" and "suddenly." Once it takes a physical form, "this minute" becomes something that can be possessed, something she can call "—oh mine—how mine—."[2] But this apparent possession is an illusion. The very physicality that seems to make possession possible also opens it up to the possibility of division: a minute can be split, the years give way to fissures, even the instant admits of fractions. The speaker's emerging awareness of time's infinite divisibility causes her to observe that time is "moving now so / differently."[3] Perhaps time is slowing down, as it is divided into smaller and smaller units. In any case, "the now" is not where—or when—she thought it was, and evades her grasp, even as she reaches for it.

The experience of time in this poem comports with Henri Bergson's observations in *Time and Free Will*. Bergson argues that we cannot quantify or measure time except insofar as we imagine it as space. To count moments of time, he says, "We involuntarily fix at a point in space each of the moments which we count."[4] For, as Bergson observes, "How could we split it up into fractions whilst affirming its unity, if we did not regard it implicitly as an extended object, one in intuition but multiple in space."[5] This is exactly what the speaker does in Graham's poem: she tries to turn moments into physical objects that can be located, felt, and possessed. But despite the sense of physical presence that the poem attributes to the present moment, the speaker's awareness of the instant's infinite divisibility leads her to assert: "there is no fire, there is no / room, actually there is nothing."[6] In what follows, the idea of the room that is not there becomes paradoxical figure for the elusiveness of the present: she registers the experience as "the roomlessness of this your *suddenly*."[7] Just as a room is not a substantial thing, but rather empty space defined by physical boundaries, the present is not a thing in itself with any real substance, but an impression created by temporal boundaries—the division of time into years, days, hours, minutes.

Up until this point, Graham has been recording an experience of what is often called "subjective time," but by the end, she asserts that even the most objective, scientific measures of time are similarly illusory:

> the daylight now is pouring itself,
> though it is not pouring anything at all or into
> anything at all because it's just the planet
> turning again and again into and out of the
> dark which is not itself actually dark
> at all.[8]

Light cannot "pour itself" because it has no physical substance; this is a metaphor we have invented. Graham goes as far as to deny the transcendent reality of categories like day and night, insisting on their phenomenological quality, as impressions we perceive as a result of the earth's rotation, depending on where we are. Even day and night are categorical divisions we have invented so that we might grasp time.

And yet, the poem tells us, "you" can still "start carving the nothing, you can test your strength / against the nothing." This is, in one sense, an invitation for all of us to keep doing what we are doing: dividing up time in order to comprehend it. As Bergson acknowledges, we cannot help but "materialize time." But Graham's injunction also points to an analogy between time and poetry. The meter and rhythm are often described in temporal terms. The page is a different kind of space, but space nonetheless; it allows us to freeze a moment and study it. A line of verse is divisible, like a unit of time, which Graham aptly demonstrates by means of enjambment within phrases and even within words, like "for- / ever." And these divisions, between feet and between lines, are significant; they are an essential part of the way poets make meaning. Poems are like rooms: spaces defined by arbitrary boundaries—hence the word *stanza*, Italian for "room." Graham's interest in the power of boundaries to give form to abstractions like time helps make sense of her decision to justify the lines of the poem along the right-hand margin. The poem also offers a meditation on human mortality: a life is defined, to some extent, by its end. That is, death circumscribes a life's extent and thus determines its shape. In the same way, the right margin—the end of the line, rather than the beginning—is the ordering principle of this poem, a meditation organized around endings rather than beginnings.

Likewise, the playwrights I will discuss in this chapter, Beckett and Yeats, use verse to "test [their] strength against the nothing," to carve insubstantial time into something with a physical shape, such that it can be manipulated. But, in the process, they never let the audience lose sight of "the now": our experience of time as both substance and nonsubstance, and the fact that this room, the temporal frame, has been constructed out of the "roomlessness" of time. In doing so, they are part of the lyric tradition of creating an experience of suspended moment via the incantatory elements of lyric poetry.

This self-conscious manipulation of time is certainly not limited to the lyric. In fact, it is one of the hallmarks of postdramatic theater that would emerge in the late twentieth century. Postdramatic theater, as theorized by Lehmann, rebels against the conventions of and assumptions behind what he calls the "Aristotelian dramatic tradition"—not just the realism of the late nineteenth and early twentieth century, but the whole theatrical tradition in the West, from Aeschylus to Brecht. One essential strategy of this traditional theater, according to Lehmann, is "to prevent the appearance of time as time."[9] Postdramatic theater, by contrast, seeks to make the audience conscious of time. Lehmann explains:

> For only an experience of time that deviates from habit provokes its explicit perception, permitting it to move from something taken for granted as a mere accompaniment to the rank of a theme. Thus, a new phenomenon in the aesthetics of theatre is established: the intention of utilizing the specificity of theatre as a mode of presentation to turn *time as such* into an object of aesthetic experience.[10]

He goes on to identify four techniques that typify the postdramatic treatment of time: duration, repetition, visualization, and simultaneity. The goal behind all of these different aesthetic strategies is to puncture the "fantasy of continuity" that traditional drama strives to preserve.[11]

Two of these techniques are of particular interest to me here: duration and repetition. The plays I will consider in this chapter cultivate both, but they do so by drawing upon lyric techniques. Lehmann contends that under the Aristotelian regime, realist drama "was able to incorporate" lyric elements "without losing its dramatic character."[12] But it seems to me that once verse was rejected by the realist theater of the late nineteenth century, it became possible to reintroduce poetry as an anti-realistic—and therefore, potentially postdramatic—element in a play. In *Poetry and the Fate of the Senses*, Susan Stewart observes, "Speech in a poem, like speech in the face-to-face communication of everyday life, is articulated in time. But unlike speech oriented toward conversational purposes, speech in a poem is not absorbed in time"; therefore, she claims, poets can "counter that temporal absorption" with "[a]ttention to the material elements of form"—just as we saw it working against absorption into plot in the last two chapters.[13] Beckett and Yeats use lyric strategies to draw the audience's attention to time. In *Rockaby*, Beckett gives time a solid form, slowing down the action of the play until it approaches a tableau. Similarly, in *Purgatory*, Yeats carves time into the shape of a circle, an endless, repetitive cycle. Although neither is universally classified as postdramatic, they share in common the use of lyric enunciation—via what I will call the ritualistic elements of lyric—to cultivate a sense of lyric temporality, which works against the plays' fictional elements like plot and character development.

Allow me one note about my terms before I dive in: "ritual" used to be a fashionable way of talking about theater, among both critics and practitioners.

During the 1970s, experimental performance groups began to use the term to describe theater that draws the audience in as participants. Critics took up this way of talking about theater, warranted by an origin myth which traces all forms of theater back to primitive rituals.[14] Richard Schechner—founder of both The Performance Group (which would become the Wooster Group) as well as what we now call performance studies—uses the word to mean any theatrical action that is "a manifestation rather than a communication."[15] But his contemporary Anthony Graham-White objected to the expansive application of a concept from anthropology beyond its technical meaning as a "performance on behalf of [...] a group or community that expresses or enforces some of its deepest values at a time (usually) of change," and offered the word "ceremony" as an alternative for critics who want to talk about a "patterned form of social expression" or a "recurrent act of symbolic communication."[16] I will be talking about theatrical action that is "a manifestation rather than a communication," but theorizing it in lyric, rather than theatrical terms. In lyric theory, especially in the work of Greene, von Hallberg, and Culler, rituality refers to a poem's bid to make something happen, to constitute an "event of language," as Culler says.[17] Greene defines lyric ritual as

> the poem's office as directions for a performance—a script, that is, compounded of sounds that serve referential or expressive purposes in nonpoetic contexts, other sounds (such as "hey-nonny-noonny" or "oba-la-la") that have no other contexts, and the patterns that organize these sounds in the reader-auditor's experience.[18]

In fact, he considers the "dialectical play" of ritualistic and fictional elements to be the essential feature of the lyric.[19] Beckett and Yeats, in their verse dramas, set up exactly this dialectic, between ritual and fiction, creating a scant fiction and using fictional elements to advance that plot, in alternation with ritualistic elements that obstruct or undermine the plot's progress.

Samuel Beckett's *Rockaby*: "Time she stopped"

Beckett's plays are often described as "poetic," but only rarely classified as verse drama. In radio plays like *Embers* (1959), *Rough for Radio I* (1961), and *Cascando* (1962), as well as the television play *Eh Joe* (1966), however, regular pauses serve the same function as line breaks, telling the actor when to take a breath, and guiding the actor or director toward certain groupings of words or clauses. *Rockaby* is the rare example of a play with true line breaks, although it is not often called a verse play. Ruby Cohn scans its lines as "rough dimeter"; most have two stresses, but the overall number of syllables is flexible, ranging from two to six.[20] Enoch Brater goes as far as to call *Rockaby* "a lyrical drama," an indication that the play has more in common with lyric poetry than just the use of verse.[21] Indeed, Beckett uses incantatory repetition a la lyric, which works in his play to subvert plot by rendering time as a cycle rather than succession of events.

Written in 1980 for a festival in his honor at State University of New York, Buffalo, in 1981, *Rockaby* features many of the hallmarks of Beckett's style: a single actor on an almost-bare stage, shrouded in darkness and engaged in compulsive speech and constrained movement, all described in exacting detail by Beckett in extensive stage directions. The character, identified only as "woman in chair" or "W," is carried slowly forward and back by a rocking chair while listening to a recording of her own voice ("V").[22] As in *Krapp's Last Tape* (1958) and *That Time* (1976), Beckett uses sound recording technology to create a double for the character on stage. Like *Waiting for Godot* and *Happy Days*, the play can be divided up into sections, in which the same action and speech is repeated, almost exactly. If *Godot* is "a play in which nothing happens, twice," as Vivian Mercier famously quipped, *Rockaby* is a play in which nothing happens four times.[23] Each of the iterations, which Cohn calls "movements," begin when the woman says "More," which triggers the rocking chair and the recording. Then, after another 50 or 60 lines of the recording, the rocking and recording come to a stop, the final line echoing as the stage lights fade. After a long pause, the cycle begins again: the lights come up, the woman in the chair cries for "More," and both rocking and recording resume.

Based on V's recorded monologues, the audience can reconstruct an adumbrated narrative of W's life. The first monologue describes her "going to and fro" out in the world, seeking "another like herself."[24] At some point, she realized it was "time she stopped" this search, and so she retreated to her home, according to the second monologue, and started looking out her window for "one other living soul / at her window / gone in like herself."[25] Eventually, she lost hope of finding even that, and began to look only for "one blind up."[26] Finally, in the last monologue, V describes the woman putting down the blind, walking down the stairs, and sitting down in her rocking chair to wait for death. In light of this backstory, the audience might be tempted to classify *Rockaby* as one of Beckett's more conventional dramas—especially compared to other plays from this period, like *Quad*. It does achieve a kind of psychological realism, insofar as it represents a character's state of mind through symbolic action.[27]

But while the monologues may seem confessional at first, even with the distance created by the third-person pronouns, the fact that they are presented as recordings—a thing made, not overheard—undercuts any assumption that they are artless self-disclosure. W is less like a traditional dramatic character and more like what Culler calls "effects of voicing" or what Greene calls a "person-representation"—that is, the impression of a fictional character created by a text. It is an example of Beckett's tendency, identified by Charles Lyons, "to present an illusion of character, sustained by the physical presence of the actor, and then [...] to dissolve the spectator's belief in the authenticity of that image."[28] The play never even confirms that the woman described in the recorded monologues is W, although we are led to accept V's fragmentary lines as W's backstory. Beckett gives us just enough fiction within the recordings to tempt us to interpret "W" as a conventional dramatic character, but gives phenomenal force to a staged ritual that threatens to undermine the fiction.

In fact, Beckett never clarifies the relationship between what we see on the stage and what we hear in the recording. This ambiguity manifests in at least three ways: in terms of character, as I have just observed; with respect to temporality, which I will turn to in a moment; and, ultimately, the hermeneutic status of the dramatic action itself. In all three cases, interpretation turns on whether one takes these elements to be mimetic (part of a dramatic fiction that represents something that might happen in the real world), or ritualistic (those elements that are in excess of or contradictory to the story V tells). Here I am drawing on Greene's account of the tension between fiction and ritual in lyric discourse. Fictional elements exist in all literary forms, even the lyric, but in lyric discourse, Greene argues, fiction must contend with ritual, which works against narrative plot and sometimes character development. In *Rockaby*, the recorded monologues invite the audience to interpret the play as fiction by piecing together a narrative to make sense of a character and her life. But the play itself enacts a ritual, one that cannot be fully accounted for by mimetic interpretation, and several of what Greene would identify as ritual elements come through even in the recordings.

Let's consider the action on stage. In what Lehmann calls the Aristotelian dramatic tradition, a play depicts something that might happen in real life, whether or not these actions have some kind of significance on top of their mimetic function. The behavior of the actor might reveal a character's emotional state, or it might have a broader meaning that applies to human nature more generally. In either case, action is mimetic first, symbolic second. What we have in *Rockaby*, by contrast, is action that is essentially symbolic. This is why I find it helpful to approach at least this Beckett play as a kind of postdramatic theater. There is no real-life precedent for a woman listening to a recording of her own voice over and over again, while an automated rocking chair rocks her to sleep. In fact, we might call the action of the play a staged symbol—figurative language that has been embodied in performance. Matthew Wagner's reading of the dagger scene in *Macbeth* could be helpful here. Wagner argues that, in the famous scene in Act II, Scene 1, the force of Macbeth's apostrophic address of the dagger is such that "the psychology of our anti-hero is secondary to the theatrical phenomenon of making *that which doesn't exist* present and real in the material world."[29] Certainly, Macbeth's hallucination reveals the extent to which "this bloody business" has affected his "heat-oppressed brain," but the psychological insight the audience gleans about Macbeth from this episode is not sufficient to account for Shakespeare's choice to use apostrophe, rather than third-person description or even the self-address that quickly gives way to second-person at the beginning of the speech ("Is this a dagger which I see before me, / The handle toward my hand? Come, let me clutch thee").[30] Along similar lines, Culler urges readers of lyric poetry to move beyond a simplistic understanding of apostrophes "as intensifiers, as images of invested passion"; he identifies three additional "levels of reading," all of which involve a poetic attempt "to will a state of affairs," to make something happen through language.[31] Macbeth's apostrophe makes something happen: it makes the dagger real to us. It works because, as Culler observes with respect to lyric apostrophe, its "presuppositions are deeply embedded, asserted more forcefully because they are not what the sentence asserts."[32] In the context of a theatrical production, Macbeth's apostrophe, according to Wagner, draws the audience's attention to the essential magic of the theater, its ability to make a world out of words. But insofar as it enacts an impossible act of address with no visible confirmation of its success, this particular apostrophe approximates lyric ritual.

Likewise, in *Rockaby*, the dramatic import of the character's speech is secondary to the lyric event of language that speech enacts. The recordings, although they supply much of the detail that contributes to the illusion of dramatic fiction, are themselves a kind of incantation. Brater, who goes as far as to call V "the voice of lyric poetry," argues that "Sound [. . .] structures sight in *Rockaby*"—his way of saying that the language comes first, dictating the mimetic action on the stage, not the other way around.[33] The plot of the play, such as it is, realizes in performance what the voice says in the recording, so that "woman seated on stage slowly becomes the image created by her own inner voice."[34] It is not a matter of words representing human behavior, but of human bodies manifesting the words.

Brater's reading is further warranted by the play's thematic treatment of self-address. The recordings mention seven times the unnamed woman talking "to herself / whom else" in an effort to become "her own other."[35] This attempt to invent an interlocutor parallels Harry Dernier's acts of address in the Walcott play discussed in Chapter Two. Presumably, the act we see before us on the stage—her constrained colloquy with herself via recording—is the means by which she becomes "her own other." But the timeline is unclear. Do these lines describe the action we see on stage? In other words, did this woman, at some point in the past, record her own voice to play back? Or is V describing an instance in which the woman spoke to herself in a more conventional sense at some point in the past? In other words, are we to interpret these lines reference to the ritual or to the fiction? This temporal confusion is the second manifestation of the tension between ritual and fiction, as I mentioned. Nothing in the play establishes the length of time between the events described in the recording and the moment the recording was made—the moment of enunciation—or the temporal relationship between the recording and the action we see on stage, for that matter. Should we assume that the recording is somehow simultaneous with the action on stage, spoken in an identical moment of enunciation? Or was it recorded in the past, to be replayed at the later moment we see on stage? If the latter is the case, it is the only instance I know of in which the lyric act of enunciation takes place somehow before the fictional moment it is in tension with it. Greene has given a name to the temporal distance between a lyric utterance and whatever it represents: the "lyric interval." He explains:

> Lyric interval is reckoned in the accumulation of deictic elements scattering through a poem or sequence—temporal and personal inflections in nouns and verbs, spatial discriminations in adverbs and demonstratives, and so forth—and other indexes of recension, such as singular or plural objects that may particularize or conglomerate the speaker's vision, and rhythms that may imply immediacy or removal. Interval is seldom a fixed distance drawn between a lyric utterance and its objects; it often varies throughout the utterance. Local oscillations will tell much about a how a poem works fictionally, and

will entertain purposes shared with other types of nonlyric fiction, while shifts toward immediacy may figure an irruption of the ritual mode into fictional discourse.[36]

He argues that "the reckoning of a poem's interval, even if carried out implicitly or instinctively, is vital to the relative assessment of ritual and fictional modes carried out in every act of interpretation."[37] In *Rockaby*, temporal markers like "till," "in the end," and "close of a long day" establish specific moments on a narrative timeline: in the first two recorded monologues, the moment when she gives up "going to and fro" and retreats inside her house, behind her window and in the third and fourth recordings, it is the moment when she closes the blinds and retreats to her rocking chair. This kind of temporal precision is possible only within the recordings, which function as a kind of enclosure for a fictional mode within the larger ritual structure of the play. As the audience of the play, aware of both the ritual and the fiction, we wonder: Is "the end" a moment that took place at some point in the past, or is it the moment we see staged before us?

Like the tension between dramatic character and lyric speaker—which, as I argued in Chapter Two, radio verse drama inherits from Victorian dramatic monologue—the tension between these two temporal orders is a feature of many lyric poems. Stewart has observed the paradoxical way in which deictics, which in other contexts provide for spatial and temporal orientation, become, in lyric discourse, unhinged from time and place and iterable, moving from "context dependence into the figuration of context independence."[38] This iterability is possible because "Deixis fuses form, expression, and theme as one event in place and time" becoming "its own location" in space as it constitutes an event in time.[39] Stewart describes the disorienting impression that emerges from these ambiguous deictics as a kind of vertigo, an inability to reckon the spatial distances or temporal interval. This tension is only intensified when lyric is put on the stage, where the real time of performance can lend phenomenological force to the now in which the characters speak In *Rockaby*, Beckett exacerbates the audience's feeling of vertigo—which is, medically speaking, a clash of the senses—by pairing a visible body on the stage in the now of performance with an audible voice that speaks out of a different moment of enunciation, experienced by the audience as a single moment in time.

Eventually, a pattern develops: fictional time slows to a stop, giving way to the timeless present of lyric enunciation, as dramatic action ossifies into tableau. But each time this happens, fictional time once again irrupts into suspended time, and the cycle repeats itself. Theater scholars have observed that this kind of cyclical temporality in postdramatic performance art serves to undercut linear or progressive views of history. According to Vanden Heuvel, Beckett uses repetition and "recursive plot structures" to disrupt "linear plot progression" "as a means to enact dramatically the entropy that burdens his characters."[40] Entropy—which is, scientifically speaking, not just randomness but the dissipation of energy—is nowhere more obvious than in *Rockaby*, where the random repetitions and recursions suggest a kind of erosion of memory and logic at the end of life.

This cyclicality is inscribed at all levels of the play, down to the rocking chair itself. The visual effect of this back-and-forth motion is amplified by the lighting, since the actress's face moves in and out of the light as the chair rocks forwards and back. The chair itself is not supposed to make a sound, according to Beckett's instructions, but the recorded voice supplies the aural rhythm, in the form of short lines of flexible dimeter that match up, more or less, with the motion of the chair. In the first performance of the play, at the Center Theater in Buffalo, Billie Whitelaw begins each line as the chair rocks back and ends the line as comes back forward, creating a synchrony between the visual rhythm created by the motion of the rocking chair and the aural rhythm of the recorded voice.

To achieve this effect in her recorded delivery, Whitelaw moved her hand—sometimes back and forth like a metronome, sometimes like a conductor, sometimes sweeping, sometimes trembling—to regulate the speed of her delivery.[41]

Verse—especially short, spare lines of dimeter—lends itself to slow delivery. Whereas longer sentences might encourage the speaker to speed up delivery, short phrases, chopped up by line breaks, force a performer to slow down. The potential pause at the end of each line disrupts the natural flow of speech, can be used to make the audience conscious of the time that is passing. As in Graham's poem, the segmentation of time makes us aware of its passage, gives it a form that allows us to study it. Whitelaw reinforces this effect with her monotone delivery. Like the mechanical motion of the chair, her voice in the recording sounds robotic.[42] She explains in her autobiography that Beckett himself told her "not to be afraid to make it sound monotonous."[43] In fact, the goal was "to get as close to *white sound* as possible."[44] At the very end of the play, Whitelaw eliminates all variations in pitch, delivering all the syllables in perfect monotone. As she repeats the final lines—"Rock her off" and "Stop her eyes"—the rhythm of delivery—long-short-long—approaches that of Morse code.[45] Whitelaw modulates the timbre of her voice so that it sounds like a low

Figure 8 *Rockaby* (1982). Pictured: Billie Whitelaw. Reproduced with permission from photographer, Irene Ikner Haupt.

whine or squeak, not unlike the squeaking of a rocking chair—a sound otherwise absent, as per Beckett's instructions, in this production. Regardless of whether the audience hears the taps of Morse code or the squeaks of a rocking chair, the impression—thanks to the defamiliarizing effect of Whitelaw's delivery—is that of inarticulate noise, not human speech.

Lehmann points out that postdramatic theater often portrays the "physical, motoric act of speaking or reading of text itself as an *unnatural, not self-evident* process."[46] This is part of the "autonomization" of language I discussed in Chapter Four, the process by which "language appears not as the speech of characters—if there are still definable characters at all—but as an autonomous theatricality."[47] Of interest to us here is Lehmann's claim that one of the effects of this autonomization of language is to draw the audience's attention to the passage of time. And certainly, as a member of the audience of *Rockaby*, one is aware of how slowly the voice speaks, how long the pauses last, how much time has passed. It is almost impossible to get absorbed in the action and forget that one is watching a play.

The play is also a good example of what Lehmann calls the "aesthetic of repetition," another related feature of postdramatic theater. We see this repetition in the visual rhythm of the rocking chair and the aural rhythm recordings. Rocking, like so much of the action in Beckett's plays, is a kind of motion without progress. The woman in the chair is like May in *Footfalls*, who ritualistically paces back and forth across the stage, exactly nine steps each time, while counting off her steps.[48] As in *Rockaby*, we get the sense that this cyclical motion correlates with the motion of her thoughts. Near the end of the play, May asks, in what seems to be a dialogue with herself: "Will you never have done? [Pause.] Will you never have done ... revolving it all? [Pause.] It? [Pause.] It all. [Pause.] In your poor mind. [Pause.] It all. [Pause.] It all."[49] The woman in *Rockaby* also seems to be "revolving it all" as she rocks back and forth.

This sense of cyclical return is reinforced by the repetitions of words and phrases. Out of 247 total lines, there are only 88 distinction formulations; the rest are repetitions. Some are repetitions of entire lines as well as anaphoric repetitions of initial words ("all eyes / all sides").[50] There are also involuted repetitions that take place over a series of adjacent lines, as in: "for another / another like herself / another creature like herself / a little like."[51] Brater observes that "lines are rotated, made to formulate new allegiances with other words, then recombined in a different way before reassuming the original shape in which we first encountered them."[52] It is as if the voice is circling around something, getting closer and closer, but always delaying a precise, direct expression of the truth of the matter. The voice then returns to the beginning, and goes through the same lines again, making only a few small changes this time through. By the third iteration—which Whitelaw calls a "stanza"—of the first movement, V drops ten of the original seventeen lines from the first stanza. In light of what we can surmise about the woman, this decay might indicate forgetfulness or senility, but it could also be an analogue for the hazy snatches of thought we have all experienced while drifting off to sleep. The latter is the effect that the Schneider production seems to be going for: when Whitelaw opens her eyes wide and cries "More," she resembles a small child waking up with a start to discover, and immediately protest, that she is no longer being rocked.

In each of the four monologues, time subtly—almost imperceptibly—recedes. Note that the dropped lines in the second and third stanzas tend to be the ones that contain past-tense verbs ("came," "said"). Beckett eschews verb tense with help from the verse itself, which allows sentences and phrases to be cut and spliced without the grammatical connective tissue that prose requires. Jonathan Kalb likens the play to "an extended predicate that refuses to resolve; we wait and wait for an active verb but keep hearing appositives, new participles, and what seem like new subordinate clauses."[53] There is an explanation, along mimetic lines, for this drift into a fuzzy, tense-less present: the woman in the chair, and the audience along with her, might be losing track of time as she falls asleep. This is consistent with Bergson's observation that sleep is the closest we get to an experience of pure duration. But there is more to this shift from past to present. The disappearance of temporal markers signals a departure from the realm of narrative time and arrival in a lyric moment. That is, the recordings become less and less a story about something that happened in the past and more and more a ritual incantation in the present, approaching what Culler calls "iterable *now* of lyric enunciation."[54] At the end of the final monologue, the recorded voice begins to issue commands—"rock her off," "fuck life"—commands that the play itself seems to be obeying, as if the performance is a embodied realization of the poem's attempt to "will a state of affairs."

Time slows down for the audience too. Verse allows for flexibility in terms of tempo, as the director and actor can choose how long to pause between lines. In the case of *Rockaby*, the exact speed of delivery is one of the few things Beckett does not stipulate in his copious stage directions. The whole play is only 247 lines—and short ones at that—but depending on the speed of delivery and the length of the pauses, performances can range from 10 to 20 minutes.[55] The many repetitions and recursions exacerbate the audience's sense that time is dragging. Whitelaw recalls, upon first reading the script, "I couldn't quite work out the tempo, but it would have to go slowly. However, from past work with Sam, I knew that there is slow and slower and graduations of slowest."[56] As in Graham's poem, where time seems to stop as she becomes aware of the "fractions here inside the / instant," Beckett achieves a similar effect by cutting sentences and phrases into smaller and smaller "graduations"—slowing the passage of time to a standstill.

As time slows to a stop, the scene approaches tableau. The recording fades, the rocking slows to a stop, the woman in the chair falls asleep. Kalb describes *Rockaby* as a "meticulously sculpted tableau, that remains nearly motionless the entire time, allowing spectators to meditate on its metaphoric significance while a flow of words emanates from the stage, guiding meditation."[57] For most of the play, this tableau forms and dissolves, repeatedly, as ritual and fiction vie for supremacy. In each iteration of the cycle, W approaches the release from time that comes with death, then shrinks from it.[58] But even this rhythm comes to a stop at the end of the play, when W's "head slowly sinks, come[s] to rest" before the final fade out of the spotlight.[59] The ritual mode ultimately prevails, consigning the fictional mode to the not-quite-hermetically sealed enclosure of the recordings.

W.B. Yeats's *Purgatory*: "not once but many times"

It is not only in postdramatic theater, and toward postdramatic ends, that playwrights suspend and dilate moments in time; it exists in Modernist verse drama as well. As early as 1914, in *Three Travellers Watch a Sunrise*, Wallace Stevens does something similar, halting the passage of stage time the moment before the sun comes up, which delays the revelation of the body of a hanged man. The most systematic exploration of the temporal implications of lyric rituality in Modernist verse drama is W.B. Yeats's late play *Purgatory* (1938). Like *Rockaby*, *Purgatory* undermines notions of chronological time by staging ritualistic action within a fictional plot and foregrounding the iterability of that ritual.

As with *Rockaby*, *Purgatory* is deceptively simple. A.S. Knowland and Richard Taylor call it Yeats's most accessible play, perhaps because, as veteran Yeats director Robert McNamara observes, it is "closest to realism."[60] In this short play, Yeats's second-to-last, an "Old Man" brings a "Boy," his son, to a desolate spot, with only a "ruined house" and a "bare tree."[61] Eventually, it comes to light that this is the estate where the Old Man was born and raised, the ancestral home of his aristocratic mother. The house burned down fifty years before, when the now-Old Man was sixteen years old; his father "killed the house," according to the Old Man, first by "squander[ing]" the mother's money, then burning it down while drunk.[62] In retribution, the Old Man stabbed his father and left the body to burn in the house. Since then, he has returned to the spot at least once, possibly more.

Although the plot and characters can be interpreted conventionally, the play also contains ritual elements that tend to work against the dramatic fiction. The use of verse, for example, foregrounds a sense of ritual from the beginning. The play's flexible four-beat line—almost iambic tetrameter, but for the frequent anapestic substitutions—allows the characters to move seamlessly between realistic, casual speech and a more formal register. Critics sometimes classify *Purgatory* as one of Yeats's Noh plays, because of these stylized elements. While it is not as close an imitation of medieval Japanese theater as *At the Hawk's Well* (1916) or *The Dreaming of the Bones* (1919), it does incorporate several features from *mugen noh* (usually translated as "dream play" or "ghost play").[63] In a typical *mugen noh*, a traveling monk or priest, the *waki*, is called upon to make a sacrifice on behalf of a ghost or spirit, the *shite*. Yoko Sato has traced the parallels between *Purgatory* and a specific *mugen noh* play called *Motomezuka* (sometimes translated as "The Maiden's Tomb" or "The Grave Sought"), in which the monk seeks the grave of a young woman who decided to commit suicide rather than choose between two suitors.[64] The structure is similar to that of *Purgatory*: in the first part, the monk looks for the grave; in the second, he sees a vision of the events from her life; and in the third, he prays for her to release him from torment. Notice the progression from present to past to future, which is typical of *mugen noh*. Kunio Komparu explains:

> Time in the play does not always progress in an ordinary, orderly, and proper flow from past to future; rather, the time of right now is interrupted as the situation demands by memories of the past, and this creates a 'present' that is viewed as corresponding to our own consciousness of actual time and that carries forward the dramatic action.[65]

In contrast to other *mugen noh*, as Sato notes, *Motomezuka* has an ambiguous ending: the monk fails to free the spirit of the young woman from her torment. Perhaps it was this lack of resolution that drew Yeats to adapt this particular play.

In Yeats's play, there is additional ambiguity: it is not clear whether it is the Old Man or his mother who is being tormented in this purgatory. Natalie Cohn Schmitt enumerates three possible interpretations: "that the dead do, in fact, return; that they are images of the old man's misery; that they are manifestations of the remorse of the mother, dead and 'dreaming back' through her passion."[66] The Old Man insists that it is his mother, driven "by remorse," who comes back to this place in order to "live / Through everything in exact detail."[67] Even though he too has returned to the scene of a past transgression—the murder of his father—he insists that it is his mother, and not himself, who is reliving past sins. He claims that the souls in purgatory "come back / To habitations and familiar spots," in order to:

> Re-live
> Their transgressions, and that not once
> But many times; they know at last
> The consequence of those transgressions
> Whether upon others or upon themselves;
> Upon others, others may bring help,
> For when the consequence is at an end
> The dream must end [...][68]

This is not how purgatory works in the Christian tradition; as Eliot observes, "there is no hint, or at least no emphasis upon Purgation."[69] Compared to the *Commedia*, Yeats's purgatory more closely resembles Dante's hell than his purgatory: in the *Inferno*, the damned reenact their sins over and over, stuck in a world where time does not advance, whereas the souls in *Purgatorio* move forward in time as they progress toward purgation. And so, the characters in Yeats's play are more like the souls in Dante's hell: damned to a world in which time stands still, where they relive the past as if it is the present, over and over again.

And yet, the Old Man understands himself to be an instrument of his mother's purgation and release, like the *waki* in *mungen noh*. He presents himself as a man possessed, the means by which she compulsively and remotely reenacts her past. I say "remotely" because the script never calls for her to be physically present on stage; the most we see of her is a shadow of a young woman in a lit window—and this apparition, unlike the later appearance of the Old Man's father, is never confirmed by the Boy. By the end of the play, however, it becomes clear that the Old Man is reliving, if only in his imagination, the night he killed his father as well as the night he was conceived, when he cries, "My father and my son on the same jack-knife!" before stabbing his son.[70] His final prayer, shortly after the murder, suggests that his actions have been driven as much by his own compulsive desire to relive his past transgressions as he is by his mother's vicarious will:

> O God!
> Release my mother's soul from its dream!
> Mankind can do no more. Appease
> The misery of the living and the remorse of the dead.[71]

The Old Man posits a mysterious form of remote possession, in which his mother "animate[s] that dead night" and forces him to participate in events from her life.[72] We might say that this remote possession parallels the theater itself. Certainly there is an analogy between the mother coercing the Old Man's actions and speech and the playwright scripting a character's movements and lines. Exhorting his mother's shadow, "Do not let him touch you!", he resembles the rebellious literary creations in Flann O'Brien's *At Swim-Two-Birds* (1939) who chafe under the narrator's authorial control.[73] It seems likely that Yeats was reflecting on the power and perils of the theater at this point near the end of his career, given the retrospective, metatheatrical poems like "The Circus Animal's Desertion" and "Man and the Echo" published alongside *Purgatory* in his final collection. But if he merely wanted to point out the force exercised by the playwright, then why obscure the agency of the playwright's analogue, as Yeats does with the Old Man's mother? The play never resolves the question of whether the mother is forcing the Old Man to return to this place, conjure the scene, and murder his son.

Furthermore, the apparition itself is a product of words rather than mimetic action, which makes me think that the compulsion we see in the play is as much an analogue for lyric possession as it is for theater. In a production that follows Yeats's stage directions closely, the audience would never see the face of the father or mother, much less the act of consummation the Old Man laments, except insofar as they imagine it, guided by the Old Man's words. Moreover, it is speech acts that "animate" the "dead night" from the past.[74] The conjuration begins when the Old Man exhorts his son to "Listen to the hoof beats! Listen, Listen!"[75] The son never hears these hoofbeats, and there are no stage directions to indicate that Yeats intended the audience to hear them either. Although some productions make use of sound effects here, the only sound called for in the script is the Old Man saying "Beat! Beat!", like a ritual invocation.[76] The choice of the word "beat," as opposed to an onomatopoetic approximation on the sound of a horse at full gallop, invokes the sound as both aural and physical sensation, like the "beat" of a line of iambic tetrameter. The Old Man is not just describing what he hears but replicating the phenomenological experience of his own hallucination for the boy and the audience. The goal here, according to Schmitt, as in all of Yeats's drama, is not "to show characters having the religious experience, but to provide that experience for his audience."[77] Perhaps this is why Yeats was so drawn to Noh, which is supposed to be an experience or encounter rather than a spectacle.[78]

The Old Man also uses acts of address more typical of lyric poetry to conjure the scene from the past. His first line—"Study that house"—is the first of many imperatives in the play, and most of these commands are related to perception.[79] Like his insistent repetition of the word "Beat," these are attempts to direct his son's senses, so that the son will see and hear the apparitions. And they act as instructions for the audience as well. By the end of the play, his son is dead, but the Old Man is still issuing orders, telling us to "Study that tree." In addition to these commands, the Old Man asks questions, inviting his son to participate in imagining the scene with prompts like, "What is it like?"[80] Direct address, whether in the imperative or the interrogative mood, has a kind of force that description does not, compelling us to answer or obey. Making a similar point, Culler observes that the lyric "enlists us in a process in ways that other texts do not," via acts of address that invite a response or through rhythm that we experience bodily.[81] This lyric conscription can happen even in a dramatic context, when the commands and questions are enunciated in heightened, ritualistic language—especially in verse.

After this invocation, the Old Man begins to describe the scene on the night of his conception. As he says "This night is the anniversary / Of my mother's wedding night," the window of the burned-out house lights up for the first time.[82] Up until this point, the Old Man has been narrating the story of his mother and father's marriage in past tense, but now he switches to present, describing the scene as if it is happening before his very eyes. At first, it seems like the Old Man is using the narrative present to create a sense of immediacy and excitement. But then, as he begins to incorporate deictics like "this night" to refer to the parents' wedding night, he collapses two moments in time, previously separated by at least sixty-seven years. The overall effect of the switch to what Culler calls the "deictic apparatus of the here-and-now of enunciation" is like the sudden "irruption of the ritual mode into fictional discourse" which Greene has identified as an essential feature of lyric discourse.[83] The Old Man, for his part, seems to believe that

149

he is in both times at once, as he alternates seamlessly between commands addressed to his mother ("Do not let him touch you!") and to his son ("Go fetch Tertullian").[84] Knowland says, "for one brief and superbly effective dramatic moment life in time and life in eternity meet as the Old Man sees in the deeps of his mind his mother and father lying upon the mattress begetting himself."[85] There is precedent for this collapsing of past and present in *mugen noh*. Peter Nicholls explains:

> A peculiarity of this type of Noh is that its main action takes place in the present of the play's performance and simultaneously in the past of stylized recollection (the dream of the *waki*). The visionary second part of the play thus links the manifestation of the god or spirit with the irruption of the past in the present, making the point of greatest intensity that in which time flows back on itself and two moments are, as it were, superimposed or grafted together.[86]

But insofar as the "stylized recollection" is spoken rather than acted out in gesture and dance, the closer analogue for the play's temporality is that of lyric poetry. The moment in which the play takes place—"this night"—has been constructed via speech act: the use of the present tense, deictics, and apostrophe. And because "this night"—which paradoxically encompasses the night of his conception, the night in which the house burned down and he murdered his father, and the night when he murders his son—exists in language, rather than actual fact, it can transcend the normal rules of chronological time. Consider the Old Man's apostrophes addressed to his mother, both when he implores her to spurn his father's advances and later when he prays to be released from his misery. Both are impossible acts of address, and, like lyric apostrophe, they represent attempts to "will a state of affairs" through language. Optative rather than representative, such utterance adds to the ritual character of his speech.

Although the son rebuffs his father's commands and questions at first, his resistance caves when he sees a figure appear in the lit window. For the original Abbey Theatre Festival production, Yeats's daughter Anne made a window by cutting a hole directly in the painted backdrop and covering the opening with gauze; the actors playing the mother and father "stood very vague behind," Anne Yeats herself reported.[87] Other productions—such as the 2018 Blue Raincoat Theatre Company production, staged outdoors against the backdrop of an eighteenth-century country house in Sligo—use a physical edifice with a window, where an actor stands, lit from behind.

Either way, the actors appear as two-dimensional images than three-dimensional bodies on the stage. This allows the son to fill in the three-dimensional details when he exclaims, "A body that was a bundle of old bones / Before I was born. Horrible! Horrible!"[88] The Old Man has succeeded in "impos[ing] his vision on the Boy," exercising an "authority," Knowland observes, derived from physical as well as imaginative prowess.[89] The audience occupies a position similar to that of the son, *vis-à-vis* the dream-vision: we never see the body itself, only the shadow, but we can imagine it, thanks to the son's visceral description of it as "a bundle of bones." This is even more true for readers: we populate the scene using the information the Old Man has given us, as if we are following a script that guides our interpretation. It is as if our imagination has been hijacked, just as the son's has, by the Old Man's poetic incantation. We have all been drawn in against our will.

In a 2015 production of the play at the University of Baltimore, the set design and costumes played up this sense that the vision is a hallucination generated by language. The stage was littered with open books and pleated accordions of paper, creating a visual motif of paper and print. All this print around the edges frames the scene within a world made of words. The actress playing the mother wore a corset made of newspaper, suggesting that she too is a figment of words.

In fact, we might say there is a kind of contagion of lyric possession going on. The Old Man, allegedly, has been compelled by his mother to imagine this moment he never witnessed, and then to participate in conjuring it. The son, as a result of his father's powerful invocation of the figures from the past, gets drawn in, not only seeing the figure in the window but adding in details of his own. We too are drawn in, even more so after the son is killed, and the Old Man continues to speak in the second person—either to us or to himself, in an act of triangulated address more typical of lyric poetry than drama. Thus, our imagination is scripted by the son, whose imagination has been scripted by the Old Man, who claims the whole ritual has been orchestrated by the mother. This is one way of accounting for Yeats's decision to leave open the three interpretive possibilities Schmitt identifies; it allows him to present the hallucination as something the characters—and the audience—both suffer and perpetuate.

I call this possession lyric, as opposed to theatrical, because it resembles the way that lyric "enlists" us, to repeat Culler's formulation, as the "I" that enunciates the poem as well as the audience that receives it. Just as the reader of the lyric, according to Culler, "lend[s] phenomenal form to something like a voice," Yeats's Old Man acts as his mother's mouthpiece.[90] As Greene explains,

> Lyric is utterance uniquely disposed to be re-uttered. In performance it may be not only compulsory but coercive discourse, for the nature of lyric's ritual dimension, simply stated, is to superimpose the subjectivity of the scripted speaker on the reader, and that substitution can entail a kind of violence.[91]

For an example of a lyric sequence that flexes the coercive power of the ritualistic elements of lyric, Greene looks to lyric possession's unapologetic partisan, Walt Whitman. In "Song of Myself, 47," Whitman asserts this coercion as a *fait accompli*:

> I follow you whoever you are from the present hour
> My words itch at your ears till you understand them.

And later, he explains:

> (It is you talking just as much as myself, I act as the tongue of you,
> Tied in your mouth, in mine it begins to be loosen'd.)[92]

This is apparently the *modus operandi* of the Old Man's mother in *Purgatory*, who has forced her son to speak the words that realize her vision, at least according to the Old Man. Although we, as members of the audience, do not feel the coercive power of the Old Man's ritual as keenly as we might if we were readers of a lyric poem like Whitman's—it is, after all, a staging of the structure of lyric enunciation, not a lyric poem *per se*—we do experience attenuated, evanescent version of this possession as a result of the ritualistic elements of the play.

The Old Man is doomed to repeat the ritual over and over again, like a reader who returns, again and again, to give voice to a compelling lyric poem. When he kills his son at the end of the play, he reassures himself that the ritual is over, that he has "finished all that consequence" such that his mother can be released from the cycle of remorse.[93] Only moments later, however, he hears the hoofbeats again, and realizes that the ritual must be reenacted "not once but many times."[94] What he hoped would be a decisive act—murdering his son—ends up being ineffectual as a means to overcome the compulsion to reenact his and his mother's transgressions. Although the script does not call for this, in many stage productions, the actors playing the son, the father, and the mother stand up and return to their original places, and even begin playing their roles again, from the top. In the University of Baltimore production, this resetting of the cast was accompanied by a clunking sound of mechanical gears moving back into place, a sound effect previously used to mark the beginning of the ritual. According to the play's director Kimberley Lynne, this sound was intended to suggest the machinery of purgatory moving back to its starting position, like an amusement park ride. When the audience saw the ostensibly dead characters stand and heard the sound of the purgatorial machine resetting itself, Lynne reports, "people screamed."[95]

This infinitely repeatable moment approximates the "iterable *now*" of lyric enunciation.[96] As such, it is another example of lyric temporality. Culler traces back to Sappho the lyric's penchant for "presenting itself as an event in a time that repeats."[97] Von Hallberg observes that it is lyric's musicality that makes it uniquely "available for repetition, as ordinary discourse is not."[98] Both agree that it is the ritualistic elements that make the lyric iterable. In Yeats's play, from the moment the Old Man switches to ritual invocation in the present tense, we have entered the realm of lyric temporality, a moment that can be repeated over and over again.[99] In his discussion of the ritual mode in lyric sequences, Greene claims that repetition necessarily implies the impossibility of completion, a cycle that will never end.[100]

Although both *Purgatory* and *Rockaby* feint toward dramatic fiction, ritual eventually prevails over plot. And so, in one sense, they resemble a great deal of postdramatic theater, insofar as they subvert traditional notions of plot and even—in the case of Beckett—character. Certainly, they cultivate a similar temporal aesthetic: durational to the point of tableau, repetitious to the point of circularity. But they can be distinguished from other postdramatic approaches insofar as the rituals they use to cultivate this temporal aesthetic come from lyric poetry—they are the very structures of lyric address. *Rockaby* stages something like triangulated address using the sound recording technology to make it possible for a disembodied speaker to talk to herself. In *Purgatory*, characters are compelled to speak poetry, occupying the role of the speaker as if possessed by it—in effect, staging what happens whenever a reader becomes the enunciator of a lyric poem.

I call them "stagings of lyric address" to designate the extent to which they are primarily events of language, embodied in performance, as opposed to imitations of rituals that are in essence physical action. But there are obvious ambiguities in both of these plays. Yeats's Old Man intends to execute a physical action, a ritual killing, at the climax of his ritual invocation of his mother. But, if he is to be believed, and he is the medium rather than the orchestrator of this ritual, then the real show is the possession—the words his mother puts in his mouth—which he attempts to put a stop to by killing his son.

This opens up for us a key distinction that can be made between dramatic ritual and lyric ritual. Dramatic ritual takes place *in a place*, whereas lyric ritual, on the other hand, happens in discourse. Greene offers the following test to distinguish between fiction and ritual, which we can apply to make a distinction of our own between dramatic and lyric ritual:

> One way to consider whether a work of literature realizes the phenomenon of fiction is to see how readers have become involved with the world it evokes. Fictions, lyric or otherwise, tend to give the illusion of occurring in a knowable place, while ritually oriented poems are supposed to happen anywhere the reader or auditor might be.[101]

Using this heuristic, we can classify *Rockaby*—and many other Beckett plays, for that matter—as lyric ritual. But *Purgatory* is trickier. The Old Man has returned to a specific place, the ruins of the Big House of an aristocratic family of the Irish ascendency. But his mother, the one ostensibly scripting his words and actions, is somewhere else, a mysterious purgatory that communicates with this site, but exists elsewhere. If purgatory both is and is not a physical place on earth, then the ritual she orchestrates from purgatory both is and is not physical.

The association of the past with a particular place anticipates the subject of the next, and final, chapter. So far, my focus has been on the phenomenology of time in verse drama—that is, the experience of time that these plays construct for the audience. But Yeats's play has already cued up another kind of time: history. And so, I turn now to a more systematic consideration of anachronism, those moments when the past or the future breaks through in the present, which has been both a curse and a boon for verse drama in its revivalist phase.

CHAPTER 6
ANACHRONISM

Since its premiere in 2014, Mike Bartlett's play *King Charles III*, a modern-day pastiche of Shakespearean history play, has proven prescient in some respects. With the death of Elizabeth II, Charles has ascended the throne and taken the regnal name Charles III. And his son Harry has left the royal family, at the urging of his wife, as his fictional counterpart threatens to do in the play. Bartlett calls his speculative portrayal of Britain's royal family a "future history play." His term draws our attention to his resuscitation of an old form, the history play, to comment on current events and make predictions about the future. I begin with Bartlett's future history play because it demonstrates the way that anachronism in verse drama can be made to cut both forward and backward. Plays like *King Charles III* foreground their affinities with theater of the past, and leverage this mastery of form and content from another period to shore up the playwright's authority in the present. What is remarkable about the plays I will discuss in this chapter is the frequency with which both retrospective and prospective anachronism coexist and even work together. It is as if unmooring the play from its specific moment in history allows the playwright to float outside of time and perceive past, present, and future more clearly.

In Heaney's *The Cure at Troy*, for example, the past is made to speak to the present via anachronism. The play, an adaptation of Sophocles' *Philoctetes*, is set during the Trojan War, but it contains references to the 1981 hunger strike in which Bobby Sands and nine other Irish Republican prisoners died, and the 1972 murder of Jean McConville, by the Provisional IRA. His chorus seems to stand outside of time, ranging freely among past, present, and future. In this way, he leverages anachronism to gain for himself the authority of a prophet, who can anticipate the day when "[t]he longed-for tidal wave / Of justice can rise up, / And hope and history rhyme."[1]

Where does this authority come from? It seems to me that these anachronistic verse plays of the twentieth and early twenty-first century follow the pattern identified by Susan Stewart, that of the "distressed genre." In *Crimes of Writing*, Stewart observes that the late seventeenth and early eighteenth centuries saw the rise of several "new antiques": the epic, the fable, the proverb, the fairy tale, and the ballad. These "literary imitations of folklore" all involved an "attempt to recoup the voice of orality in all its presumed authenticity of context."[2] These deliberately "distressed genres" represent the "hope to *enter* time, to re-create" and ultimately "to *transcend time*."[3] She claims that the "nostalgia for oral forms is a nostalgia for the presence of the body and the face-to-face, a dream of unmediated communication that, of course, could never be approximated even in the oral—a dream of an eternalized present, a future-past."[4] The author of a new antique asserts his or her freedom from constraints of time: he or she can go back in time, revive a form from the past that is contingent on its historical context, and give it new life in a new context. This is, in a certain sense, what all of the modern and contemporary verse dramatists are doing: taking a form with a "superb and unsurpassable past—but no possible future" (to quote Wilfrid Wilson Gibson again) and giving it new life in the twentieth century.[5]

Distressed genres, according to Stewart, share in a common "rejection of the present" that "operates on the level of form, theme, and intention."[6] But a rejection of the present does not always imply a preference for the past. Joyelle McSweeney is an example of a contemporary verse playwright whose use of anachronism is motivated not by reactionary nostalgia but by a thoroughgoing progressivism. In her essay, "Justice Absconditus, or Why I Write Verse Plays," McSweeney argues that anachronism in the theater can serve as an "occult lens" by which to perceive and portray the future.[7] By way of explanation, she offers her own experience in postindustrial America shortly before the Great Recession as an analogy:

> The Rust Belt, "left behind", "behind the times" due to the decline of US manufacturing, somehow hosts a sped-up experience of time. You see ruin here—early and permanent. [...] You see it here ... and then, suddenly, it is 2008 and happening everywhere: Athens, Floria, Argentina, the UK, Connecticut. Global financial collapse.[8]

South Bend Indiana, ostensibly "stuck in the past," turns out to be a portent of things to come. Like the Rust Belt, her plays seem anachronistic—not only does she embrace verse, but she also makes use of all kinds of old-fashioned tropes like epithets, apostrophe, and puns. These conventions, far from making her work conventional, imbue her plays with a sense of dark foreboding and play a role in the "counterspell" she sees herself as casting with verse drama.[9]

Anachronism

In this chapter, I will consider four plays that cultivate and thematize this kind of prophetic anachronism. In all four cases, the return to (or of) the past serves to shore up a character's or the playwright's authority, as someone who can see or even travel to other places and times. Gertrude Stein's *The Mother of Us All* thematizes prophetic authority directly, featuring Susan B. Anthony standing alone as the one true prophet amongst a panoply of nineteenth-century American would-be visionaries. But like her Old Testament antecedents, her witness is ignored by those who want to instrumentalize her voice for their own causes, reinforcing her pessimism about the future of her cause and undercutting the other characters' progressive view of history. In *The Strange Undoing of Prudencia Hart*, anachronism takes the form of nostalgia. David Greig's titular protagonist is no prophetess—merely an antiquarian, fascinated by medieval literature. Her preference for the past is at first ironized, but eventually comes to serve her well, in an existential battle for her soul. If Stein's Susan B. is an Old Testament prophet, Greig's Prudencia is a Romantic poet, affirming the power of poetry to overcome the powers of hell and mortality itself. Indeed, the Romantic notion of the poet-prophet underpins all the plays considered here; but the plays make use of this seemingly backward-looking inspiration to make pronouncements that speak to their contemporary moment, and to audiences today. Tony Harrison, in both *The Common Chorus* and *The Trackers of Oxyrhynchus*, conflates historical periods in order to deliver an indictment of a political situation in his own time. But his is a postmodern anarchism, where texts exert a power of their own, sometimes at the expense of the characters' agency or the playwright's. This oracular authority emanates not from the person of the playwright, but from the words themselves. In this respect, all of these anachronistic verse plays are like lyric poetry.

Susan B. Anthony as Prophetess in Gertrude Stein's *The Mother of Us All*

In *The Mother of Us All*, Stein and Thomson try to capture the spirit of nineteenth-century America, as it is expressed in its great movements. Rodney Lister has described it as an opera that fundamentally portrays "the political optimism of Americans and their conviction that through their votes they can shape their fate and history."[10] The play also distinguishes between an orator and a prophet—during a period of American history in which the two were often intertwined. The "mother" of the title is Susan B. Anthony. She stands out from the many fathers in the play: founding fathers like John Adams, Susan B.'s father Daniel, and even Stein's own father. Stein portrays Susan B. as the one real prophet among a host of rhetoricians, who alternately court and reject her. Like a true prophet, she delivers indictments and predictions that pique not only her contemporaries, but also the audience.

The libretto for *The Mother of Us All* includes a mix of prose and verse. And yet, even some of the prose passages sound like verse because of their periodic rhymes; for example, Susan B. says, "Yes I know, they love me so, they tell me so and they tell me so, but I, I do not tell them so because I know [. . .]."[11] It is easy to imagine a lineated version of this speech, with line breaks after the rhyme words, even if readers might quibble over which are end rhymes and which are internal.

The opera has two acts and an interlude, but no real historical or even narrative arc. As Bay-Cheng observes, it "at first appears to be an episodic history, but it is not a linear retrospective."[12] It does not stage the political events themselves—rallies, ratifications, or elections—but rather the characters' conversations about these events. Act I introduces an eclectic cast of characters that spans American history, including politicians like Daniel Webster, as well as Stein's own friends.[13] Lister calls it "a pageant," which captures the way that characters appear on stage and converse with one another, in different combinations, and then disappear again, without these episodes ever coalescing into a storyline.[14] All of these characters were engaged—positively or negatively—with one of the great nineteenth-century political causes: abolition, suffrage, temperance, etc. The characters themselves seem to conflate these causes, or treat them as interchangeable. At one point, Thaddeus Stevens tells Susan B.:

> We all know that whatever happens we all can depend upon you to do your best for any cause which is a cause, and any cause is a cause and because any cause is a cause therefore you will always do your best for any cause, and now you will be doing your best for this cause our cause the cause.[15]

Although he uses the language of logical syllogism, his reasoning is circular. The implication is that politicians support causes like abolition because they want to be involved in some movement, any movement. To his rambling thank-you, Susan B. responds with the tongue-in-cheek,

"Because"—suggesting that she is aware of the shallow motivations behind most of her allies' involvement in her cause.

While Stevens uses circular logic to conflate his cause with hers, Susan B. insists on distinguishing them. In an earlier scene, she asks a "Negro Man" if he would exercise his right to vote even if his wife could not, to which he responds, "You bet."[16] When Stevens insists that "humanity comes first"— that is, the law must grant human rights to slaves first, before granting civil rights to women—she replies, "You mean men come first."[17] All of this works to create a sharp contrast between Susan B. and the men around her, who proclaim themselves the "Chorus of the V.I.P.s."[18] To be a V.I.P. means: "we have special rights, they ask us first and they wait for us last and wherever we are well there we are everybody knows we are there, we are the V.I.P. Very important persons for everybody to see."[19] This is an obvious send-up of the self-importance of these political figures, but Stein also draws attention to their interchangeability:

Thaddeus S.   When they all listen to me.
Andrew J.   When they all listen to him, and by him I mean me.
Daniel Webster   By him I mean me.
Thaddeus S.   It is not necessary to have any meaning I am he he is me I am a V.I.P.[20]

The V.I.P.s compete to assert themselves as the foremost authority, even though they are all interchangeable—a strange assertion, given the starkly opposed political beliefs of, say, Stevens and Johnson. So, when the fictional Thaddeus S. asserts their equivalence, he must be referring to something somehow more essential than anything they said or did, something more like an attitude or disposition they share: namely, that they all want everyone to listen to them and respect their authority.

The V.I.P.s also think of themselves as prophets. Webster's first lines echo several passages from the Bible, but the counterpoint sung by the rest of the characters insists that he is "not Daniel in the lion's den."[21] Later in the opera, presumably after the passing of the Fourteenth Amendment, Daniel Webster asks Susan B., "why should you want what you have chosen, when mine eyes, why do you want that the curtain may rise, why when mine eyes, why should the vision be opened to what lies behind."[22] He begs her to accept what progress has been made by abolitionists, rather than insist on women's suffrage, a more dubious prospect. Evoking the "Battle Hymn of the Republic," he sees universal male suffrage as the realization of the promised "coming of the glory of the Lord"—which is why his harangue ends with a vision of "the gorgeous ensign of the republic, still full high advanced, its arms and trophies streaming in their original luster."[23]

Yet it is Susan B., and not Webster, who truly possesses prophetic authority. The most powerless characters go to her with their questions, and everyone, even the V.I.P.s, admits that she speaks with authority. She alone issues prophetic criticism of the behaviors of her contemporaries. And like the prophets of old, when she issues prophetic indictments, her listeners recoil—even her fellow suffragettes. At one point, after prophesying their eventual triumph, Susan B. cuts short Anne's celebration with this prediction: "By that time it will do them no good because having the vote they will become like men, they will be afraid [. . .]."[24] When Anne asks why she refrains from making these pronouncements publicly, Susan B. replies, "because if I did they would not listen" but instead "revenge themselves."[25] When Donald Gallup offers to help her, if she will let him, she asks, "if I do and I annoy you what will you do," a question he avoids answering.[26] Like Tiresias in *The Waste Land*, who "perceived the scene, and foretold the rest," she can predict how things will go.[27] Just as the typist and the "young man carbuncular" are types that Eliot's Tiresias is familiar with, these V.I.P.s are a type that Susan B knows well.[28] Over and over again, men ask for or offer help, but their good will lasts only as long as Susan B. is willing to say what they want to hear. Hence Stein's interchangeable treatment of figures as different as Webster, Stevens, and Johnson: the details of who they are, where they are from, and what cause they champion are merely variations on a type.

The causes are the same, the politicians are the same, and all of American history is the same cycle repeated over and over. To underscore this point, Stein collapses the events of the nineteenth century (and early twentieth) into what Bay-Chang describes as a "continuous present."[29] In this "continuous present," John Adams and Susan B. Anthony become contemporaries, and Daniel Webster lives to see women get the vote. History appears not as a succession of different events, but rather "a single moment, played over and over again."[30] There is no development, no progress. Not even the Fourteenth Amendment is portrayed as a substantive change for the good; the characters refer to this achievement periphrastically—and ironically—as "[writing] the word male into the constitution."[31] But only Susan B. seems to recognize this lack of progress. When the chorus praises her achievements, Susan B. replies sarcastically, repeating their phrase "so successful" so as to puncture the celebratory mood.[32]

As Bay-Chang observes, this "single moment, played over and over again" is similar to the temporality of Stein's poems. And indeed, Stein has confirmed that her plays, like her poetry, are attempts to portray a person or a thing without recourse to narrative. Story is one of the "things over which one stumbles" when watching a play, she says in "Plays"; Stein believes it contributes to the disjunction between what is happening to the characters on stage and what the audience is experiencing.[33] The heart of the problem is, according to Stein, that the "emotion" and "sensation" of the audience is "always either behind or ahead of the play at which you are looking and to which you are listening."[34] Stein confesses a preference for foreign-language theater because "the manners and customs [...] created a thing in itself, and it existed in and for itself as the poetical plays had that I used so much to read, there were so many characters just as there were in those plays and you did not have to know them they were so foreign."[35] In other words, she can enjoy the sound and the spectacle, without worrying about understanding the characters and their stories. Like melodrama, she experiences it as "a very simple direct and moving picture."[36] She tries to recreate this experience in her portrait poems and her landscape plays; she explains, "All these things might have been a story but as a landscape they were just there and a play is just there."[37] Based on these experiments, Stein concludes, "anything that was not a story could be a play."[38] In *The Mother of Us All* too, Stein attempts to turn history itself, something that "might have been a story," into a timeless scene that, like a lyric poem, is "just there."

In apparently presenting a distinct historical episode, the final scene seems at first to be an exception to this non-narrative approach to history. It takes place in Congressional Hall apparently sometime after the passage of the Nineteenth Amendment in 1921, and the stage directions call for a replica of Adelaide Johnson's marble statue of Anthony, Stanton, and Lucretia Mott to appear on stage. Susan B. no longer appears—the real Anthony died in 1906—but her voice seems to speak from the statue. Other deceased historical figures like Adams and Webster do appear, although they too would have been dead by this time. We are still in a kind of ahistorical present, then, in which Susan B. is a ghost. This ghostly presence gets the last word, in an authoritative, if ironically repetitive, speech. It begins with what seems like a reflection on their progress: "We cannot retrace our steps, going forward may be the same as going backward. We cannot retrace our steps, retrace our steps. All my long life, all my life, we do not retrace our steps, all my long life."[39] As if to negate any implications of progress, she says "but," and then stops, for what the stage directions call "a long silence."[40] This turns

Staging the Lyric

out to be the first in a series of silences that punctuate and fragment her remarks. When she speaks again, her reflections start to dissolve into self-doubt. She wonders aloud, "do I want what we have got [...]."[41] All this is surprisingly honest for a speech on the "glorious" occasion of the installation of this sculpture in her honor. It is also discouragingly pessimistic about the possibility of progress: all the time they thought they were "going forward," they may have been in reality "going backward," she suggests. These prophetic pronouncements are liable to discourage the audience too—especially if they are voiced by the hero of women's suffrage, the Mother of Us All. The play forces us to ask ourselves—whatever cause we champion—have our efforts been "the same as going backward"? Do we want "what we have got" after all? Have women, as Susan B. predicts, "become like men," craven and defensive, believing that rights are a zero-sum good? These questions are strikingly resonant, and potentially troubling, even now.

Lyric Possession in David Greig's *The Strange Undoing of Prudencia Hart*

The creators of *The Strange Undoing of Prudencia Hart*, playwright David Greig and director Wils Wilson, conceived of it as a "theatre ballad"—a storytelling performance in verse. The play is not written in ballad meter; most of it is rhyming couplets, without a standard length. Its balladness instead emerges from the context in which it is set: a pub. Since its very first performance, it has almost always been staged in a bar or pub, in keeping with Greig's and Wilson's desire to cultivate the atmosphere of a "magical lock-in," with drinking, live music, singing, and audience participation.[42] In its invocation of the ballad tradition, *Prudencia Hart* is reminiscent of Arden's plays. As in *Live Like Pigs*, Greig's play begins with traditional Scottish ballad, "The Twa Corbies"—a move that puts the ballad forward as the encapsulation of the whole of the dramatic action.[43] Although not every scene begins with a ballad, there are several more in the course of the play, including "The Bonnie Lass o' Fyvie," "The Rolling Hills of the Borders," and "Down by Blackwaterside"—and an Irish reel and jig set to boot.

The play takes place in Kelso, a small town on the border between Scotland and England, the region whence many of these ballads hail. Prudencia travels there to deliver a paper on the topography of Hell in the border ballads at an academic conference in folk studies. Her antiquarian approach is derided as old-fashioned by the other presenters, who study contemporary pop culture or approach the ballad form with a more critical and progressive methodology. Her antagonist, Colin Syme, tells her, "Your problem is you persist / Like—I don't know—some kind of romanticist / With a sort of old fashioned ethnographic notion of 'collecting' / Or 'protecting' / Ballads."[44] To Colin and the other conference attendees, Prudencia is stuck in the past. What was trendy in Arden's day, during the revival of the 1950s and '60s—and could be subsumed into his Leftist political project at that time—is a quaint antiquarian interest by Prudencia's time.

The criticisms of Prudencia's nostalgia sound a lot like criticisms of modern verse drama, also called antiquated, backward-looking, and decadent. The revival of verse drama, like the revival of the ballad, often seems to be predicated on the existence of anachronistic places from which verse drama can be retrieved and revived in mainstream, metropolitan theater. These anachronistic spots might be colonies on the periphery of the empire or diasporic ghettos within the metropolitan center—communities that by virtue of race, class, ethnic, or religious differences have not been entirely absorbed into modern society and therefore retain some of their "primitive" or "premodern" culture. Walcott points out, in "The Poet in the Theatre," "without any academic urging, without any sense of siege or nostalgic aggression, verse ignores the centre and continues exuberantly in provincial or ghetto theatre, in rap, in rock music, and in that second-rate expression of exuberance—the stage musical."[45] It seems to me that many metropolitan writers—in England and the United States—think of these provincial and subaltern cultures as a kind of incubator, from which they can "recover" verse drama and reintroduce it to mainstream audiences.

The Irish Literary Revival is a prime example. Ireland in particular becomes a foil for English culture—more poetic, more primitive, more romantic than the seat of empire to its east. Morra observes that the "negative social and cultural connotations" of verse are unique to English theater, and verse drama has not suffered the same decline in Scotland, Ireland, and Wales.[46] The Revival began, in the late nineteenth century, with scholarly and antiquarian interest in Ireland's Gaelic heritage. Writers like Yeats, Synge, and Lady Gregory began to write poetry, fiction, and drama based on Irish mythology and history. With the success of their plays at the Abbey Theatre, they came to be portrayed as rescuers not only of ancient Irish legends but also poetic drama. In 1937, looking back on the Revival, Harley Granville-Barker claimed, "it is, I think, to the example of the Abbey Theatre, Dublin, that we chiefly owe the more fruitful approach to the theater of the English poet-dramatists to-day."[47] He credits Yeats as an influence on Eliot, Masefield, Auden, and Isherwood. Masefield, speaking for himself, claimed Synge as his primary inspiration:

> Listening to Synge's play [...] made me feel what a wealth of fable lay still in the lonely places in England. [...] We had not become alive to its presence: we were dead to it: and much of the theatre of that time was dead in consequence. [...] The thought occurred to some of us younger Englishmen that some of us might find, in the English country, subjects as moving, fables as lively [...][48]

The rural peripheries thus came to be fetishized as a kind of mythic source of inspiration, with Ireland as the *locus classicus*, or, rather, a *locus hibernicus*.

This narrative of recovery from provincial obscurity surfaces even in the work of more radical writers like Arden, as we saw in Chapter Three. In Arden's plays, verse is the chosen mode of expression of those who cannot assimilate into English society, from Scotsmen to gypsies. And so, when Prudencia Hart travels to the border to present a paper on the border ballads, she is like the Old Man in *Purgatory* returning to his ancestral estate. Kelso is a portal to the past, as well as a venue for poetic inspiration. After they get snowed in, Prudencia jumps at the chance to attend a trad session at the Kelso Folk Club, and she persuades Colin to stay, in the hopes of gaining "a real insight / Into the authentic folk expression of a Borders town."[49] Her prizing of "authentic folk expression" supports Colin's diagnosis of her Romantic sensibility: she, like Wordsworth, wants an authentic representation of the way real people speak to each other.

In addition to the liminal geographical setting, it is set at a liminal time of year: the winter solstice. The pub's landlord convenes the event with the following announcement:

> Ladies and Gentleman—
> It's Midwinter's Eve—
> Can you sort out the microphone, Steve?
> Call it solstice, call it Yule,
> Call it the last day of term at school
> Call it what you like—it's that moment when
> We look back at the past then forward again
> And then leap—jump over time's crack
> Between looking forward and looking back,

A fractional second of universal stil
When what "was" is, and what is—is "will"
And all time and everything stops
Even the ticking of the clocks
A midnight's moment, when past and future kiss.[50]

Once again, we encounter a play that takes place in a suspended moment, when the clocks stop. The dull folk session then transforms into a Saturnalian karaoke night, a drunken revelry which seems to exist outside of normal chronological time—much like the Airman's fall in Sayers's *The Just Vengeance* or the temporal slowdown as the woman in the chair approaches death in Beckett's *Rockaby*. This temporal distortion lasts only for the time it takes for the clocktower to chime twelve times for midnight. But it expands radically for Prudencia, who wanders out of the pub into the snow, and gets kidnapped by the devil and taken to hell.

For Prudencia, her time at the devil's bed-and-breakfast feels like thousands of years. Over time, she moves from disbelief to curiosity about her surroundings—at which point she spends a few centuries reading and cataloguing all of the ballads in his library—then becomes bored and then despondent, and finally hatches a plan for escape. Each scene in hell ends with a variation on the following refrain:

She falls through years.
Years and Years.
She falls from wild curiosity into a routine of work.
She is caught.[51]

This refrain creates an episodic rhythm of brief vignettes depicting an interaction between the Devil and Prudencia, between which hundreds of years are supposed to have passed.

Prudencia eventually escapes the Devil's clutches by seducing him—not by direct sexual advances, which he spurns, but with help from the ballads she knows so well. Making her case to the Devil, she observes:

All this time we've existed in prose
Which is interesting
Because—as every author knows—
If you surrender your thought to metre
You surrender yourself to the poem's beat, or

> Rhyme or formula or words or sound,
> The author is lost and creation found,
> The poem finds itself—its own *autonomia*[52]

But slowly his lines begin to conform to the patterns of rhyme and meter in spite of his efforts. It is only when she convinces him to "give [himself] over to the rhyming couplet," that he relents and she seduces him.[53] Then, while he sleeps, she escapes from the bed-and-breakfast, back into the snowy night in Kelso. The rhythm of poetry forces him to take a human form, in spite of his instance that "Formlessness is more the norm-al thing for me."[54] In fact, his insistence on his own formlessness is a defensive tactic, like his refusal to speak in rhyme, but it too ultimately fails. It seems that in poetry, Prudencia has the upper hand, even over the devil, such that even after she escapes, he pines for her.

The power Prudencia wields in this scene is a species of what Von Hallberg calls "lyric power." Von Hallberg, following Montaigne, believes "poetry expresses power more than truth," and that power is "produced by the formal, and in particular musical, resources" of verse.[55] He observes that "[r]eaders stay with poems [...] because shapely sounds drawn them on," like a kind of hypnosis.[56] In the play, Prudencia uses "shapely sounds" to entice the devil, exercising a power even he is powerless to resist.

But hers is a power predicated on surrender: she talks about giving herself to the rhythm of the poem, and to the agency of the form itself. As Prudencia tells the devil, "The tighter the form the less control / We have over meaning or, you might say, soul."[57] This paradoxical way of talking about poetic prowess—as power that comes from a kind of surrender or possession—is a common refrain in lyric discourse. It dates back at least to Sir Philip Sidney's "Defense of Poesy," in which Sidney invokes the Roman tradition of the poet-prophet. Sidney observes that the Romans called poets *vates*, the same word they used for diviners and prophets. The Roman *vates* was closer to a medium, possessed by what Sidney calls "heart-ravishing knowledge."[58] Sidney explains:

> Although it were a very vain and godless superstition, as also it was to think that spirits were commanded by such verses—whereupon this word charms, derived of *carmina*, comes—so yet serves it to show the great reverence those wits were held in, and altogether not without ground, since both the oracles of Delphos and Sibylla's prophecies were wholly delivered in verses; for that same exquisite observing of

number and measure in words, and that high-flying liberty of conceit, proper to the poet, did seem to have some divine force in it.[59]

This kind of possession is uniquely inscribed in the ballad's mode of enunciation. In a ballad, as Susan Stewart observes, "the ballad singer performs all the parts of a play as if inhabited by the characters, yet within a presentation of physical person that remains constant throughout"—as if he or she is "spoken through" rather than speaking.[60] And so, Stewart claims, "Of all the singers of Western lyric, the ballad singer is the one must radically haunted by others."[61] This is true of Prudencia, as well as the performers of Greig's play. They too give themselves over to this power, in order to overpower us.

Poetic Possession in Tony Harrison's *The Common Chorus* and *The Trackers of Oxyrhynchus*

If the use of these antique forms can facilitate something akin to possession, then the playwrights who use them open themselves up to substantial risk—of loss of control, even dissolution of self. Tony Harrison thematizes these potential hazards in several adaptations of classical Greek drama from the late '80s and early '90s. In *The Common Chorus* and *The Trackers of Oxyrhynchus*, anachronism becomes a vector through which another time and place contaminates, even takes over, the action. In *The Common Chorus*, the present encroaches upon the past, puncturing the theatrical illusion of anachronism and resisting the lesson of history. In *The Trackers of Oxyrhynchus*, it is the opposite: the past infiltrates the present, eventually overriding the character's will. In both cases, there is give and take between past and present. The porous temporal setting allows Harrison to comment on contemporary issues like war and poverty, in a voice made more authoritative by its comprehension of the whole of history.

In *The Common Chorus*, Harrison adapts not one but two Greek plays: Part I is Aristophanes' comedy, the *Lysistrata*, and Part II is Euripides' tragedy, the *Trōiades* ("The Trojan Women"). Both parts highlight the parallels between the protests made by women from the past—against the Peloponnesian War in Aristophanes and the Trojan War in Euripides—and Greenham Common Women's Peace Camp, a group of women protesting the storage of cruise missiles at the Royal Air Force base at Greenham Common in the '80s. Harrison explains that he "imagined them played and performed by the women of the peace camp at Greenham Common for the benefit of the guards behind the wire."[62] The play begins at Greenham Common, with three guards, assigned to keep watch over the silos at RAF Greenham Common, jawing with one another and heckling the female protestors on the other side of the fence. The plot of the *Lysistrata* is embedded in the contemporary context as a kind of play-within-a-play, performance art put on by the women protestors for the edification of the RAF and American troops stationed at the base. Like the women in the *Lysistrata*, Harrison's protestors swear to go on a sex strike until peace is negotiated. By the end of the first act, it looks like it might work. Then the women are arrested by a police inspector—like many of their real-life analogues at Greenham Common—and part II takes a turn toward the tragic. The rest follows the plot of *The Trojan Women*, as Hekabe, Andromache, Cassandra, and Helen, played by Greenham protestors, learn of and lament their fate at the hands of the victorious Greeks.

Despite the more obvious parallels between the disarmament protests at Greenham Common and the situation in the *Lysistrata*, the original inspiration, according to Harrison, came from *The Trojan Women*, the moment when Hekabe takes solace in knowing their story will be retold. Harrison translates her speech as follows:

> BUT if they hadn't brought us down so low,
> face down in the dust, we'd disappear for ever.
> Whereas now we are stories everyone will tell.[63]

In the essay that prefaces the print edition of the play, Harrison observes, "Every time the play is played through history in all its versions the 'mortals' become 'later'. And we are the latest mortals now. We are in that long line of 'later mortals' first addressed in 415 BC as if from the present suffering of the Trojan Women of centuries before."[64] The play is the medium by which these women from the past speak to people in the present, and their laments are the means by which Harrison offers his own plea to end nuclear disarmament. In this way, the anachronism of *The Trojan Women* is something found rather than invented by Harrison.

He adds to the anachronism in the first half of the play, creating a temporally porous setting in which characters from different times and plays come and go, interacting with one another and highlighting parallels between ancient Greece and modern Britain. At one point, Lysistrata tells the guards, who have been heckling their performance, "Look, we're trying to pretend that this is ancient Greece. / I wish you'd give us just a little bit of peace."[65] Later, when they mention the missiles, she insists, "Those weapons haven't been invented yet. / We're still in the age of shields and swords."[66] These lines acknowledge the incursions of Harrison's contemporary moment, while trying also to hold that time at bay. Nor is this incursion merely a matter of the guards' noncompliance; the other women protestors commit similar anachronistic lapses. Lysistrata has to remind a fellow protestor, "Christ isn't born yet. It's BC four-eleven."[67] These frequent, and ultimately ineffectual, protests against the present suggest the insufficiency of the protestors' amateur theatricals to achieve peace. Ultimately, theater itself is paltry in the face of present circumstances—and the same might be said for the Peace Camp itself, another performance that fails to achieve its ends.

Near the end of the play, as the chorus of Trojan women, still dressed as Grenfell Common protestors, is keening for their dead, Harrison inserts one more reference to his contemporary moment. The chorus likens the British response to the weapon housed at the base to the Trojan response to the wooden horse left by the Greeks: "JUST AS WE ALL SAID HURRAY / TO THE WOODEN HORSE FROM THE USA." In this transhistorical epic simile, the British are not aggressors in an imperial war, but credulous facilitators of American aggression, complicit in their own destruction.

Ultimately, the play is pessimistic, insofar as the parallels across time and culture all confirm the inevitability and ubiquity of war. But there is a kind of paradoxical hopefulness about the play. Acknowledging the tendency of history to repeat itself, Lysistrata declares:

Since 1945 past and present are the same.
And it doesn't matter if its "real" or a play—
imagination and reality both go the same way.
So don't say it's just a bunch of ancient Greeks.
It's their tears that will be flowing down your cheeks.[68]

This could be discouraging to someone like Lysistrata—or Harrison himself—who hopes to see the end of the cycle of violence. But she reframes this recurrence as a testament to the power of theater. She has faith that the ancient Greeks will speak to, and eventually speak through, their latter-day audience. In speaking through them, they infiltrate the very bodies of their contemporary counterparts, to such an extent that Greek tears will flow down twentieth-century cheeks. Their plays allow the past to enter the present via a kind of bodily possession.

That *The Common Chorus* was never performed does work to undercut this affirmation of theater's power, to some extent. No cast ever gave voice to Harrison's script; no audience of "later mortals" cried ancient Greek tears. And so, I must turn to another of Harrison's plays, where the past succeeds in invading—and possessing—the present. *The Trackers of Oxyrhynchus* was also intended for a single performance in a specific location: the ancient stadium in Delphi (Greece) on July 12, 1988.[69] It is an adaptation of a lost satyr play by Sophocles called *Ichneutae* ("The Tracking Satyrs"). A fragment of the *Ichneutae* was discovered in 1907 by Bernard Grenfell and Arthur Hunt among the papyri at Oxyrhynchus, in Egypt. Harrison's play begins not with the satyrs themselves, but with the two archaeologists, Grenfell and Hunt, who are "trackers" of lost papyri. It is clear, however, from the beginning of the play, that one of the trackers, Grenfell, has become the tracked. His colleague Hunt explains:

> I worry about Grenfell. Only last year
> he said the god Apollo was shouting in his ear.
> Apollo pursuing him. Grenfell couldn't rest
> Till he became, I have to say, almost literally possessed.
> He viewed the way our names were in conjunction—
> Grenfell-Hunt as an Apollonian injunction.[70]

The audience will see Apollo hounding Grenfell moments later. In the meantime, Grenfell and Hunt discover a lost paean of Pindar among the papyri, and the chorus has begun to chant the words of Pindar's poem. When Grenfell reads the word "Apollo," he is "transfixed" and begins "listening for the god in his ear."[71]

This moment in Harrison's play reminds me of a similar moment near the end of Heaney's *The Cure at Troy*, written two years later. In *The Cure at Troy*, Hercules uses the chorus as his mouthpiece; they become "ritually claimant" and speak "as Hercules." This too is a kind of possession, but not a violation, as in some other plays that stage divine possession. The bystander to this scene is the character Philoctetes, but he experiences Hercules' speech inside his head—not in the mouth of the chorus. In this respect, Philoctetes is like Grenfell.[72] But Grenfell also resembles Heaney's chorus, as he too becomes the mouthpiece of a god. In the revised script used for the National Theatre production, it happens immediately upon the discovery of Pindar. In the original performance at Delphi, the possession progressed more slowly. The chorus's chant acts as a kind of ritual invocation; when the paean ends, an image of Apollo, taken from a pottery fragment discovered at Delphi, appears on the screen behind the actors, and a voice begins to chant the opening lines of his play *Ichneutae* from behind the screen, "as if from the distant past."[73] At this point, Grenfell, "frozen in rapt attention" starts to be "taken over by APOLLO."[74] He begins talking to himself in "a frantic dialogue" in rhyming couplets.[75] Here Harrison is taking advantage of a coincidence of history: that the fragment discovered by the historical Grenfell and Hunt is a play about Apollo, the god of prophecy, who was said to communicate with human beings via possession. Like the Roma, the oracle at Delphi, a woman known as the *Pythia*, received divine revelation in an ecstatic state. Her ravings would then be interpreted by the male *prophetai* for the benefit of the person seeking Apollo's counsel—in dactylic hexameter, as Herodotus renders it.[76]

Unlike the *Pythia*, Grenfell tries to resist being possessed. In the National Theatre script, the stage directions describe Grenfell as "horrified that the voice of APOLLO came out of his mouth."[77] Eventually, Apollo, still speaking through Grenfell, resorts to torturing him by forcing him to repeat the same incomplete line over and over: "απαντα χρηστα καί … something …"[78] Grenfell, speaking for himself, laments, "I can't get that phrase from my brain."[79] Many of us experienced something similar: a line we cannot quite remember that still gets stuck in our head. Grenfell's experience also approximates the phenomenon of lyric possession we saw in Yeats's *Purgatory*. Compulsions like this can be a function of the material dimension of language: a sound that catches your ear or a rhythm that gets stuck in your body. This perhaps explains why Harrison foregrounds the materiality of Sophocles' verse—evoking the sound and rhythm of the Greek, without translating it to English, and projecting the image of the fragment onto the backdrop.

But sometimes lines get stuck in our heads because they are like the *punctum* of a photograph, that detail that both "attracts" and "distresses" the viewer, according to Roland Barthes.[80] For Barthes, the punctum is always an accident, something the photographer could not have staged. Culler applies the concept to lyric poetry, although in the lyric context the *punctum* is often intentional on the part of the poet. Culler uses Barthes's term to designate the word or phrase in a poem that sticks with you not because of what it means but because it bothers you. It could be a single word that clashes with the diction of the rest of the poem, or a grammatical construction that does

Staging the Lyric

not quite work. These moments—whether intended to bother the reader or not—are like photographic *puncta* insofar as we experience them as both appealing and annoying at the same time. In this situation, it is not only the materiality of language that entices us but also a sense that there is a meaning just outside of our reach, the impression of semantic content tantalizing us to exercise our interpretive machine. In Grenfell's case, it is the missing word, marked by the placeholder "something," that bothers him. The missing word irritates him on an intellectual and a sensory level: the former insofar as the missing word prevents him from understanding the meaning of the line, the latter insofar as the ellipsis disrupts the rhythm of the line. Grenfell keeps coming back to it, as if thinking hard enough will help him remember the words of a play he has not read. Harrison's framing of this perseveration as a function of something supernatural—possession by a god—testifies to the coercive power of verse. Sometimes having a poem (or song) in your head does feel like an external force compelling you to enunciate the poem again and again. That it is Apollo, the god of poetic inspiration, that does the possessing is another clue pointing in this direction.

Eventually, Silenus, the leader of satyrs—played by the actor who plays Hunt—teaches the audience to chant some of these fragments, so that they too get the chance to participate in giving voice to these words from the past. The stated purpose of this chant is to call the satyrs on the stage. In addition, the chant also facilitates a communion of human beings from the past and the present, as the words of the audience are "echoed by the ancient voices of the 8000 ghosts at the ancient Pythian Games," according to the stage directions.[81]

The satyrs enter, and the play shifts to a classical satyr play. At first, the action follows the plot of Sophocles' satyr play in depicting a group of satyrs, led by Silenus, searching for Apollo's lost cattle. Harrison supplements the fragment, which consists of a few lines of dialogue between Apollo and Silenus, with details and plot points from other ancient texts, like the *Homeric Hymn to Hermes*. Harrison's satyrs locate the thief, Hermes, and discover that he has used the cattle to make strings for his newly invented instrument, the lyre. The satyrs are initially terrified of the lyre and its music, but eventually grow curious and want to try it out. Apollo rebuffs them, saying: "You don't need lyres. Your days proceed / from one need satisfied to the next need."[82] Apollo insists upon a hierarchy, "a fixed scale in creation" with Olympian Gods at the top and primitive creatures like crustaceans at the bottom.[83] Even though they can speak, satyrs are "almost at the bottom but not quite," Apollo says, because they are "stuck between animal and human status." Music, which is, according to Apollo's definition, "half-human, half-divine," is too high for them.[84] He enforces this hierarchy by reminding the satyrs of Silenus' brother Marsyas, whom he flayed alive for playing the *aulos*.

As the play continues, Harrison hints at a parallel between Apollo's hierarchy of creation and the class hierarchy in contemporary Britain. Just as the ancient Athenians distinguish the high art of tragedy from the low art of the satyr play, Harrison's contemporaries distinguish between the high art of poetry and the low art of popular music. As part of this analogy, the satyrs are stand-ins for the British working class, while the audience is addressed as the Apollonian elite.[85] Silenus reveals, "Unlike my poor flayed brother, Marsyas, / I never yearned to move out of my class."[86] This complacency earns him the moniker "Uncle Tom" from the "new generation" of satyrs, who by this time have returned to the stage dressed as "football hooligans." The satyrs' "brutish" music is represented by "ghetto-blasters wrapped in gold foil," distributed to the satyrs as a reward for their help.[87] As Silenus looks on sadly, they spray-paint graffiti, litter the stage with beer cans, slash the backdrop, and burn the papyrus fragments Grenfell and Hunt so carefully sorted at the beginning of the play, fulfilling the role the Apollo assigned to them.

The National Theatre production ends with an additional scene in which the satyrs return "dressed like the South Bank homeless."[88] By this point, the parallels with the contemporary Britain are obvious. They build a "crate city" out of the modular crates used first by Grenfell and Hunt to store papyri and later by the satyrs to construct the Theatre of Dionysus, and they sleep under "papyrus duvets."[89] This "crate city" recalls Cardboard City, a homeless settlement in London's Waterloo train station in the 1980s and 1990s, a gesture toward the rise in homelessness in the UK during this time.

In this way, *The Trackers of Oxyrhynchus*, like *The Common Chorus*, demonstrates one of the affordances of anachronism in verse drama: it creates a temporal porousness that allows not only the characters but the playwright too, to condemn the injustices and excesses of the present. Like the Old Testament prophets, Stein's Susan B., Greig's Prudencia, and Harrison's Lysistrata, Hekabe, and Silenus comprehend a broader swath of history than their own, which gives them the authority to speak not only to their contemporaries but to us later mortals. This is not nostalgic anachronism. Nor is it part of a unified ideological project, like the antique genres Stewart gives an account of in *Crimes of Writing*. As is the case with so many of the features of modern and contemporary verse drama, its position in between lyric poetry and theater allows it to be put to a variety of uses.

CONCLUSION

Verse Drama after the Internet

So far, I have endeavored to show the ways in which English-language playwrights, from the modernist era to the present, have imported features from lyric poetry in order to disrupt the conventions of realist theater from the nineteenth century. The experiments with voice in the first two chapters work against realist portrayals of character by exposing the noncoincidence of voice and identity. The plays in the second section treat language as potentially resistant material, not a transparent medium of communication, thereby putting pressure on the dramatic conventions that underwrite communication and understanding between characters within a play, and between theater-makers and their audiences. And in the last section, we saw two different ways verse dramas undermine the conventions by which time and chronology are represented in theater, conventions that goes back further than the nineteenth century—all the way back to Aristotle's *Poetics*, in fact. Along the way, we have observed a few cases in which performance puts pressure on lyric conventions: Plath's and Walcott's radio plays, and Laurens's *The Three Birds*. Given that rebellion against realism is a defining feature of postdramatic theater, many of these verse plays might be classified within this movement. And yet, the genealogies traced in the foregoing chapters reveal that these efforts to challenge realist notions of character, communication, and time predate postdramatic theater proper; they are present in the plays of Stein, Yeats, Eliot, Williams, Auden, and Barnes in the first half of the century. What we see then, in verse drama over the course of a century or so, is an ever-expanding rebellion, which begins by pushing back against nineteenth-century realism but eventually broadens its target to the entire Western tradition of theater. If, as Johnson argues in *The Idea of Lyric*, in ancient Greek drama "lyric exists to serve dramatic ends," then in twentieth-century verse drama, lyric exists to serve antidramatic ends.[1]

The experimental impulse I have been at pains to tease out of modernist verse plays has hitherto been subsumed under the heading of modernist anti-theatricalism, as theorized by Puchner in *Stage Fright*. He points out that what modernist theater defines itself against is "a particular form of mimesis at work in the theater," that uses "human performers as signifying material."[2] The uneasy relationship between bodies on the stage and words on the page troubles the modernist playwright, but does not lead to a rejection of performance. Instead, Puchner argues, it becomes a "productive force" within theater.[3] Verse drama, insofar as it hybridizes a highly textual genre of literature, the lyric, with performance, facilitates this anti-theatrical theater. But it does more than that. For one thing, it extends beyond the period of modernist anti-theatricalism. And in the second half of the twentieth century, verse drama gets taken up as part of what might be considered the opposite dynamic. Whereas modernist anti-theatricalism puts its trust in texts rather than bodies as the signifying material of theater, antitextual theater stages self-consciously embodied and evanescent performances that undermine the authority of—and sometimes the audience's faith in—language. That verse drama plays a part in these apparently opposed projects is a testament to the flexibility that comes with its newly invented hybridity in the twentieth century.

So, what's next for verse drama, the most textual of performance arts and most bodily of literary forms? Among other things, it is uniquely well suited for theater in the digital age, as playwrights ask new questions about the relationship between voice and embodiment, given the rise of a virtual world, generated and conducted via text. Perhaps I should not call them new, as many of these questions will be familiar from the preceding chapters—it's the answers that are different. Now verse dramatists want to know: is it possible for language to produce a voice without a human subject? Playwrights have already used verse to render ambiguous who is speaking and how many speakers there are: think of Stein's *Ladies' Voices* (1916) or Sarah Kane's *4.48 Psychosis* (2000). In Kane's plays, "character and language slightly disengage from one another," Dan Rebellato observes, as a result of the unattributed lines of verse in the script.[4] Caryl Churchill does something similar in *Love and Information* (2013), a series of 57 short scenes with unknown and changing participants. As in *4.48 Psychosis*, the lines are not attributed to characters. The script even includes, in an appendix titled "Random," a list of "Optional" lines—math facts, Google trivia, tabloid headlines—that can be inserted at any point in the play, as if their context and speaker did not matter.[5] I take this to be a kind of send-up of the way we receive information today: depersonalized, often unattributed, cut off from the relevant context.

Playwrights like Joyelle McSweeney and Khadijah Queen explore the relationship between embodiment and subjectivity online. The internet is for McSweeney what the radio was for Walcott and Plath: a medium that simultaneously—paradoxically—embodies and disembodies language, allowing for a thematic meditation on the relationship between the physical and the textual. McSweeney refers to her approach as "posthumous poetics," a term that designates any language that survives and proliferates outside of the author's control. An example is the eponymous "dead youth" in *Dead Youth, or The Leaks* (2013); they are the victims of what McSweeney calls "collateral murder," caused by unethical labor practices, environmental disasters, police brutality, hate crimes, drug trafficking, and war. They are able to live on in her plays with the help of digital technology. As one dead youth explains, "I'm dead so I can live two places: everywhere and on the Internet."[6] *The Commandrine* (2004) features another group of "unwittingly posthumous" characters, a group of dead sailors, who continue to follow their routine of "chores and drills made up largely of word games" even though their ship is at the bottom of the ocean.[7] The eponymous Commandrine asks the audience, "What does it mean that they continue their routine / down there, without a sprite, without a soul?"[8] Their wordplay is apparently not the work of human consciousness, then, but the product of mechanical processes that continue even after death. In this way, *The Commandrine* stages the automatic production of figurative language, independent of a controlling human consciousness. The games they play, as well as the lists produced by the dead youth in *Dead Youth*, are dictated by the material properties of language; they follow patterns of rhyme, meter, assonance, and consonance, like the plays in Chapter Four.[9]

Queen's play *Non-Sequitur*, according to the playwright herself, "explores the relationship between body and text/speech, how the body mediates thought, feeling and perception, enacting unconscious drives and performing/interacting with stereotypes in absurd, unexpected ways."[10] She turns these drives and stereotypes into characters: some are personified types ("The Habitual Justifier," "The Tiger Mom"), others inhuman concepts ("The 40% Discount," "The Weekend Yoga Class"), and a few fall somewhere in between ("White Appropriation"). Given that the humor and pathos of the play is embedded in the names of the dramatis personae, a feature of the script not usually voiced in performance, Queen's play poses a challenge for performers. In the 2015 production by Fiona Templeton's company The Relationship, a narrator, seated on stage through the play, announced each character's name every time they spoke. One thing Queen seems to be getting at is the power of unwilled forces like institutional racism to dictate our thoughts and actions, despite our attempts to suppress them. She is also interested in the way these nonvolitional forces play out online. So, some scenes are set in virtual locations, rather than physical places: for example, one scene takes place "[i]nside multiple social and dating apps on a smartphone."[11] Some of the characters are human personae from the internet ("The Eharmony Skeptic," "The In-App Purchaser") while others are inanimate phenomena ("The Online Payments"). By turning virtual phenomena into characters, Queen highlights the way the internet allows for the creation of speaking subjects. These range from invented social media personae to artificial intelligence so sophisticated that it passes for human. Her portrayal of "The Online Payments"—who keeps saying lines like "your payment was rejected"—for instance, registers the experience of becoming frustrated with an automated response, as if it were a human being with a will.

In addition to the new stagings of disembodied voices and text-generated subjectivity, twenty-first-century verse plays also evoke recent changes in the way we experience time, thanks to the internet. In *Love and Information*, unattributed lines of dialogue become fragments of data, "bombard[ing] us with information" as happens in daily life, as Seda Ilter observes.[12] In the 2012 production of *Love and Information* at the Royal Court Theatre, director James Macdonald staged the play at the fastest possible pace. Actors delivered their lines quickly, and the transitions between scenes were sudden and abrupt. They were able to get this effect by closing and then opening a screen in front of the sterile, white room in which the action took place, "evoking how we jump from one page to another when we surf on the internet [...] or simultaneously engage with multiple media platforms," Ilter speculates.[13] The use of verse facilitates this pacing, just as we saw with Beckett, although with the opposite effect.

Another example of a play that imitates fast-paced exchange of information in the digital age and "treat[s] meaningful information as data," to quote Bill Blake, is *Shuffle* (2010), the work of the New York-based theater company Elevator Repair Service, known for its stage adaptations of famous works of literature at breakneck speed.[14] Elevator Repair Service has staged verse dramas this way in the past (Shakespeare's *Measure for Measure* in 2017), but *Shuffle* is based on novels: Fitzgerald's *The Great Gatsby*, Hemingway's *The Sun Also Rises*, and Faulkner's *The Sound and the Fury*. The actors read from a script generated in real time by a program that pulls passages from the novels at random. As the text is relayed to the actors via devices concealed behind books, it is also projected onto the wall for the audience to see, so that "the words themselves are conspicuous" according to

Blake.[15] The goal is not to communicate what the novels say; instead, as we saw in *Nayatt School*, it is a staging of language *as language*. Jason Farman has pointed out that it is not immersion but the "continual oscillation between the material and the digital" that most engages audience, presumably because it draws their attention to the material through which the experience is mediated.[16] Although the excerpts come from prose novels, I would argue that the algorithmic excerpting functions somewhat like lineation: it chops up the prose in bite-size pieces, much like the bits of dialogue and "random" facts in *Love and Information*.

But unlike *Love and Information*, *Shuffle* is not meant to be a rebuke. Blake considers it a playful celebration of the discoveries and connections that emerge when we treat literature as data. In this sense, *Shuffle* shares in the pleasure and fun McSweeney derives from the word games in her plays. But, as Blake admits, there is an "implicit moral" here, about the algorithms that structure our experience of the world—and increasingly of art—without our knowledge.[17]

It is clear from these examples why theater practitioners like McSweeney and Lech have insisted on the term "verse drama," even with all of its negative connotations. It is the act of combining the lyric with performance—putting verse in the mouths of embodied characters—that opens up these questions about the intersection of the textual world and the physical world that can take place on the stage or the page, whether that page is in a book or on the web.

NOTES

Introduction

1. Kasia Lech, "Five Reasons Why Verse is the Language for Theatre in the 2020s," *Theatre Times*, March 12, 2021.
2. Harley Granville-Barker, *On Poetry in Drama* (London: Sidgwick and Jackson, 1937), 3–4.
3. J.C. Trewin, *Verse Drama since 1800* (New York: Cambridge University Press, 1956), 5.
4. Glenda Leeming, *Poetic Drama* (New York: St. Martin's, 1989), 1.
5. Wilfrid Wilson Gibson, "Some Thoughts on the Future of Poetic-Drama," *Poetry Review* 3 (1912): 119.
6. Christopher Fry, "Why Verse?" *Vogue*, March 1955: 166.
7. For a discussion of the early history of verse drama in the United States, including the conflict over poetic drama among the members of the Provincetown Players, see Donna Gerstenberger, "Verse Drama in America: 1916–1939," *Modern Drama* 6, no. 3 (1963): 309–22.
8. Nora Sayre, "The Poets' Theatre: A Memoir of the Fifties," *Grand Street* 3, no. 3 (1984): 93.
9. Ibid., 95.
10. Since 1986, the Poets' Theatre has produced an Eliot centennial (1988), Beckett's *Stirrings Still* (1989), *Beckett Woman: Not I, Footfalls, Rockaby, Come & Go* (2015), Edgar Lee Masters's *Spoon River Anthology* (2015), and Martha Collins's *Blue Front* (2015).
11. William G. McCollom, "Verse Drama: A Reconsideration," *Comparative Drama* 14, no. 2 (1980): 99, accessed September 4, 2023, www.jstor.org/stable/41152885.
12. Derek Walcott, *The Poet in the Theatre* (London: The Poetry Book Society, 1990), 3.
13. Charles Martin, "The Three Contemporary Voices of Poetry," *The New Criterion* (April 2004): 35, accessed September 4, 2023, https://newcriterion.com/issues/2004/4/the-three-voices-of-contemporary-poetry.
14. Joel Brouwer, "The Possibility of a Poetic Drama," "Harriet Books" (blog), *Poetry Foundation*, July 2009, https://www.poetryfoundation.org/harriet/2009/07/the-possibility-of-a-poetic-drama.
15. Walcott, *Poet in the Theatre*, 2.

Notes

16. R.C. Churchill, "Age of Eliot," *Concise Cambridge History of English Literature* (Cambridge: Cambridge University Press, 1970), 908.
17. Octavio Paz, *Children of the Mire: Modern Poetry from Romanticism to the Avant-garde*, trans. Rachel Phillips, (Cambridge, MA: Harvard University Press, 1991), 3–4.
18. Michael Goldman, *On Drama: Boundaries of Genre, Borders of Self* (Ann Arbor, MI: University of Michigan, 2000), 34.
19. Edward Moore, "Preface," *The Gamester*, Project Gutenberg, accessed September 4, 2023.
20. Jacob Tootalian, "Without Measure: The Language Of Shakespeare's Prose," *Journal For Early Modern Cultural Studies* 13, no. 4 (2013): 48.
21. Harrison and, more recently, Richard O'Brien have experimented with the democratic potential of verse on the stage. See O'Brien's reflections on his attempts to put verse to egalitarian ends, in "Community and Conflict: a Practitioner's Perspective," *Connotations* 27 (2018): 120–54.
22. Denis Donoghue, *The Third Voice* (Princeton, NJ: Princeton University Press, 1959), 5.
23. Stendhal, *Racine and Shakespeare*, trans. Guy Daniels (London: Alma Classics, 2019), 9.
24. Ibid., 92.
25. Joseph Wood Krutch, *Modernism in Modern Drama* (Ithaca, NY: Cornell University Press, 1953), viii, 5.
26. Derek Miller, "Realism," *Ibsen in Context* (London: Cambridge University Press, 2021), 43.
27. Stine Brenna Taugbøl, "Henrik Ibsen's Use of Metre in His Verse Dramas," *Ibsen Studies* 9, no. 1 (2009): 19.
28. Quoted in Miller, "Realism," 39.
29. Henrik Ibsen, *Correspondence of Henrik Ibsen*, trans. and ed. Mary Morison (New York: Haskell House, 1970), 367.
30. Mads B. Claudi observes a stagnation of the lyric during the 1840s, that resulted in the widespread belief that it was backward-looking. At the same time, drama was gaining cache as literature, not just entertainment (*Ibsen in Context*, 30).
31. Walcott, *Poet in the Theatre*.
32. Ibid.
33. Ibid.
34. W.B. Worthen, *Print and the Poetics of Modern Drama* (London: Cambridge University Press, 2005), 6, 55.
35. G.W.F. Hegel, *Aesthetics: Lectures on Fine Arts*, trans. T.M. Knox (London: Oxford University Press, 1998), 1038.
36. Virginia Jackson, *Dickinson's Misery* (Princeton, NJ: Princeton University Press, 2005), 6.

Notes

37. Ibid., 8.
38. Ibid., 9.
39. T.S. Eliot, "The Possibility of Poetic Drama," in *The Sacred Wood* (New York: Barnes and Noble, 1928), 66.
40. William Archer, *The Old Drama and the New* (Boston: Small, Maynard and Company, 1923), 4.
41. Ibid., 5.
42. Ibid.
43. Gareth Lloyd Evans also presents poetic drama as a hybrid, uniting the temporal realm of man with the transcendent realm of divinity; see *The Language of Modern Drama* (London: Rowman and Littlefield, 1997).
44. T.S. Eliot, *The Three Voices of Poetry* (Cambridge University Press, 1954), 6–7.
45. Ibid., 29.
46. Ibid, 25, 27.
47. Ibid, 6–7.
48. Ibid., 7.
49. Martin, "Three Contemporary Voices," 34.
50. Eliot, *Three Voices*, 12.
51. Ibid.
52. Natalia Cecire, *Experimental* (Baltimore, MD: Johns Hopkins University Press, 2019). Experimental writing, Cecire argues, "does not *do experiments*" but rather "performs epistemic virtues" (23).
53. Fry, "Why Verse," 137.
54. Quoted in Tony Harrison, *Collected Film Poetry* (London: Faber, 2007), 16.
55. Heidi R. Bean, *Acts of Poetry: American Poets' Theater and the Politics of Performance* (Ann Arbor, MI: University of Michigan Press, 2019), 10.
56. This paradoxical idea of an "experimental tradition" is inspired by Marjorie Perloff's identification of an "avant-garde tradition" in American poetry; see *Differentials* (Tuscaloosa, AL: University of Alabama Press, 2004) and "Language Poetry and the Lyric Subject" in *Critical Inquiry* 25, no. 3 (1999): 405–34. Cecire, however, argues that this continuity is an illusion created by Language poets.
57. Martin Puchner, *Stage Fright* (Baltimore, MD: Johns Hopkins University Press, 2011).
58. Erika Fischer-Lichte, "The Avant-Garde and the Semiotics of the Antitextual Gesture," trans. James M Harding, in *Contours of the Theatrical Avant-Garde* (Ann Arbor: University of Michigan: 2000), 82.
59. Sarah Bay-Cheng and Barbara Cole, *Poets at Play: An Anthology of Modernist Drama* (Selinsgrove, PA: Susquehanna University Press, 2010), 18.
60. Worthen, *Print and the Poetics of Modern Drama*, 3.

Notes

61. Hans-Theis Lehmann, *Postdramatic Theatre*, trans. Karen Jurs-Munby (New York: Routledge, 2006), 145.
62. Lehmann, *Postdramatic Theatre*, 18.
63. Claire Warden, *British Avant-garde Theatre* (London: Palgrave MacMillan, 2012), 24.

Chapter 1

1. Aristotle, *Poetics*, trans. Stephen Halliwell (Chapel Hill, NC: University of North Carolina Press, 1986), 4.
2. Plato, *The Republic of Plato*, trans. Allan Bloom. 2nd Ed. (New York: Basic Books, 1991), 3.394c.
3. Friedrich Nietzsche, *The Birth of Tragedy and the Genealogy of Morals*, trans. Frans Golffing (New York: Doubleday, 1956), 56.
4. Ibid., 55.
5. John Herington, *Poetry into Drama* (Berkeley, CA: University of California Press, 1985), x.
6. William Shakespeare, *Henry V*, in *Arden Shakespeare Third Series Complete Works*, eds Richard Proudfoot, Ann Thompson, David Scott Kastan and H.R. Woudhuysen (London: The Arden Shakespeare, 2020), I.15–16.
7. Lloyd Evans avers that Eliot is only able to write poetic drama because he believes in the "integrated reality of God's created universe" (24).
8. Claire Warden, *British Avant-Garde Theatre* (London: Palgrave MacMillan, 2012), 142.
9. W.R. Johnson, *The Idea of the Lyric* (Berkeley, CA: University of California Press, 1982), 182.
10. *The Family Reunion* is based on Aeschylus' *Oresteia*, *The Cocktail Party* on Euripides' *Alcestis*, *The Confidential Clerk* on Euripides' comedy *Ion*, and *The Elder Statesman* on Sophocles' *Oedipus at Colonus*.
11. T.S. Eliot, *The Rock* (London: Faber, 1934), 7.
12. Ibid.
13. Randy Malamud, *Where the Words Are Valid: T.S. Eliot's Communities of Drama* (London: Greenwood Press, 1994), 41.
14. David Ward, *T.S. Eliot Between Two Worlds* (London: Routledge, 2015), 180.
15. T.S. Eliot, *The Three Voices of Poetry* (Cambridge University Press, 1954), 12.
16. Ibid.
17. Ibid., 19.
18. Ibid.

Notes

19. Ibid., 12–13.
20. T.S. Eliot, *Murder in the Cathedral* (New York: Harcourt, 1935), 19.
21. Ibid., 18.
22. Eliot, *Three Voices of Poetry*, 28, 32.
23. T.S. Eliot, *The Family Reunion*, in *Collected Plays* (London: Faber, 1963), 74.
24. Ibid., 88.
25. Ibid.
26. T.S. Eliot, *Poetry and Drama* (New York: Faber, 1950), 35.
27. Ibid., 33–4.
28. Richard Lattimore, *Complete Greek Tragedies*, vol. III (Chicago: University of Chicago Press, 1992), vii.
29. Albert Weiner, "The Function of the Tragic Greek Chorus," *Theatre Journal* 32, no. 2 (1980): 208.
30. Pius XII, *Mystici Corporis Christi* [Encyclical Letter on the Mystical Body of Christ], The Holy See, June 29, 1943, sec 1.
31. Ibid.
32. Dorothy L. Sayers, *The Just Vengeance* (Eugene, Oregon: Wipf and Stock, 2011), 27. Although the play was very well received by audiences (including the Queen) and Sayers considered it "the best thing I've done" (quoted in Barbara Reynolds, *The Passionate Intellect*: Dorothy L. Sayers' Encounter with Dante Kent, OH: Kent State University Press, 1989, 97), this play has received very little critical attention. It was staged once, and then broadcast once by the BBC on March 30, 1947. Barbara Reynolds gives it the most thorough treatment in *The Passionate Intellect*. Janice Brown also considers it in *The Seven Deadly Sins in the Work of Dorothy L. Sayers* (Kent, OH: Kent State University Press, 1998).
33. Ibid., 27–8.
34. Sayers uses the name "Persona Dei" for Christ throughout the play. This may be because Sayers was trying to appease the Lord Chamberlain, who at the time was tasked with the censorship of theatrical productions; he gave her special permission to have a Christ figure in the play despite existing laws against the depiction of Christ on the stage.
35. The 750th anniversary would have been 1945, but the production was postponed until the summer of 1946 because of the war.
36. Sayers, *Just Vengeance*, 28.
37. Ibid.
38. Norah Lambourne, "Recollections of Designing for the Religious Plays of Dorothy L. Sayers," *Costume* 25, no. 1 (1991): 2.
39. W.H. Auden, *On the Frontier* (New York: Random House, 1938), 114.
40. Sayers, *Just Vengeance*, 30.

Notes

41. Ibid., 31–4.
42. Ibid., 30.
43. Ibid.
44. Eric Csapo gives an example from the entrance of the chorus in Aristophanes' The Woman at the Thesmophoria; see "Imagining the Shape of Choral Dance" in *Choreutika: Performing and Theorizing Dance in Ancient Greece* (Rome: Fabriio Serraeditore, 2017). Since, as Csapo observes, "choruses are well-drilled, even if they are amateurs," the self-instructions in Aristophanes' play "have no obvious function [...] other than to mark the imitation of cultic music," which is likely what Aristophanes is parodying (122).
45. Sayers, *Just Vengeance*, 30.
46. Ibid., 42.
47. Ibid.
48. Ibid., 84.
49. Ibid.
50. Ibid., 94.
51. This moment has its own liturgical parallel: the practice of having the congregation read the lines of the crowd during the reading of the Passion account on Palm Sunday.
52. Ibid., 88.
53. Ibid.
54. Neal A. Lester, Ntozake Shange (New York: Garland, 1995), 67; P. Jane Splawn, "'Change the Joke[r] and slip the joke': Boal's 'Joker' system in Ntozake Shange's for colored girls ... and spell #7," *Modern Drama* 41, no. 3 (1998): 389.
55. Ntozake Shange, *for colored girls* who have considered suicide, when the rainbow is enuf (New York : MacMillan, 1977), xv.
56. Cheryl Clarke, *"After Mecca": Women Poets and the Black Arts Movement* (New Brunswick, NJ: Rutgers University Press, 2005), 95.
57. David Savran, *The Playwright's Voice* (New York: Theatre Communications Group, 1999), 195.
58. Shange, *for colored girls*, 1.
59. Ibid., 2–3.
60. Ibid., 2.
61. Ibid., 3.
62. Ibid.
63. Culler, *Theory of the Lyric* (Cambridge, MA: Harvard University Press, 2015), 186.
64. John Timpane, "'The Poetry of a Moment': Politics and the Open Form in the Drama of Ntozake Shange," *Studies in American Drama*, 1945-Present 4 (1989): 91.

65. Ibid., 99.
66. Shange, *for colored girls*, 2.
67. Ibid., 4.
68. Ibid., 16.
69. Sarah Mahurin, "'Speakin Arms' and Dancing Bodies in Ntozake Shange," *African American Review* 46, no. 2 (2013): 335.
70. Ibid., 336.
71. Ibid., 339.
72. Shange, *for colored girls*, 15.
73. Joyelle McSweeney, "Justice Absconditus, or Why I Write Verse Plays," *Fanzine* October 8, 2017.
74. Thomas Hobbes, *Leviathan*, ed. Richard Tuck (Cambridge: Cambridge University Press, 1996), 114.
75. Shange, for colored girls, 52.
76. Ibid.
77. Timpane, "The Poetry of a Moment," 92.
78. Mary Holland, "Field Day's Tenth Birthday," program notes for *The Cure at Troy*, Stephen Rea and Bob Crowley, directors (Guildhall, Derry, Northern Ireland, 1990), 12.
79. Seamus Heaney, *The Cure at Troy* (New York: Farrar, Straus, and Giroux, 1991), 77.
80. Ibid., 1.
81. Ibid., 2.
82. Ibid.
83. Ibid.
84. Ibid.
85. Ibid.
86. Seamus Heaney, *The Redress of Poetry* (New York: Farrar, Straus and Giroux, 1995).
87. Heaney, *Cure at Troy*, 2.
88. This is one of the original instances of the deus ex machina device, after Aeschylus' *Eumenides*. Both predate Euripides' development of the stage machinery.
89. Ibid., 78.
90. Ibid.
91. See David Grene's introduction to his translation of *Philoctetes* for an overview of the responses to the play's ending, in Sophocles II, ed. David Grene and Richard Lattimore (Chicago: University of Chicago Press, 1969).

Notes

92. Heaney, *Cure at Troy*, 77.
93. Ibid.
94. Ibid., 81.
95. Ibid., 78.

Chapter 2

1. Northrop Frye, *Anatomy of Criticism* (Princeton, NJ: Princeton University Press, 1957), 250.
2. Jonathan Culler, *Theory of the Lyric* (Cambridge, MA: Harvard University Press, 2015), 187.
3. Ibid., 186.
4. Ibid., 187; Paul de Man, "Lyrical Voice in Contemporary Theory: Riffaterre and Jauss," in *Lyric Poetry: Beyond New Criticism*, ed. Chaviva Hosek and Patricia Parker (Ithaca, NY: Cornell University Press, 1985), 55.
5. Helen Vendler, *Soul Says* (Cambridge, MA: Harvard University Press, 1995), 3.
6. Ibid., 2–3.
7. Robert von Hallberg, *Lyric Powers* (Chicago: University of Chicago, 2008), 42–3.
8. Ibid., 43.
9. Theodor Adorno, "Lyric Poetry and Society," trans. Shierry Weber Nicholson, in *The Lyric Theory Reader*, ed. Virginia Jackson and Yopie Prins (Baltimore, MD: Johns Hopkins Press, 2014), 343.
10. Olena Kalytiak Davis, *The Poem She Didn't Write and Other Poems* (Port Townsend, WA: Copper Canyon Press, 2014), 8.
11. Roland Greene, *Post-Petrarchism* (Princeton, NJ: Princeton University Press, 1991), 14.
12. Davis, *The Poem She Didn't Write*, 12.
13. Percy Bysshe Shelley, *The Complete Poetical Works of Percy Bysshe Shelley*, ed. Thomas Hutchinson (London: Oxford University Press, 1956).
14. Donald McWhinnie, *The Art of Radio* (London: Faber, 1959), 174.
15. Leslie Wheeler, *Voicing American Poetry: Sound and Performance from the 1920s to the Present* (Ithaca, NY: Cornell University Press, 2008), 39; Steven Connor, *Dumbstruck: A Cultural History of Ventriloquism* (London: Oxford University Press, 2000), 35.
16. See Jeffrey Lyn Porter, "Samuel Beckett and the Radiophonic Body: Beckett and the BBC," *Modern Drama* 53, no. 4 (2010): 431–46; James Jesson, "'White World, Not a Sound': Beckett's Radioactive Text in *Embers*," *Texas Studies in Literature and Language* 51, no. 1 (2009): 47–65. Barry McGovern argues that the voices in stage plays like *Not I* and *The Unnameable* are radio voices too; see "Beckett and

Notes

the Radio Voice," in *Samuel Beckett: 100 Years*, ed. Christopher Murray (Dublin: New Island, 2006), 132-44.

17. William Waters, *Poetry's Touch* (Ithaca, NY: Cornell University Press, 2003), 1.
18. Culler, *Theory of the Lyric*, 186.
19. John Ashbery, *Your Name Here* (New York: Farrar, Straus and Giroux, 2000), 3.
20. Culler, *Theory of the Lyric*, 223.
21. For speculation on the date of composition, see John Thieme's *Derek Walcott* (Manchester, UK: Manchester University Press, 1999), 42. More on the production history of *Harry Dernier* can be found in Henry Swanzy, *The Selected Diaries*, ed. Chris Campbell, Michael Niblett, and Victoria Ellen Smith (Leeds, UK: Peepal Tree Press, 2023).
22. Swanzy's diary does not indicate whether the problem is the recording quality or the complexity of Walcott's script (65-8).
23. Ann Spry Rush, *Bonds of Empire* (New York: Oxford University Press, 2001), 170.
24. See Eric Falci, *The Cambridge Introduction to British Poetry, 1945-2010* (London: Cambridge University Press, 2015); Peter J. Kalliney, *Commonwealth of Letters* (New York: Oxford University Press, 2013), 4.
25. Glyne A. Griffith. *The BBC and the Development of Anglophone Caribbean Literature, 1943-1958* (New York: Palgrave Macmillan, 2016), 2.
26. Derek Walcott, *Harry Dernier* (Bridgetown, Barbados: Advocate, 1952), 4.
27. Ibid., 1.
28. Ibid., 1.
29. Ibid., 2.
30. William Shakespeare, *Hamlet*, in *Arden Shakespeare Third Series Complete Works*, ed. Richard Proudfoot, Ann Thompson, David Scott Kastan and H.R. Woudhuysen (London: The Arden Shakespeare, 2020), V.1.189-91.
31. Ibid., 187-8.
32. The name Quant recalls the character in Auden's *The Age of Anxiety*, written four years prior, and sharing its concerns with isolation and interest in the radio. Auden's exploration of mirrored selves anticipates Harry's wish that Quant be "the other me. Harry's split personality," which may explain Walcott's choice of the name.
33. Walcott, *Harry Dernier*, 4.
34. Jonathan Culler, "Apostrophe," in *The Pursuit of Signs* (Ithaca, NY: Cornell University Press, 2002), 143.
35. Walcott, *Harry Dernier*, 5.
36. I hear echoes of Milton's Satan when Harry calls God "Thunderer" (as Satan does in Book VI of *Paradise Lost*) and attempts to invert the relationship between creator and creation (as Satan does in Book V).

Notes

37. W.B. Yeats, *The Yeats Reader*, Revised Edition, ed. Richard J. Finneran (New York: Scribner, 2002), 149.
38. Johnson, *Idea of Lyric* (Berkeley, CA: University of California Press, 1982), 3.
39. Walcott, *Harry Dernier*, 10.
40. Gauri Viswanathan argues that English literature itself was invented as an academic subject for the purposes of educating colonial subjects; see *The Masks of Conquest* (New York: Columbia University Press, 1989).
41. In this production, Penelope Lee played the Wife, Jill Balcon played the Secretary, and Janette Richer played the Girl. This production was aired a second time on September 13. A second production, with Jill Balcon reprising her role and new actors Barbara Jeffords and Rosalie Shanks playing the Wife and the Girl, was aired on the BBC Third Programme on June 9, 1968.
42. Martin Shuttleworth, "Review of *Three Women*," *Listener*, August 30, 1962, 329.
43. Alexis Soloski, "Giving Voice to Sylvia Plath's Pregnant Women," *New York Times*, September 26, 2010, 7.
44. Shaw's production later traveled to the Edinburgh Festival Fringe and the 59E59 Theaters in New York City in 2010.
45. Quoted in Soloski, "Giving Voice," 7.
46. In the limited edition of the play printed by Turret Books in 1968, the Secretary is named Secy, which could be an abbreviation of "secretary," but there is some warrant for interpreting it as a nickname. In a letter to her mother in June 1962, Plath identified Ingmar Bergman's *The Brink of Life* (1958) as an inspiration to the play, and that film features a similar character named Cecilia (Sylvia Plath, *Letters Home*, ed. Aurelia Schober Plath, New York: Harper and Row, 1975, 456).
47. Sylvia Plath, *Three Women* (London: Turret Books, 1968), 9.
48. Ibid., 9–10.
49. Burns Singer, "Review of *Three Women*," *Listener*, August 30, 1962, 330.
50. Herbert Tucker, "Dramatic Monologue and the Overhearing of Lyric," in *Lyric Poetry: Beyond New Criticism*, 228.
51. Tucker, "Dramatic Monologue," 229–30.
52. Ibid., 228.
53. Leslie Wheeler, *Voicing American Poetry: Sound and Performance from the 1920s to the Present* (Ithaca, NY: Cornell University Press, 2008), 2.
54. Alexandra Keller, "Shards of Voice: Fragments Excavated toward a Radiophonic Archaeology," in *Experimental Sound and Radio*, ed. Allen S. Weiss (Cambridge, MA: MIT Press), 25.
55. Ibid.
56. Allen S. Weiss, "Radio Icons, Short Circuits, Deep Schisms," in *Experimental Sound and Radio*, 4.
57. McWhinnie, *Art of Radio*, 26.

Notes

58. Derek Furr, *Recorded Poetry and Poetic Reception from Edna Millay to the Circle of Robert Lowell* (New York: Palgrave Macmillan, 2010), 2.
59. Keller, "Shards of Voice," 22.
60. See Linda Bamber's *Comic Women, Tragic Men* (Stanford, CA: Stanford University Press, 1982), 72, for a discussion of Hamlet's "sex nausea."
61. Walcott, *Harry Dernier*, 7.
62. Shakespeare, *Hamlet*, III.1.121.
63. Walcott, *Harry Dernier*, 8.
64. Plath, *Three Women*, 10.
65. Ibid., 9.
66. Ibid., 13.
67. Ibid., 14.
68. Elin Diamond, "(In)Visible Bodies in Churchill's Theatre," *Theatre Journal* 40, no. 2 (1988): 191.

Chapter 3

1. Anthony Easthope, "Problematizing the Pentameter," *New Literary History* 12, no. 3 (1981): 476.
2. Richard O'Brien, "Community and Conflict: a Practitioner's Perspective," *Connotations* 27 (2018): 120–54. Accessed September 7, 2023. www.connotations.de/article/richard-o-brien-a-practioners-perspective-on-verse-drama/" 123.
3. Michael Billington, *State of the Nation: British Theatre since 1945* (London: Faber, 2007), 27.
4. See also Michael Sidnell's *Dances of Death: The Group Theatre of London in the Thirties* (London: Faber, 1984).
5. Laurence Binyon, "The Return to Poetry," *Rhythm* 1, no. 4 (1912): 1–2.
6. Brenda Murphy, *The Provincetown Players and the Culture of Modernity* (Cambridge: Cambridge University Press, 2005), xiii.
7. See Colin Chambers, *The Story of the Unity Theatre* (New York: St. Martins, 1989), 317.
8. Irene Morra, *Verse Drama in England, 1900–2015*, (London: Bloomsbury, 2016), 11.
9. Ibid., 12.
10. Billington, *State of the Nation*, 26.
11. Ezra Pound, *The Cantos of Ezra Pound* (New York: New Directions, 1989), 532.
12. Timothy Steele, *Missing Measures* (Fayetteville, AR: University of Arkansas Press, 1990), 29.

Notes

13. Ibid., 34–40. Ben Glaser has traced the vestiges of counted meter in modern poetry, even in free verse; see *Modernism's Metronome* (Baltimore, MD: Johns Hopkins University Press, 2020).
14. Bertolt Brecht, *Brecht on Theatre*, ed. and trans. John Willett (New York: Hill and Wang, 1992), 115.
15. Brecht, *Brecht on Theatre*, 117.
16. Ibid., 119.
17. Walter Benjamin, *Understanding Brecht* (New York: Verso, 1998), 115. Bruce Gaston argues that this play is as much a response to Shakespeare's history plays as it is an adaptation of Marlowe's play; see Gaston, "Brecht's Pastiche History Play: Renaissance Drama and Modernist Theatre in *Leben Eduards Des Zweiten Von England*," *German Life and Letters* 56, no. 4 (2003): 344–62.
18. Brecht, *Brecht on Theatre*, 190.
19. Ibid., 191, 188.
20. Ibid., 192.
21. T.S. Eliot, *Poetry and Drama* (New York: Faber, 1950), 77, 79.
22. See Brian Vickers, *The Artistry of Shakespeare's Prose* (London: Methuen, 1968), Ralph Berry *Shakespeare and Social Class* (Atlantic Highlands, NJ: Humanities Press International, 1988), and George Steiner *The Death of Tragedy* (New Haven, CT: Yale University Press, 1980) for variations on this argument. Elsewhere, shifts from verse to prose and prose to verse functions as a signal of a change in emotion or psychological state. See, for example, George T. Wright, *Shakespeare's Metrical Art*, (Berkeley, CA: University of California Press, 1988); and Russ McDonald, *Shakespeare and the Art of Language* (New York: Oxford University Press, 2001). O'Brien insists that the use of a shared line of iambic pentameter has the opposite effect: it unifies characters across class divisions.
23. Barton R. Friedman identifies several marks of the "imprint of the Henriad" in his essay "*On Baile's Strand* to *At the Hawk's Well*: Staging the Deeps of the Mind," *Journal of Modern Literature* 4, no. 3 (1975): 626. Declan Kiberd calls it a "thinly disguised reworking" of *Richard II* in "*On Baile's Strand*: W. B. Yeats's National Epic," *Princeton University Library Chronicle* 68, no. 1–2 (2007): 261.
24. The first published version calls the Fool and the Blind Man Fintain and Barach, and they speak in prose. See *On Baile's Strand Manuscript Materials*, ed. Jared Curtis and Declan Kiely (Ithaca, NY: Cornell University Press, 2014).
25. W.B. Yeats, *The Yeats Reader*, ed. Richard J. Finneran (New York: Scribner, 2002), 180.
26. Ibid. The Young Man's lines, and Cuchulain's final speech, are consistent across the published and performed versions of the play, despite Yeats's significant revisions to the first half of the play between its first run at the Abbey in 1904 and the subsequent version published at the end of 1906.
27. Ibid., 189.

Notes

28. Ibid., 191.
29. It was published in 1917 in a volume called *Four Plays for Dancers*, which include three other Noh-inspired plays: *The Only Jealousy of Emer, The Dreaming of the Bones*, and *Calvary*. Later plays like *The Death of Cuchulain* (1935) and *Purgatory* (1939) are not close imitations of Noh, but do evince its continued influence.
30. Yeats, *Yeats Reader*, 221.
31. Yeats, "Certain Noble Plays of Japan," in *Essays and Introductions* (New York: Collier Books, 1961), 222.
32. Ibid., 223.
33. Yeats, *Yeats Reader*, 219–220.
34. The delivery may be modelled on Noh chant, just as the movements are modelled on Noh dance. Carrie Preston mentions that Yeats learned about utai, a Noh chanting technique, from Itō Michio, who played the Hawk in a later production. See Preston, *Learning to Kneel* (New York: Columbia, 2017), 77.
35. Ibid., 64.
36. Yeats, "Certain Noble Plays," 225.
37. Edward Mendelson, *Later Auden* (New York: Farrar, Straus, and Giroux, 1999), 242.
38. W.H. Auden, *Collected Poems* (New York: Vintage Books, 1991), 449.
39. Ibid.
40. Beth Ellen Roberts notices that this alliterative pattern occasionally infiltrates the prose narration; see *One Voice and Many* (Newark, DE: University of Delaware Press, 2006), 70.
41. Anthony Hecht, *The Hidden Law: The Poetry of W.H. Auden* (Cambridge, MA: Harvard University Press, 1998), 294.
42. Mendelson, *Later Auden*, 243.
43. Richard Hoggart, *Auden: An Introductory Essay* (New Haven, CT: Yale University Press, 1951), 194; Alan Ross, "Third Avenue Eclogue," in *The Modern Movement: A TLS Companion*, ed. John Gross (Chicago: University of Chicago Press, 1992), 138.
44. Quoted in Seamus Perry, "Auden's Forms," in *W.H. Auden in Context*, ed. Tony Sharp (London: Cambridge University Press, 2013), 369.
45. Auden, *Collected Poems*, 454.
46. Steele notes that in Anglo-Saxon poetry, "sentences conclude more often at mid-line breaks than at line endings"; see *All the Fun's in How You Say a Thing* (Columbus, OH: Ohio University Press, 1999), 247.
47. Roberts, *One Voice and Many*, 44.
48. Auden, *Collected Poems*, 464.

Notes

49. Ibid., 485.
50. Ibid., 487.
51. Ibid., 489.
52. Alan Jacobs, "Introduction," *The Age of Anxiety* (Princeton, NJ: Princeton University Press, 2011), xxxix.
53. Judith Malina, "Remembering Jackson Mac Low," *Performing Arts Journal* 27, no. 2 (2005): 76.
54. The production itself he described as "not very successful, but certainly interesting"; see John Ashbery, "Interview: Poet in the Theatre," *Performing Arts Journal* 3, no. 3 (1979): 19.
55. Daniela Caselli, *Improper Modernism: Djuna Barnes's Bewildering Corpus* (Burlington, VT: Ashgate, 2009), 221.
56. Meryl Altman, "*The Antiphon*: 'No Audience at All'?", in *Silence and Power: A Reevaluation of Djuna Barnes*, ed. Mary Lynn Broe (Carbondale, IL: Southern Illinois University Press, 1991), 272.
57. Quoted in Caselli, *Improper Modernism*, 221–2.
58. See production history in Philip Herring, *Djuna: The Life and Works of Djuna Barnes* (New York: Viking, 1995), 346.
59. Julie Taylor argues that Barnes began working on the play as early as 1936. See "Revising *The Antiphon*, Restaging Trauma; Or, Where Sexual Politics Meets Sexual History," *Modernism/modernity* 18, no. 1 (2011): 126.
60. Goody avoids coming down on one side or the other, classifying the play's meter as "Shakespearean-Jacobean free verse," in *Modernist Articulations: A Cultural Study of Djuna Barnes, Mina Loy, and Gertrude Stein* (New York: Palgrave Macmillan, 2007), 2.
61. Louise de Salvo argues that the play itself is an act of revenge on Barnes's part for the crimes her family perpetrated on her as a child.
62. Caselli, *Improper Modernism*, 197.
63. Barnes, *The Antiphon*, in *Selected Works of Djuna Barnes* (New York: Farrar Straus and Cudahy, 1962), 194.
64. Dudley Fitts, "Discord and Old Age: THE ANTIPHON. By Djuna Barnes," *New York Times*, April 20, 1958.
65. Marie Ponsot, "Careful Sorrow and Observed Compline," *Poetry* 95, no. 1 (1959): 48.
66. George P. Elliott, "Review: A Libretto: And Two Millstones of Our Time," *The Hudson Review* 11, no. 2 (1958): 311.
67. "The Antiphon" (review), *Times Literary Supplement*, April 5, 1958, 182.
68. Alex Goody, "'High and Aloof': Verse, Violence, and the Audience in Djuna Barnes's *The Antiphon*." *Modern Drama* 57, no. 3 (2014): 359.
69. Altman, "No Audience at All," 273.

70. Barnes, *The Antiphon*, 81–2.
71. Ibid., 102.
72. Barnes, *The Antiphon*, 104.
73. Ibid., 96, 126.
74. Ibid., 210.
75. Ibid., 83.
76. Goody argues that her theatrical references are part of her critique of violence as spectacle, while Altman argues that they contribute to her critique of the theatricality of interpersonal interaction.
77. Barnes, *The Antiphon*, 15.
78. Ibid., 38.
79. Ibid., 213.
80. Ponsot, "Careful Sorrow," 48.
81. Ibid., 214.
82. I should note that Auden collaborated with Brecht on an adaptation of Webster's *The Duchess of Malfi* in 1946.
83. John Arden, "Building the Play," *Encore* July-August 1961: 22.
84. John Arden, *Plays: One* (London: Methuen, 1994), 227.
85. John Arden, "Telling a True Tale," in *Drama Criticism Developments Since Ibsen: A Casebook*, ed. Arnold P. Hinchcliffe (New York: Macmillan, 1979), 127.
86. Arden, *Plays: One*, 9.
87. Brecht, *Brecht on Theatre*, 190.
88. Georg Gaston, "An Interview with John Arden," *Contemporary Literature* 32, no 2 (1991): 155.
89. Ibid.
90. The first folk revival took place at the turn-of-the-century, and was associated with more conservative figures like Francis J. Child and Cecil Sharp, who recorded, categorized, and standardized ballads and folk songs from the British Isles and North America. These early revivalists often downplayed or censored scandalous elements in their source material, producing more wholesome versions of traditional songs. The midcentury folk revival began as a more progressive, socialist movement.
91. Michael Brocken, *The British Folk Revival: 1944–2002* (London: Routledge, 2003), 41.
92. James Porter, "ballad," in *Grove Music Online* (London: Oxford University Press, 2001).
93. James Hodgson, *The Social Conflict* (London: Methuen, 1972), 149.
94. Arden, *Plays: One*, 19.

Notes

95. Ibid., 53.
96. Ibid., 41.
97. Ibid., 54.
98. Ibid., 119.
99. Mary Burke, *Tinkers: Synge and the Cultural History of the Irish Traveller* (London: Oxford University Press, 2009), 198.
100. Quoted in Burke, *Tinkers*, 199.
101. Arden, *Plays: One*, 124.
102. Brecht, *Brecht on Theatre*, 201.
103. Arden, *Plays: One*, 127.
104. Ibid., xvii.
105. Ibid., 148.
106. Ibid., 119.

Chapter 4

1. Edward Mendelson, *Later Auden* (New York: Farrar, Straus, and Giroux, 1999), 243.
2. Northrop Frye, *Anatomy of Criticism* (Princeton, NJ: Princeton University Press, 1957).
3. Jonathan Culler, *Theory of the Lyric* (Cambridge, MA: Harvard University Press, 2015), 8.
4. Robert Von Hallberg, *Lyric Powers* (Chicago: University of Chicago Press, 2008) 4–5.
5. Mutlu Konuk Blasing, *Lyric Poetry: The Pain and the Pleasure of Words* (Princeton, NJ: Princeton University Press, 2007), 2.
6. W.B. Worthen, *Print and the Poetics of Modern Drama* (London: Cambridge University Press, 2005), 45.
7. Ibid., 55.
8. Kathleen George, *Rhythm into Drama* (Pittsburgh: University of Pittsburgh Press, 1980), 30.
9. T.S. Eliot, *Poetry and Drama* (New York: Faber, 1950), 13.
10. Following *Nayatt School*, this would become a recurring feature of Wooster Group shows. See Andrew Quick, *The Wooster Group Workbook* (New York: Routledge, 2007), 11.
11. It is worth remembering that *The Cocktail Party*, like all of Eliot's later plays, is itself a very loose adaptation, of Euripides' *Alcestis*. See R.G. Tanner, "The Dramas of T. S. Eliot and Their Greek Models," *Greece & Rome* 17, no. 2 (1970): 123–4.

Notes

12. Quick, *Wooster Group Workbook*, 9.
13. Michael Vanden Heuvel, *Performing Drama / Dramatizing Performance* (Ann Arbor, MI: University of Michigan, 1991), 128–9.
14. Lenora Champagne, "Always Starting New: Elizabeth LeCompte," *The Drama Review* 25, no. 3 (1981): 23.
15. Quick, *Wooster Group Workbook*, 9.
16. *Nayatt School* itself became the object of scrutiny, when the Wooster Group revisited the material for show called *Since I Can Remember*. In her program note, director Elizabeth LeCompte calls it a "reanimating" of *Nayatt School*; in the show itself, Kate Valk calls it a "piece on top of a piece."
17. T.S. Eliot, *The Cocktail Party* (New York: Harcourt, 1950).
18. Vanden Heuvel, *Performing Drama / Dramatizing Performance*, 126.
19. In *Since I Can Remember*, Kate Valk reveals that these "demented doctor scenes" were inspired by Arch Oboler's *Drop Dead*, a record of horror stories Gray listened to.
20. David Savran, *Breaking the Rules: The Wooster Group* (New York: Theatre Communications Group, 1998), 49.
21. See Spaulding Gray, "Children of Paradise: Working with Kids," *Performing Arts Journal* 5, no. 1 (1980): 66–7.
22. Savran, *Breaking the Rules*, 52.
23. Antonin Artaud, *The Theater and its Double*, trans. Mary Caroline Richards (New York: Grove Press, 1958), 84–5.
24. Ibid., 89.
25. Hans-Theis Lehmann, *Postdramatic Theatre*, trans. Karen Jurs-Munby (New York: Routledge, 2006), 145.
26. Artaud, *Theatre and its Double*, 89–91.
27. Joanna Laurens, "Make it up," *The Guardian*, December 11, 2003.
28. Joanna Laurens, *The Three Birds* (London: Oberon Books, 2001), 5.
29. Ibid., 64.
30. Ibid., 13.
31. Ibid., 13.
32. Saskia Leggett, "Avian Greeks keep sex within the nest," *Yale Daily News*, February 10, 2006, B7.
33. Laurens, *Three Birds*, 16.
34. Ibid., 20.
35. William Wordsworth, *Lyrical Ballads, with Other Poems* (London: Longman and Rees, 1800), xxxiii–xxxiv.
36. Laurens, *Three Birds*, 22.

Notes

37. Ibid., 31.
38. Ibid.
39. Ibid.
40. Ibid., 32.
41. Ibid., 36.
42. Ibid., 37.
43. In this respect, Laurens's adaptation is similar to Ovid, where Philomela speaks only after she is raped.
44. Ibid.
45. Ibid., 44.
46. Ibid., 51.
47. Ibid., 47.
48. Claire Warden, *British Avant-Garde Theatre* (London: Palgrave MacMillan, 2012), 4.
49. Gertrude Stein, *Lectures in America* (Boston: Beacon Press, 1957), 111.
50. Ibid., 115–16.
51. Gertrude Stein, *Last Plays and Operas* (Baltimore: Johns Hopkins Press, 1949), 337.
52. Ibid., 344.
53. Ibid., 348.
54. James F. Schaefer, "An Examination of Language as Gesture in a Play by Gertrude Stein," *Literature in Performance* 3, no. 1 (1982): 2.
55. Williams himself acknowledges Coward as an influence, but several critics have posited Pirandello as the more decisive influence. See Thomas Kilroy, "Brecht, Beckett, and Williams," *Sagetrieb* 3, no. 2 (1984): 84.
56. William Carlos Williams, *Many Loves and Other Plays* (Norfolk, CT: New Directions, 1961), 92.
57. Ibid.
58. Ibid., 3.
59. Sarah Bay-Cheng and Barbara Cole, *Poets at Play: An Anthology of Modernist Drama* (Selinsgrove, PA: Susquehanna University Press, 2010), 213.
60. Williams, *Many Loves*, 93.
61. Bay-Cheng, *Poets at Play*, 216.
62. Williams, *Many Loves*, 4.
63. Beck and Malina founded Living Theatre in 1947. In the early days, they performed several verse plays, including a staged reading of Stein's *Ladies' Voices* (1951), full productions of Stein's *Doctor Faustus Lights the Lights* (1951), Kenneth Rexroth's *Beyond the Mountains* (1951), Eliot's *Sweeney Agonistes* (1952), John Ashbery's *The Heroes* (1952), and Auden's *Age of Anxiety* (1954).

Notes

64. Bertolt Brecht, *Brecht on Theatre*, ed. and trans. John Willett (New York: Hill and Wang, 1992), 212.
65. Ibid., 43.
66. Ibid., 45.
67. Marvin Carlson, "Alternative Theatre," in *The Cambridge History of American Theatre*, vol. III, ed. Don B. Wilmeth and Christopher Bigsby, (Cambridge: Cambridge University Press, 2000), 253.
68. Terrell W. Marrs, "The Living Theatre: History, Theatrics, and Politics," PhD diss., (Texas Tech University, 1984), 102.
69. Williams, *Many Loves*, 93.
70. Eleanor Berry, "Williams' Development of a New Prosodic Form: Not the 'Variable Foot,' But the "Sight-Stanza," *William Carlos Williams Review* 7, no. 2 (1981): 23.
71. Berry, "Williams' Development," 26.
72. Ibid., 23.
73. Ibid., 25.
74. Williams *Many Loves*, 93.
75. Kilroy, "Brecht, Beckett, and Williams," 81.
76. Brecht, *Brecht on Theatre*, 213.
77. Kilroy, "Brecht, Beckett, and Williams," 86.
78. For history of the Living Theatre production and its reception, see David A. Fedo, "The William Carlos Williams-Julian Beck Correspondence and the Production of 'Many Loves,'" *William Carlos Williams Newsletter* 3, no. 2 (1977): 12–17.
79. Williams, *Many Loves*, 9.
80. Heidi R. Bean, *Acts of Poetry: American Poets' Theater and the Politics of Performance* (Ann Arbor, MI: University of Michigan Press, 2019), 86.
81. Christopher Innes, "Text, Pre-Text/Pretext: The Language of Avant-Garde Experiment" in *Contours of the Theatrical Avant-Garde*, 62.
82. Williams, *Many Loves*, 90.
83. Bill Blake, *Theatre and the Digital* (London: MacMillan, 2014), 59.
84. Lehmann, *Postdramatic Theatre*, 33.

Chapter 5

1. Jorie Graham, "I Catch Sight of the Now," in *To 2040* (Port Townsend, WA: Copper Canyon Press, 2023), 38.

Notes

2. Ibid.
3. Ibid.
4. Henri Bergson, *Time and Free Will* (New York: Harper and Row, 1960), 79.
5. Ibid., 81.
6. Graham, "I Catch Sight," 38.
7. Ibid.
8. Ibid., 39.
9. Lehmann, *Postdramatic Theater*, 161. Others have argued that all theater seeks to make the audience aware of time as time. See Ian Rabey's *Theatre, Time, and Temporality* (Chicago: University of Chicago Press, 2016), 43, where he argues "a theatrical performance is a specifically heightened and demonstrative awareness of time." Matthew Wagner makes a similar argument in *Shakespeare, Theatre, and Time* (London, Routledge, 2012), 4, attending to the way that Shakespeare's work "sharpens our awareness of different, often conflicting schemes of time, and of the 'thickness' of the present, past, and future."
10. Lehmann, *Postdramatic Theater*, 156.
11. Ibid., 161.
12. Ibid., 22.
13. Susan Stewart, *Poetry and the Fate of the Senses* (Chicago: University of Chicago, 2002), 83.
14. See Richard Schechner, *Between Theater and Anthropology* (Philadelphia: University of Pennsylvania Press, 1985) for the most significant articulation of this approach to theater. For a comprehensive overview and a rebuttal, see Eli Rozik's *Roots of Theatre* (Iowa City, IA: University of Iowa Press, 2002).
15. Richard Schechner, "Drama, Script, Theatre, and Performance" *The Drama Review* 17, no. 3 (1973): 7.
16. Anthony Graham-White, "'Ritual' in Contemporary Theatre and Criticism." *Educational Theatre Journal* 28, no. 3 (1976): 320–1.
17. Jonathan Culler, *Theory of the Lyric* (Cambridge, MA: Harvard University Press, 2015), 223.
18. Roland Greene, *Post-Petrarchism* (Princeton, NJ: Princeton University Press, 1991), 5.
19. Ibid.
20. Ruby Cohn, *A Beckett Canon* (Ann Arbor, MI: University of Michigan Press, 2005), 361. Cohn reveals that the earliest draft of the play was written in prose "punctuated by dots and dashes," but he switched to verse by the first typescript (360).
21. Enoch Brater, "Light, Sound, Movement, and Action in Beckett's *Rockaby*" *Modern Drama* 25, no. 3 (Fall 1982): 345.
22. Samuel Beckett, *The Complete Dramatic Works* (London: Faber, 2005), 435.

Notes

23. Vivian Mercier, "The Uneventful Event" *Irish Times* February 18, 1956, 6.
24. Beckett, *Complete Dramatic Works*, 435.
25. Ibid., 439.
26. Ibid.
27. A 2021 production of the play by EgoPo Classic Theater highlighted the parallels between the psychological state of this character and that of many people during the COVID-19 pandemic and lockdown. "Out-Becketting Beckett," according to one review, these socially-distanced performances took place in different locations around Philadelphia, each attended by one audience member at a time watching through a window and listening to the recording in headphones (Jillian Ashely Blair Ivey, "Time She Stopped: EgoPo Classic Theater presents Samuel Beckett's Rockaby." *Broad Street Review* March 15, 2021).
28. Charles R. Lyons, "Perceiving 'Rockaby'—As a Text, As a Text by Samuel Beckett, As a Text for Performance," *Comparative Drama* 16, no. 4 (Winter 1982): 300.
29. Wagner, *Shakespeare, Theatre, and Time*, 44.
30. William Shakespeare, *Hamlet*, in *Arden Shakespeare Third Series Complete Works*, ed. Richard Proudfoot, Ann Thompson, David Scott Kastan and H.R. Woudhuysen (London: The Arden Shakespeare, 2020), II.i.46–60.
31. Jonathan Culler, "Apostrophe," in *The Pursuit of Signs* (Ithaca, NY: Cornell University Press, 2002), 138–9.
32. Ibid., 141.
33. Brater, "Light, Sound, Movement, and Action," 345.
34. Ibid., 348.
35. Beckett, *Rockaby*, 441.
36. Greene, *Post-Petrarchism*, 157.
37. Ibid.
38. Stewart, *Poetry and the Fate of the Senses*, 152.
39. Ibid.
40. Michael Vanden Heuvel, *Performing Drama / Dramatizing Performance* (Ann Arbor, MI: University of Michigan, 1991), 79.
41. *Rockaby*, directed by Daniel Labeille (New York: Pennebaker Hegedus Films, 1982).
42. Although her delivery is largely affectless, Whitelaw does make a few lines more expressive; these are usually moments when the voice quotes what others have said.
43. Billie Whitelaw, *Billie Whitelaw . . . Who He?: an Autobiography* (New York: St Martin's Press, 1996), 174.
44. Ibid., 175.
45. Beckett, *Complete Dramatic Works*, 442.

Notes

46. Lehmann, *Postdramatic Theater*, 147.
47. Ibid., 18.
48. The plays are so similar as to warrant frequently double-billing (the 2021 production at London's Jermyn Street Theatre), or tripled-billing with *Not I*, Whitelaw's other play (Lisa Dwan's virtuosic performance at the Royal Court Theatre in 2015), although Beckett himself preferred that they not be staged together.
49. Beckett, *Complete Dramatic Works*, 403.
50. Ibid., 435.
51. Ibid.
52. Brater, "Light, Sound, Movement, and Action" 346.
53. Jonathan Kalb, *Beckett in Performance* (London: Cambridge University Press, 1991), 12.
54. Culler, *Theory of the Lyric*, 289.
55. The play *Footfalls* possesses even greater potential for temporal dilation. Beckett—despite all the other details he stipulates, down to which foot the actor ought to use first—does not proscribe a pace. In the *Beckett on Film* version, it takes about 25 minutes to stage five pages of text.
56. Whitelaw, *Billie Whitelaw*, 174.
57. Kalb, *Beckett in Performance*, 49.
58. Insofar as time seems to slow down as the character approaches death, *Rockaby* is part of a long tradition that stretches back to *The Summoning of Everyman* and includes *The Just Vengeance*. In both cases, the moment of the protagonist's death is dilated to encompass the entire action of a two-hour play.
59. Beckett, *Complete Dramatic Works*, 433.
60. A.S. Knowland, *W.B. Yeats, Dramatist of Vision* (Totowa, NJ: Barnes and Noble Books, 1983); Richard Taylor, *The Drama of W.B. Yeats* (New Haven, CT: Yale University Press, 1976), 174; Robert McNamara, interview with author, July 6, 2023. Despite the relative ease of interpretation, the possible eugenicist implications of the play, especially in light of *On the Boiler*, written the same year, have made it less appealing to stage in recent years.
61. Yeats, *Yeats Reader*, 259.
62. Ibid., 261.
63. The 1985 production at Trinity College Dublin and the 2023 Scena Theatre production, both under the direction of Robert McNamara, play up the associations with Noh, using choreographed dance, live music, and Japanese screens for backdrops.
64. Yoko Sato, "The Symbolic Structure of Yeats's 'Purgatory'" *Journal of Irish Studies* 26 (2011): 76–87.

Notes

65. Kunio Komparu, *Noh Theater: Principles and Perspectives* (New York: Weatherhill/Tankosha, 1983), 77.
66. Natalie Crohn Schmitt, "Curing Oneself of the Work of Time: W. B. Yeats's *Purgatory*" *Comparative Drama* 7, no. 4: 318.
67. Yeats, *Yeats Reader*, 263-4.
68. Ibid., 260.
69. T.S. Eliot, *The Complete Prose of T. S. Eliot: The Critical Edition, Volume 6: The War Years, 1940-1946*, ed. David E. Chinitz and Ronald Schuchard (Baltimore, MD: Johns Hopkins University Press, 2017), 83.
70. Yeats, *Yeats Reader*, 265.
71. Ibid., 266.
72. Ibid.
73. Ibid., 263.
74. Ibid., 266.
75. Ibid., 262. Schmitt argues that the spell begins the line before, when the Old Man says, "Because of what I did or may do."
76. Ibid., 263.
77. Schmitt, "Curing Oneself," 311.
78. See Kunio Komparu's *Noh Theater* for a comparison of Noh to the Japanese tea ceremony (xxi).
79. Yeats, *Yeats Reader*, 259.
80. Ibid.
81. Culler, *Theory of the Lyric*, 132.
82. Yeats, *Yeats Reader*, 263.
83. Greene, *Post-Petrarchism*, 31, 157.
84. Yeats, *Yeats Reader*, 264.
85. Knowland, *W.B. Yeats*, 235.
86. Peter Nicholls, "An Experiment with Time: Ezra Pound and the Example of Japanese Noh," *The Modern Language Review* 90, no. 1 (1995): 6.
87. John Unterecker, "An Interview with Anne Yeats" *Shenandoah* 16, no. 4 (Summer 1965): 9.
88. Yeats, *Yeats Reader*, 265. The son's lament reminds me of Harry Dernier's question, and the disgust that accompanies it: "Where did you get / Flesh to wrap you, the old carnal metaphor / Around the destructive argument of the bone, the bone?" (4).
89. Knowland, *W.B. Yeats*, 231.
90. Culler, *Theory of the Lyric*, 305.
91. Greene, *Post-Petrarchism*, 6-7.

Notes

92. Walt Whitman, *Leaves of Grass: Comprehensive Reader's Edition*, ed. Harold W. Blodgett and Sculley Bradley (New York: New York University Press, 1965): 85.
93. Yeats, *Yeats Reader*, 266. Schmitt reads the Old Man's actions as an "[attempt] to free himself and his mother from history and time and their contamination by going back to the paradisal beginnings" (312).
94. Yeats, *Yeats Reader*, 266.
95. Kimberley Lynne, interview with author, June 30, 2023.
96. Culler, *Theory of the Lyric*, 289.
97. Ibid., 16.
98. Robert Von Hallberg, *Lyric Powers* (Chicago: University of Chicago Press, 2008), 169.
99. The Old Man's compulsion to relive—and even reenact—a traumatic event from the past has inspired some critics to interpret the play in light of trauma theory. Chu He sees it as a "precursor" to a spate of "trauma plays" by Irish and Northern Irish playwrights; see "Yeats's Dreaming Back, 'Purgatory', and Trauma" *Studi Irlandesi: A Journal of Irish Studies* 11 (2021): 343.
100. Greene, *Post-Petrarchism*, 123.
101. Ibid., 195.

Chapter 6

1. Seamus Heaney, *Cure at Troy* (New York: Farrar, Straus and Giroux, 1991), 77.
2. Susan Stewart, *Crimes of Writing* (New York: Oxford University Press, 1991), 68.
3. Ibid., 69.
4. Ibid., 90.
5. Wilfrid Wilson Gibson, "Some Thoughts on the Future of Poetic-Drama," *Poetry Review* 3 (1912): 119.
6. Stewart, *Crimes of Writing*, 92.
7. Joyelle McSweeney, "Justice Absconditus, or, Why I Write Verse Plays," *Fanzine*, August 10, 2017. Web. Accessed December 30, 2023, http://thefanzine.com/justice-absconditus-or-why-i-write-verse-plays/
8. Ibid.
9. Ibid.
10. Rodney Lister, "Another Completely Interesting Opera: 'The Mother of Us All,'" *Tempo* 64, no. 254 (October 2010): 7.
11. Gertrude Stein, *Last Operas and Plays* (New York: Rinehart & Co, 1949), 76–7.
12. Sarah Bay-Cheng and Barbara Cole. *Poets at Play: An Anthology of Modernist Drama* (Selinsgrove, PA: Susquehanna University Press, 2010), 270.

Notes

13. Anthony Tommasini, *Virgil Thomson, Composer on the Aisle* (New York: Norton, 2007), 385.
14. Lister, "Another Completely Interesting Opera," 9.
15. Stein, *Last Plays and Operas*, 79.
16. Ibid., 67.
17. Ibid., 78–9.
18. Ibid., 68.
19. Ibid.
20. Ibid., 68–9.
21. Ibid., 53.
22. Ibid., 82.
23. Ibid.
24. Ibid., 81.
25. Ibid., 80.
26. Ibid., 68.
27. T.S. Eliot, *The Poems of T.S. Eliot*, ed. Christopher Ricks and Jim McCue (New York: Farrar, Straus, and Giroux, 2018), 64.
28. Ibid., 63.
29. Bay-Cheng, *Poets at Play*, 271.
30. Ibid.
31. Stein, *Last Plays and Operas*, 83.
32. Ibid.
33. Gertrude Stein, *Geography and Plays* (Boston: Four Seas, 1922), 114–15.
34. Ibid., 93.
35. Ibid., 115–16.
36. Ibid., 116.
37. Ibid., 131.
38. Ibid., 119.
39. Ibid., 87.
40. Ibid.
41. Ibid., 88.
42. David Greig, *The Strange Undoing of Prudencia Hart* (London: Faber, 2011), v.
43. The play ends with Kylie Minogue's 2001 hit "Can't Get You Out of My Head." Beginning in the doleful style of a ballad then transforming into a recognizable version of Minogue's upbeat song, accompanied by the fiddle, this final song represents a marriage of two folk forms: the ballads Prudencia loves, and the pop music Colin advocates for.

Notes

44. Greig, *Strange Undoing*, 15.
45. Derek Walcott, *The Poet in the Theatre* (London: The Poetry Book Society, 1990), 2.
46. Irene Morra *Verse Drama in England* (London: Bloomsbury, 2016), 12.
47. Harley Granville-Barker, *On Poetry in Drama* (London: Sidgwick and Jackson, 1937), 12–13.
48. John Masefield, *So Long to Learn (*New York: MacMillan, 1952), 154–5.
49. Greig, *Strange Undoing*, 20.
50. Ibid., 24.
51. Ibid., 58.
52. Ibid., 65–6.
53. Ibid., 66.
54. Ibid., 65.
55. Robert Von Hallberg, *Lyric Pow*ers (Chicago: University of Chicago Press, 2008), 4, 7.
56. Ibid., 10.
57. Ibid., 66.
58. Philip Sidney, *Miscellaneous Prose of Sir Philip Sidney*, ed. Katherine Duncan-Jones and Jan Van Dorsten (London: Oxford, 1973), 76.
59. Ibid., 76–7.
60. Stewart, *Crimes of Writing*, 121.
61. Ibid.
62. Tony Harrison, *The Common Chorus* (Boston: Faber, 1992), x. The play was commissioned by the National Theatre of Great Britain, part of a trilogy. After seeing the finished project, the National Theatre delayed production, presumably because of its criticisms of the British government and military. The third play, *Maxims* (later known as *Square Rounds*) was eventually produced by the National Theatre in 1992.
63. Harrison, *Common Chorus*, 339.
64. Ibid.
65. Ibid., 17.
66. Ibid.
67. Ibid., 23.
68. Ibid., 50.
69. The National Theatre produced a revised version of the play in 1990 at the Olivier Theatre, and in historic spaces like the ancient amphitheater in Carnuntum (Austria).
70. Tony Harrison, *Trackers of Oxyrhynchus* (London: Faber, 1990), 12.

Notes

71. Ibid., 17.
72. This is another moment that figures a chain of lyric possession, as in Yeats's *Purgatory*; see Chapter 5.
73. Ibid.
74. Ibid., 17–18.
75. Ibid., 18.
76. See *Histories* 1.47 and 7.140 for instances in which Herodotus gives the content of the oracle in verse.
77. Harrison, *Trackers of Oxyrhynchus*, 87.
78. Ibid., 21.
79. Ibid.
80. Roland Barthes, *Camera Lucida: Reflections on Photography*, trans. Richard Howard (New York: Hill and Wang, 1981), 40.
81. Harrison, *Trackers of Oxyrhynchus*, 28.
82. Ibid., 55.
83. Ibid.
84. Ibid.
85. In the National Theatre production, the audience is forced to confront that they are not part of the elite, as Apollo assumes, because they cannot read the papyrus. Addressing the crowd, he asks, "Is there a doctor ... some don from Queen's / who can tell the rest of us what all this means?" (133). When the audience remains silent, he declares, "I get it! No one reads Greek. Neither do I" (134).
86. Ibid., 68.
87. Ibid., 120.
88. Ibid., 134.
89. Ibid., 135.

Conclusion

1. W.R. Johnson, *Idea of the Lyric* (Berkeley, CA: University of California Press, 1982), 146.
2. Martin Puchner, *Stage Fright: Modernism, Anti-Theatricality, and Drama* (Baltimore, MD: Johns Hopkins University Press, 2002), 5.
3. Ibid., 13.
4. "The Work of Sarah Kane: Part Two," *National Theatre*, podcast audio, September 6, 2016.

Notes

5. Caryl Churchill, *Love and Information* (New York: Theatre Communications Group, 2013), 74–7.
6. Joyelle McSweeney, *Dead Youth, or The Leaks* (New York: Litmus Press, 2014), 26.
7. Joyelle McSweeney, "Justice Absconditus, or, Why I Write Verse Plays," *Fanzine* August 10, 2017. Web. Accessed December 30, 2023, http://thefanzine.com/justice-absconditus-or-why-i-write-verse-plays/
8. Joyelle McSweeney, *The Commandrine and Other Poems* (New York: Fence Books, 2004), 32.
9. See Sarah Berry, "Automatomorphism in Joyelle McSweeney's *Dead Youth*," *ASAP/Journal*, November 7 (2023).
10. Khadijah Queen, *Non-Sequitur* (New York: Litmus Press, 2015), 11.
11. Ibid., 69.
12. Seda Ilter, *Mediatized Dramaturgy* (London: Methuen, 2021), 9.
13. Ibid., 167.
14. Bill Blake, *Theatre and the Digital* (London: Macmillan, 2014), 40.
15. Ibid., 39.
16. Jason Farman, "Surveillance Spectacles: The Big Art Group's Flicker and the Screened Body in Performance," *Contemporary Theater Review* 19, no. 2 (2009): 182.
17. Blake, *Theatre and the Digital*, 40.

BIBLIOGRAPHY

Adorno, Theodor. "Lyric Poetry and Society." Translated by Shierry Weber Nicholson. In *The Lyric Theory Reader*, edited by Virginia Jackson and Yopie Prins, 339–50. Baltimore: Johns Hopkins University Press, 2014.
Altman, Meryl. "*The Antiphon*: No Audience at All?" In *Silence and Power: A Reevaluation of Djuna Barnes*, edited by Mary Lynn Broe, 271–85. Carbondale, IL: Southern Illinois University Press, 1991.
"The Antiphon" (Review). *Times Literary Supplement*, April 5, 1958.
Archer, William. *The Old Drama and the New*. Boston: Small, Maynard, and Company, 1923.
Arden, John. "Building the Play." *Encore* July–August 1961: 22–41.
Arden, John. *Plays: One*. London: Methuen, 1994.
Arden, John. "Telling a True Tale." In *Drama Criticism Developments Since Ibsen: A Casebook*, edited by Arnold P. Hinchcliffe, 211–15. New York: Macmillan, 1979.
Aristotle. *Poetics*. Translated by Stephen Halliwell. Chapel Hill, NC: University of North Carolina Press, 1986.
Artaud, Antonin. *The Theater and its Double*. New York: Grove Press, 1958.
Ashbery, John. "Interview: Poet in the Theatre." *Performing Arts Journal* 3, no. 3 (1979): 15–27.
Ashbery, John. *Your Name Here*. New York: Farrar, Straus and Giroux, 2000.
Auden, W.H. *Collected Poems*. New York: Vintage Books, 1991.
Auden, W.H. *On the Frontier*. New York: Random House, 1938.
Auden, W.H. *The Age of Anxiety*. Edited by Alan Jacobs. Princeton, NJ: Princeton University Press, 2011.
Bamber, Linda. *Comic Women, Tragic Men*. Stanford, CA: Stanford University Press, 1982.
Barthes, Roland. *Camera Lucida: Reflections on Photography*. Translated by Richard Howard. New York: Hill and Wang, 1981.
Bartlett, Mike. *King Charles III*. New York: Theatre Communications Group, 2014.
Bartlett, Mike. *The 47th*. London: Nick Hern Books, 2022.
Bay-Cheng, Sarah, and Barbara Cole. *Poets at Play: An Anthology of Modernist Drama*. Selinsgrove, PA: Susquehanna University Press, 2010.
Bean, Heidi R. *Acts of Poetry: American Poets' Theater and the Politics of Performance*. Ann Arbor, MI: University of Michigan Press, 2019.
Beckett, Samuel. *The Complete Dramatic Works*. London: Faber, 2005.
Benjamin, Walter. *Understanding Brecht*. New York: Verso, 1998.
Bergson, Henri. *Time and Free Will*. New York: Harper and Row, 1960.
Berry, Eleanor. "Williams' Development of a New Prosodic Form: Not the 'Variable Foot,' But the 'Sight-Stanza.'" *William Carlos Williams Review* 7, no. 2 (1981): 21–30.

Bibliography

Berry, Ralph. *Shakespeare and Social Class*. Atlantic Highlands, NJ: Humanities Press International, 1988.

Berry, Sarah. "*Automatomorphism in Joyelle McSweeney's* Dead Youth." *ASAP/Journal*, November 7, 2023. https://asapjournal.com/poetic-voice-and-materiality-automatomorphism-in-joyelle-mcsweeneys-dead-youth-sarah-berry/

Billington, Michael. *State of the Nation: British Theatre since 1945*. London: Faber, 2007.

Binyon, Laurence. "The Return to Poetry." *Rhythm* 1, no. 4 (1912): 1–2.

Blake, Bill. *Theatre and the Digital*. London: Macmillan, 2014.

Blasing, Mutlu Konuk. *Lyric Poetry: The Pain and the Pleasure of Words*. Princeton, NJ: Princeton University Press, 2007.

Brater, Enoch. "Light, Sound, Movement, and Action in Beckett's *Rockaby*." *Modern Drama* 25, no. 3 (Fall 1982): 342–8.

Brecht, Bertolt. *Brecht on Theatre*, edited and translated by John Willett. New York: Hill and Wang, 1992.

Brouwer, Joel. "The Possibility of a Poetic Drama." *Harriet Books* (blog). *Poetry Foundation*, July 2009. Accessed September 4, 2023. https://www.poetryfoundation.org/harriet/2009/07/the-possibility-of-a-poetic-drama.

Brown, Janice. *The Seven Deadly Sins in the Work of Dorothy L. Sayers*. Kent, OH: Kent State University Press, 1998.

Burke, Mary. *Tinkers: Synge and the Cultural History of the Irish Traveller*. London: Oxford University Press, 2009.

Carlson, Marvin. "Alternative Theatre." In *The Cambridge History of American Theatre*, vol. III, edited by Don B. Wilmeth and Christopher Bigsby, 249–93. Cambridge: Cambridge University Press, 2000.

Caselli, Daniela. *Improper Modernism: Djuna Barnes's Bewildering Corpus*. Burlington, VT: Ashgate, 2009.

Cecire, Natalia. *Experimental*. Baltimore, MD: Johns Hopkins University Press, 2019.

Chambers, Colin. *The Story of the Unity Theatre*. New York: St. Martins, 1989.

Champagne, Lenora. "Always Starting New: Elizabeth LeCompte." *The Drama Review* 25, no. 3 (1981): 18–28.

Churchill, Caryl. *Love and Information*. New York: Theatre Communications Group, 2013.

Churchill, R.C., ed. "Age of Eliot." In *Concise Cambridge History of English Literature*, 841–938. Cambridge: Cambridge University Press, 1970.

Clarke, Cheryl. *"After Mecca": Women Poets and the Black Arts Movement*. New Brunswick, NJ: Rutgers University Press, 2005.

Cohn, Ruby. *A Beckett Canon*. Ann Arbor, MI: University of Michigan Press, 2005.

Csapo, Eric. "Imagining the Shape of Choral Dance." In *Choreutika: Performing and Theorizing Dance in Ancient Greece*, edited by Laura Gianvittorio, 119–156. Rome: Fabriio Serraeditore, 2017.

Culler, Jonathan. "Apostrophe." In *The Pursuit of Signs*, 135–52. Ithaca, NY: Cornell University Press, 2002.

Bibliography

Culler, Jonathan. *Theory of the Lyric*. Cambridge, MA: Harvard University Press, 2015.

Davis, Olena Kalytiak. *The Poem She Didn't Write and Other Poems*. Port Townsend, Washington: Copper Canyon Press, 2014.

De Man, Paul. "Lyrical Voice in Contemporary Theory: Riffaterre and Jauss." In *Lyric Poetry: Beyond New Criticism*, edited by Chaviva Hosek and Patricia Parker, 55–72. Ithaca, NY: Cornell University Press, 1985.

Diamond, Elin. "(In)Visible Bodies in Churchill's Theatre." *Theatre Journal* 40, no. 2 (1988): 188–204.

Donoghue, Denis. *The Third Voice: Modern British and American Verse Drama*. Princeton, NJ: Princeton University Press, 1959.

Easthope, Anthony. "Problematizing the Pentameter." *New Literary History* 12, no. 3 (1981), 475–92.

Eliot, T.S. *The Cocktail Party*. New York: Harcourt, 1950.

Eliot, T.S. *The Complete Prose of T. S. Eliot: The Critical Edition, Volume 6: The War Years, 1940-1946*, edited by David E. Chinitz and Ronald Schuchard. Baltimore, MD: Johns Hopkins University Press, 2017.

Eliot, T.S. *The Family Reunion*. In *Collected Plays*. London: Faber, 1963.

Eliot, T.S. *Murder in the Cathedral*. New York: Harcourt, 1935.

Eliot, T.S. *The Poems of T.S. Eliot*, edited by Christopher Ricks and Jim McCue. New York: Farrar, Straus, and Giroux, 2018.

Eliot, T.S. *Poetry and Drama*. New York: Faber, 1950.

Eliot, T.S. *The Rock*. London: Faber, 1934.

Eliot, T.S. *The Sacred Wood*. New York: Barnes and Noble, 1928.

Eliot, T.S. *The Three Voices of Poetry*. Cambridge University Press, 1954.

Elliott, George P. "Review: A Libretto: And Two Millstones of Our Time." *The Hudson Review* 11, no. 2 (1958): 308–12.

Farman, Jason. "Surveillance Spectacles: The Big Art Group's Flicker and the Screened Body in Performance." *Contemporary Theater Review* 19, no. 2 (2009): 181–94.

Fitts, Dudley. "Discord and Old Age: THE ANTIPHON. By Djuna Barnes." *New York Times* April 20, 1958. https://www.nytimes.com/1958/04/20/archives/discord-and-old-age-the-antiphon-by-djuna-barnes-127-pp-new-york.html (accessed October 6, 2023).

Friedman, Barton R. "*On Baile's Strand* to *At the Hawk's Well*: Staging the Deeps of the Mind." *Journal of Modern Literature* 4, no. 3 (February 1975): 625–50.

Fry, Christopher. "Why Verse?" *Vogue*, March 1955.

Frye, Northrop. *Anatomy of Criticism*. Princeton, NJ: Princeton University Press, 1957.

Furr, Derek. *Recorded Poetry and Poetic Reception from Edna Millay to the Circle of Robert Lowell*. New York: Palgrave Macmillan, 2010.

Gaston, Bruce. "Brecht's Pastiche History Play: Renaissance Drama and Modernist Theatre in *Leben Eduards Des Zweiten Von England*." *German Life and Letters* 56, no. 4 (2003): 344–62.

Gaston, Georg. "An Interview with John Arden." *Contemporary Literature* 32, no 2 (1991): 147–70.

Bibliography

George, Kathleen. *Rhythm into Drama*. Pittsburgh: University of Pittsburgh Press, 1980.
Gibson, Wilfrid Wilson. "Some Thoughts on the Future of Poetic-Drama." *Poetry Review* 3 (1912): 119–20.
Glaser, Ben. *Modernism's Metronome*. Baltimore, MD: Johns Hopkins University Press, 2020.
Goldman, Michael. *On Drama: Boundaries of Genre, Borders of Self*. Ann Arbor, MI: University of Michigan, 2000.
Goody, Alex. "'High and Aloof': Verse, Violence, and the Audience in Djuna Barnes's *The Antiphon*." *Modern Drama* 57, no. 3 (2014): 339–63.
Goody, Alex. *Modernist Articulations: A Cultural Study of Djuna Barnes, Mina Loy, and Gertrude Stein*. New York: Palgrave Macmillan, 2007.
Graham, Jorie. *To 2040*. Port Townsend, WA: Copper Canyon Press, 2023.
Graham-White, Anthony. "'Ritual' in Contemporary Theatre and Criticism." *Educational Theatre Journal* 28, no. 3 (1976): 318–24. https://doi.org/10.2307/3206421.
Granville-Barker, Harley. *On Poetry in Drama*. London: Sidgwick and Jackson, 1937.
Gray, Spaulding. "Children of Paradise: Working with Kids." *Performing Arts Journal* 5, no. 1 (1980): 61–74.
Greene, Roland. *Post-Petrarchism*. Princeton, NJ: Princeton University Press, 1991.
Greig, David. *The Strange Undoing of Prudencia Hart*. London: Faber, 2011.
Harding, James M. *Contours of the Theatrical Avant-Garde*. Ann Arbor: University of Michigan: 2000.
Harrison, Tony. *The Common Chorus*. Boston: Faber, 1992.
Harrison, Tony. *The Trackers of Oxyrhynchus*. London: Faber, 1990.
He, Chu. "Yeats's Dreaming Back, 'Purgatory', and Trauma." *Studi Irlandesi: A Journal of Irish Studies* 11 (2021): 343–56.
Heaney, Seamus. *The Cure at Troy*. New York: Farrar, Straus and Giroux, 1991.
Heaney, Seamus. *The Redress of Poetry*. New York: Farrar, Straus and Giroux, 1995.
Hecht, Anthony. *The Hidden Law: The Poetry of W.H. Auden*. Cambridge, MA: Harvard University Press, 1998.
Hegel, G.W.F. *Aesthetics: Lectures on Fine Arts*. Translated by T.M. Knox. London: Oxford University Press, 1998.
Herington, John. *Poetry into Drama*. Berkeley, CA: University of California Press, 1985.
Herring, Phillip. *Djuna: The Life and Works of Djuna Barnes*. New York: Viking, 1995.
Hobbes, Thomas. *Leviathan*, edited by Richard Tuck. Cambridge: Cambridge University Press, 1996.
Hoggart, Richard. *Auden: An Introductory Essay*. New Haven, CT: Yale University Press, 1951.
Holland, Mary. "Field Day's Tenth Birthday." Program notes for Field Day Theatre Company, *The Cure at Troy*. Stephen Rea and Bob Crowley, directors. Guildhall, Derry, Northern Ireland, 1990.
Ibsen, Henrik. *Correspondence of Henrik Ibsen*. Translated and edited by Mary Morison. New York: Haskell House, 1970.

Bibliography

Ilter, Seda. *Mediatized Dramaturgy*. London: Methuen, 2021.

Ivey, Jillian Ashely Blair. "Time She Stopped: EgoPo Classic Theater presents Samuel Beckett's Rockaby." *Broad Street Review* March 15, 2021. https://www.broadstreetreview.com/reviews/egopo-classic-theater-presents-samuel-becketts-rockaby

Jackson, Virginia. *Dickinson's Misery*. Princeton, NJ: Princeton University Press, 2005.

Jackson, Virginia and Yopie Prins. *The Lyric Theory Reader*. Baltimore, MD: Johns Hopkins Press, 2014.

Jesson, James. "'White World, Not a Sound': Beckett's Radioactive Text in *Embers*." *Texas Studies in Literature and Language* 51, no. 1 (2009), 47–65.

Johnson, W.R. *The Idea of the Lyric*. Berkeley, CA: University of California Press, 1982.

Kalb, Jonathan. *Beckett in Performance*. London: Cambridge University Press, 1991.

Keller, Alexandra. "Shards of Voice: Fragments Excavated toward a Radiophonic Archaeology." In *Experimental Sound and Radio*, edited by Allen S. Weiss, 22–6. Cambridge, MA: MIT Press, 2001.

Kiberd, Declan. "On Baile's Strand: W.B. Yeats's National Epic." *The Princeton University Library Chronicle* 68, no. 1–2 (Winter 2007): 261–70.

Knowland, A.S. *W.B. Yeats, Dramatist of Vision*. Totowa, NJ: Barnes and Noble Books, 1983.

Komparu, Kunio. *Noh Theater: Principles and Perspectives*. New York: Weatherhill/Tankosha, 1983.

Krutch, Joseph Wood. *Modernism in Modern Drama*. Ithaca, NY: Cornell University Press, 1953.

Lambourne, Norah. "Recollections of Designing for the Religious Plays of Dorothy L. Sayers." *Costume* 25, no. 1 (1991): 1–17.

Lattimore, Richard. *Complete Greek Tragedies*, Volume III. Chicago: University of Chicago Press, 1992.

Laurens, Joanna. "Make it up." *The Guardian*, December 11, 2003. Accessed December 19, 2023. https://www.theguardian.com/stage/2003/dec/11/theatre3

Laurens, Joanna. *The Three Birds*. London: Oberon Books, 2001.

Lech, Kasia. "Five Reasons Why Verse is the Language for Theatre in the 2020s." *Theatre Times*, March 12, 2021. Accessed September 7, 2023. www.thetheatretimes.com/5-reasons-why-verse-is-the-language-for-theatre-in-2020s/.

Leeming, Glenda. *Poetic Drama*. New York: St. Martin's, 1989.

Leggett, Saskia "Avian Greeks keep sex within the nest." *Yale Daily News*, February 10, 2006. B7.

Lehmann, Hans-Theis. *Postdramatic Theatre*. Translated by Karen Jurs-Munby. New York: Routledge, 2006.

Lester, Neal A. *Ntozake Shange*. New York: Garland, 1995.

Lister, Rodney. "Another Completely Interesting Opera: 'The Mother of Us All.'" *Tempo* 64, no. 254 (October 2010): 2–10.

Lloyd Evans, Gareth. *The Language of Modern Drama*. London: Rowman and Littlefield, 1977.

Bibliography

Lyons, Charles R. "Perceiving 'Rockaby'—As a Text, As a Text by Samuel Beckett, As a Text for Performance." *Comparative Drama* 16, no. 4 (Winter 1982): 297–311.

MacDonald, Russ. *Shakespeare and the Arts of Language*. Oxford University Press, 2001.

Mahurin, Sarah. "'Speakin Arms' and Dancing Bodies in Ntozake Shange." *African American Review* 46, no. 2 (2013): 329–43.

Malamud, Randy. *Where the Words Are Valid: T.S. Eliot's Communities of Drama*. London: Greenwood Press, 1994.

Malina, Judith. "Remembering Jackson Mac Low." *PAJ: A Journal of Performance and Art* 27, no. 2 (2005): 76–8. muse.jhu.edu/article/183262.

Marrs, Terrell W. "The Living Theatre: History, Theatrics, and Politics." PhD dissertation. Texas Tech University, 1984.

Martin, Charles. "The Three Contemporary Voices of Poetry." *The New Criterion* (April 2004): 34–7. Accessed September 4, 2023. www.newcriterion.com/issues/2004/4/the-three-voices-of-contemporary-poetry.

Masefield, John. *So Long to Learn*. New York: MacMillan, 1952.

McCollom, William G. "Verse Drama: A Reconsideration." *Comparative Drama* 14, no. 2 (1980): 99–116. Accessed September 4, 2023. www.jstor.org/stable/41152885.

McDonald, Russ. *Shakespeare and the Art of Language*. New York: Oxford, 2001.

McGovern, Barry. "Beckett and the Radio Voice." In *Samuel Beckett: 100 Years*, edited by Christopher Murray, 132–44. Dublin: New Island, 2006.

McSweeney, Joyelle. *The Commandrine and Other Poems*. New York: Fence Books, 2004.

McSweeney, Joyelle. *Dead Youth, or The Leaks*. New York: Litmus Press, 2014.

McSweeney, Joyelle. "Justice Absconditus, or, Why I Write Verse Plays." *Fanzine*, August 10, 2017. Web. Accessed December 30, 2023. http://thefanzine.com/justice-absconditus-or-why-i-write-verse-plays/

Mendelson, Edward. *Later Auden*. New York: Farrar, Straus, and Giroux, 1999.

Mercier, Vivian. "The Uneventful Event." *Irish Times* February 18, 1956, 6.

Miller, Derek. "Realism." In *Ibsen in Context*, edited by Narve Fulsas and Tore Rem, 37–45. Cambridge University Press, 2021.

Moore, Edward. "Preface." *The Gamester. Project Gutenberg*. Accessed September 4, 2023. www.gutenberg.org/files/16267/16267-h/16267-h.htm.

Morra, Irene. *Verse Drama in England, 1900-2015*. London: Bloomsbury, 2016.

Murphy, Brenda. *The Provincetown Players and the Culture of Modernity*. London: Cambridge University Press, 2005.

Nayatt School. Composed by Spalding Gray and Elizabeth LeCompte, The Performing Garage, New York, June 4, 1978.

Nicholls, Peter. "An Experiment with Time: Ezra Pound and the Example of Japanese Noh." *The Modern Language Review* 90, no. 1 (1995): 1–13.

Nietzsche, Friedrich. *The Birth of Tragedy and the Genealogy of Morals*. Translated by Frans Golffing. New York: Doubleday, 1956.

Non-Sequitur. Written by Khadijah Queen, directed by Fiona Templeton. Theaterlab, New York City. December 10–20, 2015.

O'Brien, Flann. *At Swim-Two-Birds*. London: Dalkey Archive, 1966.

Bibliography

O'Brien, Richard. "Community and Conflict: a Practitioner's Perspective." *Connotations* 27 (2018): 120–54. Accessed September 7, 2023. www.connotations.de/article/richard-o-brien-a-practioners-perspective-on-verse-drama/

Paz, Octavio. *Children of the Mire: Modern Poetry from Romanticism to the Avant-garde*. Translated by Rachel Phillips. Cambridge, MA: Harvard University Press, 1991.

Perloff, Marjorie. *Differentials: Poetry, Poetics, Pedagogy*. Tuscaloosa, AL: University of Alabama Press, 2004.

Perloff, Marjorie. "Language Poetry and the Lyric Subject: Ron Silliman's Albany, Susan Howe's Buffalo." *Critical Inquiry* 25, no. 3 (1999): 405–34. www.jstor.org/stable/1344185.

Perry, Seamus. "Auden's Forms." In *W.H. Auden in Context*, edited by Tony Sharp, 369–80. London: Cambridge University Press, 2013.

Pius XII. *Mystici Corporis Christi* [Encyclical Letter on the Mystical Body of Christ]. The Holy See. June 29, 1943. https://www.vatican.va/content/pius-xii/en/encyclicals/documents/hf_p-xii_enc_29061943_mystici-corporis-christi.html

Plath, Sylvia. *Letters Home*, edited by Aurelia Schober Plath. New York: Harper and Row, 1975.

Plath, Sylvia. *Three Women*. London: Turret Books, 1968.

Plato. *The Republic of Plato*. Translated by Allan Bloom. Second Edition. New York: Basic Books, 1991.

Ponsot, Marie. "Careful Sorrow and Observed Compline." *Poetry* 95, no. 1 (1959): 47–50.

Porter, James. "ballad." In *Grove Music Online*. London: Oxford University Press, 2001. https://doi.org/10.1093/gmo/9781561592630.article.01879.

Porter, Jeffrey Lyn. "Samuel Beckett and the Radiophonic Body: Beckett and the BBC." *Modern Drama* 53, no. 4 (2010): 431–46.

Pound, Ezra. *The Cantos of Ezra Pound*. New York: New Directions, 1989.

Preston, Carrie. *Learning to Kneel*. New York: Columbia University Press, 2017.

Puchner, Martin *Stage Fright: Modernism, Anti-Theatricality, and Drama*. Baltimore, MD: Johns Hopkins University Press, 2002.

Queen, Khadijah. *Non-sequitur*. New York: Litmus Press, 2015.

Quick, Andrew. *The Wooster Group Workbook*. New York: Routledge, 2007.

Rabey, David Ian. *Theatre, Time and Temporality: Melting Clocks and Snapped Elastics*. Chicago: University of Chicago Press, 2016.

Radia, Pavlina. "Djuna Barnes and *The Antiphon*: From State Politics to Theatre of Ideas." *Journal of Modern Literature* 40, no. 4 (2017): 150–65. https://doi.org/10.2979/jmodelite.40.4.12.

Reinelt, Janelle. *After Brecht: British Epic Theater*. Ann Arbor, MI: University of Michigan, 1996.

Reynolds, Barbara. *The Passionate Intellect*. Kent, OH: Kent State University Press, 1989.

Roberts, Beth Ellen. *One Voice and Many*. Newark, DE: University of Delaware Press, 2006.

Rockaby. Directed by Daniel Labeille. New York: Pennebaker Hegedus Films, 1982. Film.

Bibliography

Ross, Alan. "Third Avenue Eclogue." In *The Modern Movement: A TLS Companion*, edited by John Gross, 134–8. Chicago: University of Chicago Press, 1992.
Rozik, Eli. *Roots of Theatre*. Iowa City, IA: University of Iowa Press, 2002.
Sato, Yoko. "The Symbolic Structure of Yeats's 'Purgatory.'" *Journal of Irish Studies* 26 (2011): 76–87. http://www.jstor.org/stable/23033178.
Savran, David. *Breaking the Rules: The Wooster Group*. New York: Theatre Communications Group, 1998.
Savran, David. *The Playwright's Voice*, New York: Theatre Communications Group, 1999.
Sayers, Dorothy L. *The Just Vengeance*. Eugene, Oregon: Wipf and Stock, 2011.
Sayre, Nora. "The Poets' Theatre: A Memoir of the Fifties." *Grand Street* 3, no. 3 (1984): 92–105.
Schaefer, James F. "An Examination of Language as Gesture in a Play by Gertrude Stein." *Literature in Performance* 3, no. 1 (1982): 1–14.
Schechner, Richard. "Drama, Script, Theatre, and Performance." *The Drama Review* 17, no. 3 (1973): 5–36.
Schechner, Richard. *Between Theater and Anthropology*. Philadelphia: University of Pennsylvania Press, 1985.
Schmitt, Natalie Crohn. "Curing Oneself of the Work of Time: W. B. Yeats's *Purgatory*." *Comparative Drama* 7, no. 4: 310–33.
Shakespeare, William. *Arden Shakespeare Third Series Complete Works*. Edited by Richard Proudfoot, Ann Thompson, David Scott Kastan and H.R. Woudhuysen. London: The Arden Shakespeare, 2020.
Shelley, Percy Bysshe. *The Complete Poetical Works of Percy Bysshe Shelley*. Edited by Thomas Hutchinson. London: Oxford University Press, 1956.
Shuffle, directed by John Collins. New York Public Library, New York City. May 21–22, 2011.
Shuttleworth, Martin. "Review of *Three Women*." *Listener*, August 30, 1962, 329–30.
Sidnell, Michael. *Dances of Death: The Group Theatre of London in the Thirties*. London: Faber, 1984.
Sidney, Philip. *Miscellaneous Prose of Sir Philip Sidney*. Edited by Katherine Duncan-Jones and Jan Van Dorsten. London: Oxford, 1973.
Soloski, Alexis. "Giving Voice to Sylvia Plath's Pregnant Women." *New York Times*, September 26, 2010, 7. https://www.theguardian.com/stage/theatreblog/2010/sep/28/sylvia-plath-three-women-unstageable.
Sophocles. *Sophocles II*. Edited by David Grene and Richard Lattimore. Chicago: University of Chicago Press, 1969.
Spanos, William V. *The Christian Tradition in Modern British Verse Drama*. New Brunswick, NJ: Rutgers University Press, 1967.
Splawn, P. Jane. "'Change the Joke[r] and slip the joke': Boal's 'Joker' system in Ntozake Shange's *for colored girls. . . and spell #7*." *Modern Drama* 41, no. 3 (1998): 386–98.
Steele, Timothy. *All the Fun's in How You Say a Thing*. Columbus, OH: Ohio University Press, 1999.
Steele, Timothy. *Missing Measures*. Fayetteville, AR: University of Arkansas Press, 1990.

Bibliography

Stein, Gertrude. *Geography and Plays.* Boston: Four Seas, 1922.
Stein, Gertrude. *Last Plays and Operas.* Baltimore, MD: Johns Hopkins Press, 1949.
Stein, Gertrude. *Lectures in America.* Boston: Beacon Press, 1957.
Steiner, George. *The Death of Tragedy.* New Haven, CT: Yale University Press, 1980.
Stendhal. *Racine and Shakespeare.* Translated by Guy Daniels. London: Alma Classics, 2019.
Stevens, Wallace. "Three Travelers Watch a Sunrise." *Poetry* 8, no. 4 (1916): 163-79. http://www.jstor.org/stable/20570836.
Stewart, Susan. *Crimes of Writing.* New York: Oxford University Press, 1991.
Stewart, Susan. *Poetry and the Fate of the Senses.* Chicago: University of Chicago, 2002.
Swanzy, Henry. *Henry Swanzy, The Selected Diaries - Ichabod: 1948-1958.* Edited by Chris Campbell, Michael Niblett, and Victoria Ellen Smith. Leeds, UK: Peepal Tree Press, 2023.
Tanner, R. G. "The Dramas of T. S. Eliot and Their Greek Models." *Greece & Rome* 17, no. 2 (1970): 123-34. http://www.jstor.org/stable/642754.
Taugbøl, Stine Brenna. "Henrik Ibsen's use of metre in his verse dramas," *Ibsen Studies* 9, no. 1 (2009): 19. Accessed September 4, 2023. doi.org/10.1080/15021860903118883.
Taylor, Julie. "Revising *The Antiphon*, Restaging Trauma; Or, Where Sexual Politics Meets Sexual History." *Modernism/modernity* 18, no. 1 (2011): 125-47.
Taylor, Richard. *The Drama of W.B. Yeats.* New Haven, CT: Yale University Press, 1976.
Tommasini, Anthony. *Virgil Thomson, Composer on the Aisle.* New York: Norton, 2007.
Tootalian, Jacob. "Without Measure: The Language Of Shakespeare's Prose." *Journal For Early Modern Cultural Studies* 13, no. 4 (2013): 47-60.
Trewin, J.C. *Verse Drama since 1800.* New York: Cambridge University Press, 1956.
Tucker, Herbert. "Dramatic Monologue and the Overhearing of Lyric." In *Lyric Poetry: Beyond New Criticism*, edited by Chaviva Hosek and Particia Parker, 226-43. Ithaca, NY: Cornell University Press, 1985.
Unterecker, John. "An Interview with Anne Yeats." *Shenandoah* 16, no. 4 (Summer 1965): 7-9.
Vanden Heuvel, Michael. *Performing Drama / Dramatizing Performance.* Ann Arbor, MI: University of Michigan, 1991.
Vendler, Helen. *Soul Says.* Cambridge, MA: Harvard University Press, 1995.
Vickers, Brian. *The Artistry of Shakespeare's Prose.* London: Methuen, 1968.
Viswanathan, Gauri. *Masks of Conquest.* New York: Columbia University Press, 1989.
Von Hallberg, Robert. *Lyric Powers.* Chicago: University of Chicago Press, 2008.
Wagner, Matthew. *Shakespeare, Theatre, and Time.* London: Routledge, 2012.
Walcott, Derek. *Harry Dernier.* Bridgetown, Barbados: Advocate, 1952.
Walcott, Derek. *The Poet in the Theatre.* London: The Poetry Book Society, 1990.
Ward, David. *T.S. Eliot Between Two Worlds.* London: Routledge, 2015.
Warden, Claire. *British Avant-Garde Theatre.* London: Palgrave MacMillan, 2012.
Waters, William. *Poetry's Touch: On Lyric Address.* Ithaca, NY: Cornell University Press, 2003.

Bibliography

Weiner, Albert. "The Function of the Tragic Greek Chorus." *Theatre Journal* 32, no. 2 (1980): 205–12.

Weiss, Allen S. "Radio Icons, Short Circuits, Deep Schisms." In *Experimental Sound and Radio*, edited by Allen S. Weiss, 1–7. Cambridge, MA: Massachusetts Institute of Technology Press, 2001.

Wheeler, Leslie. *Voicing American Poetry: Sound and Performance from the 1920s to the Present*. Ithaca, NY: Cornell University Press, 2008.

Whitelaw, Billie. *Billie Whitelaw . . . Who He?: an Autobiography*. New York: St Martin's Press, 1996.

Whitman, Walt. *Leaves of Grass: Comprehensive Reader's Edition*, edited by Harold W. Blodgett and Sculley Bradley. New York: New York University Press, 1965.

Williams, William Carlos. *Many Loves, and Other Plays*. Norfolk, CT: New Directions, 1961.

Wordsworth, William. *Lyrical Ballads, with Other Poems*. London: Longman and Rees, 1800.

"The Work of Sarah Kane: Part Two." *National Theatre*. Podcast audio. September 6, 2016. https://podcasts.apple.com/gb/podcast/the-work-of-sarah-kane-part-two/id1194511440?i=1000379885915.

Worthen, W.B. *Print and the Poetics of Modern Drama*. London: Cambridge University Press, 2005.

Wright, George T. *Shakespeare's Metrical Art*. Berkeley, CA: University of California Press, 1988.

Yeats, W.B. *Essays and Introductions*. New York: Collier Books, 1961.

Yeats, W.B. *On Baile's Strand Manuscript Materials*, edited by Jared Curtis and Declan Kiely. Ithaca, NY: Cornell University Press, 2014.

Yeats, W.B. *The Yeats Reader*. Edited by Richard J. Finneran. New York: Scribner, 2002.

INDEX

Abbey Theatre 2, 150, 163–4, 192n6
Abercrombie, Lascelles 73
Adorno, Theodor 50, 52, 64
Adrian, Rhys 53
Aeschylus 23, 29, 133, 184n10
   Agamemnon 24
   Eumenides 28, 187n88
Alfred, William 4
alienation effect 18, 74–6, 87–8, 91–3, 97–9
   See also Brecht, Bertolt
alliterative verse 80–1, 84, 193n40
Anderson, Maxwell 18–19
Arden, John 3, 4, 76, 126, 163–4
   All Fall Down 91
   Friday's Hiding 103
   Live Like Pigs 18, 92, 93, 94, 95–9, 162
   Soldier, Soldier 92–5, 99
Arden of Faversham 6
Aristophanes 82
   Lysistrata 167–9
   Women at the Thesmophoria 186n44
Aristotle 11, 18, 126–7, 133–4, 137
   Poetics 23, 29, 175
Artaud, Antonin 108–9
Ashbery, John 2, 51, 54, 84, 194n54, 198n63
Auden, W.H. 3, 14, 76, 91, 99, 101, 126, 164, 175, 195n82
   Age of Anxiety 18, 79–84, 189n32, 198n63
   Dance of Death 73
   On the Frontier 32
Augustine, Saint 31, 59
avant-garde 119–20
   in drama 14, 15, 19, 25, 73, 76, 99, 109, 118
   in poetry 183n56

ballad 9, 92–9, 156, 162–7, 195n90, 205n43
   ballad meter 83, 92
Barnes, Djuna 76, 99
   The Antiphon 14, 18, 84–91, 194n59
Barthes, Roland 171–2

Bartlett, Mike 4, 155
British Broadcasting Company 17, 52, 55, 60, 67, 69, 103, 185n32, 190n41
Beck, Julian 84, 121–6, 198n63
   See also Malina, Judith; Living Theatre
Beckett, Samuel 53, 125, 133–5, 137, 153, 178
   All That Fall 53
   Cascando 135
   Eh Joe 135
   Embers 53, 135
   Footfalls 143, 181n10, 202n48, 202n55
   Happy Days 136
   Krapp's Last Tape 136
   Not I 181n10, 188n16, 202n48
   Quad 136
   Rockaby 18, 134, 135–45, 154, 165, 181n10, 200n20, 201n27, 202n48
   Rough for Radio I 135
   That Time 136
   Waiting for Godot 136
Behan, Brendan 96
Bergman, Ingmar 190n46
Bergson, Henri 132–3, 144
Berkoff, Steve 4
Bernstein, Leonard 79
Binyon, Laurence 73
Black Arts Movement 25, 36, 38
blank verse 73–5, 76–7, 84–7, 92, 109, 192n22
Blue Raincoat Theatre Company 150
bourgeois tragedy 5–7
Brecht, Bertolt 18, 74–6, 93, 97, 122, 125–6, 192n17, 195n82
British New Wave 3–4
   see also Arden, John; Osborne, John; Pinter, Arnold
Broadway 37, 126
Browne, E. Martin 3, 26
   see also Mercury Theatre; Canterbury Festival

Index

Browning, Robert 9, 63–4
Byron, George Gordon 9, 119

Canterbury Festival 3, 27, 74
chorus 10, 12, 17, 23–47, 49, 69, 111–7, 155, 159–60, 169–71
Christian verse drama
   see Canterbury Festival, religious drama
Churchill, Caryl 4, 69, 176, 178–9
civil rights movements 43, 59
   in US 17, 25
class 6–8, 24, 32, 64, 76–7, 163
   in Arden 91–9
   in Elizabethan drama 76, 192n22
   in Harrison 173, 182n21, 207n85
   in Yeats 76–8, 202n60
Claudel, Paul 11, 126
closet drama 9, 14, 16, 126
   The Antiphon as 84–5, 88
   see also Romantic drama
Cold War, the 167–9, 206n62
Coleridge, Samuel Taylor 9
Confessional poetry 50–2
Cooper, Giles 53
Culler, Jonathan 49–55, 56, 58, 60–4, 101, 114, 135–8, 144, 149–51, 153, 171

dance 38, 41, 79, 105, 150
Dante 147, 185n32
D'Arcy, Margaretta 94, 98, 103
Davis, Olena Kalytiak 50–2
de Man, Paul 49–50
Doone, Rupert 3, 73
dramatic poetry 2, 9, 10, 12–13, 78
   Auden's *Age of Anxiety* 79–81
   Plath's *Three Women* 60, 67, 69
   see also Victorian dramatic monologue
Drinkwater, John 73
Dryden, John 2

Eagleton, Terry 4
Edinburgh Fringe 190n44
EgoPo Classic Theater 201n27
Elevator Repair Service 178–9
Eliot, T.S. 3, 14, 16–17, 24, 29, 41, 49, 73, 80, 83, 85, 92, 104, 126, 147, 164, 181n10, 184n7
   The Cocktail Party 18, 25, 76, 87, 104–7, 121, 184n10, 196n11
   The Confidential Clerk 25, 184n10

The Elder Statesman 25, 184n10
The Family Reunion 25, 28–9, 184n10
The Four Quartets 28, 108
"The Love Song of J. Alfred Prufrock" 114
Murder in the Cathedral 12, 25, 26–8, 74
"The Possibility of Poetic Drama" 4, 11
The Rock 12, 25–7
Sweeney Agonistes 198n63
The Three Voices of Poetry 12–3, 26–8
The Waste Land 59, 160
Elizabethan drama 1–2, 6–7, 8, 24, 75–6, 86–7, 95
   See also Kyd, Thomas; Marlowe, Christopher; Shakespeare, William
Ellams, Inua 1
epic theater
   see alienation effect; Brecht, Bertolt
Euripides 23, 29
   Alcestis 184n10, 196n11
   Ion 184n10
   Trojan Women 167–8
experimental poetry 13, 183n52
   see also avant-garde poetry
experimental theater 14, 76, 104–9, 120–1, 135, 178–9, 183n56
   see also avant-garde theater

Field Day Theatre Company 43
folk music 156, 162
   British Folk Music Revival 93, 164–5, 195n90, 205n43
Friel, Brian 43
Fry, Christopher 2, 4, 13, 24, 73, 74
   The Lady's Not For Burning 3
Frye, Northrop 12, 49, 101

Gate Theatre (London) 109
Genette, Gerard 9–10
Goethe, Johann Wolfgang von 9
Górnicka, Marta 1
Graham, Jorie 131–3
Gray, Spaulding 104–9, 121, 197n19
Gray, Terence 73
Greek drama (classical) 8, 13, 25, 167, 175, 196n11
   Aristotlean conventions 11, 126–7, 133–4, 137–8, 175
   chorus in 23–4, 29, 34, 38, 44, 89

See also Aeschylus; Aristophanes; Euripides; Sophocles
Greig, David 14, 19, 157, 162–7, 173, 205n43
Group Theatre 3, 73
Guinness, Alec 105, 108

Hardy, Thomas 2
Harrison, Tony 13, 19
   The Common Chorus 157, 167–70, 173
   Square Rounds 206n62
   The Trackers of Oxyrhynchus 157, 167, 170–3
Hamilton 1, 4
Heaney, Seamus 17
   The Cure at Troy 24, 43–7, 155, 170
Herbert, George 58–9, 101
Herodotus 171, 207n76
Heywood, Thomas 6–7
Hobbes, Thomas 41–3
Howes, Libby 107–8
Hughes, Langston 49, 52
Hughes, Ted 52

iambic pentameter
   See blank verse
Ibsen, Henrik 7–8, 103
Irish Literary Revival 2, 163–4
   See also Yeats
Isherwood, Christopher 3, 164
   On the Frontier 32

Jackson, Virginia 9–11
Jacobean drama 84–7, 194n60
   See also Heywood, Thomas; Middleton, Thomas
Jonas, Joan 106–7

Kane, Sarah 16, 176
Kreymborg, Alfred 2
Kyd, Thomas 86
Kyle, Barry 60

Language Poetry 13, 183n56
Laurens, Joanna 14, 104, 110
   The Three Birds 18, 109–17, 175, 198n43
Lech, Kasia 1, 179
LeCompte, Elizabeth 105, 197n16
Lillo, George 6–7
Littlewood, Joan 74
liturgy 89, 186n51

Living Theatre 76, 79, 84, 99, 120–6, 198n63, 199n78
Lloyd, A.L. 93, 96
Loy, Mina 2
Lyceum Theatre Edinburgh 103
Lynne, Kimberley 153
lyricization 9–12, 50

MacColl, Ewan 93
MacLow, Jackson 84
MacNeice, Louis 3, 52
Maeterlinck, Maurice 11, 126
Malina, Judith 84, 121–6, 198n63
Manahan, Anna 98
Manning, Mary 2
Marlowe, Christopher 75, 192n17
Masefield, John 3, 164
McNamara, Robert 79, 145, 202n63
McSweeney, Joyelle 14, 41, 156
   The Commandrine 119
   Dead Youth, or The Leaks 119, 176–7
Melodrama 76, 79, 161,
Mercury Theatre 27
metapoetry 51, 54
metatheater 88, 106, 120–4
Middleton, Thomas 6–7, 86
Mill, J.S. 54
Millay, Edna St. Vincent 2, 51–2, 89
Milton, John 189n36
mime 103, 116
miracle play 30
Miranda, Lin-Manuel *See Hamilton*
Modernism 55
   in theater 2, 3, 15, 18, 19, 75, 84, 91, 99, 118, 120, 126, 145, 175
   in poetry 14, 74, 80
Moore, Edward 6–7
musical theater 4, 38, 103–4, 163

National Theatre (UK) 170, 173, 206n62
New Criticism 10, 52
Nietzsche, Friedrich 23
Noh drama 77–9, 146–7, 149–50, 193n29, 193n34, 202n63, 203n78

O'Hara, Frank 2
opera 29, 88, 118,
   The Mother of Us All 157–62
Osborne, John 3, 74
Ovid 110–1, 198n43

Index

Pantomime *See* mime
Passion play 31–5
Pinter, Harold 3, 53, 104
Plath, Sylvia 51, 53, 177
  Three Women 14, 15, 18, 52, 54, 60–70, 103, 175, 190n46
Plato 11, 23
Poets' Theatre (Cambridge) 3, 181n10
Pope Pius XII 30, 35
Postconfessional poetry 50–2
postdramatic theater 18, 19, 75, 126–7, 175
  language of 16, 101
  Nayatt School as 109
  Many Loves as 118–20
  Rockaby as 138–43, 153
  temporality of 133–4
postmodernism 14–15, 126, 157
Pound, Ezra 74, 77, 80
print literature, plays as 9, 15, 102
prosody 76–77, 79–83, 84, 86–7, 94, 136, 141, 146, 166, 171, 192n13
Provincetown Players 2, 73

Queen, Khadijah 17, 176–8

radio drama 14, 17, 51–4, 69–70, 140, 175, 177, 189n32
  by Beckett 53, 135, 188n16
  See also Plath *Three Women*; Walcott *Harry Dernier*
Rea, Stephen 43
realism 5, 11, 13, 18, 31, 40, 75, 79, 84, 99–100, 101, 103–4, 133–4, 137, 146, 175
  in fiction 9
  in Ibsen 7–8
  in *Many Loves* 109–10, 120–5
recording technology 201n27
  in *Nayatt School* 105–8
  in *Rockaby* 136–45, 153
Relationship, The (theater company) 177
religious drama 3, 25–9, 30–6, 74, 184n7
  see also Canterbury Festival
Rexroth, Kenneth 76, 198n63
rhyme 46, 79, 101, 158, 162, 166, 171, 177
ritual 39, 40, 46, 116, 154, 170–1
  in *Purgatory* 145–53
  in *Rockaby* 137–45
  lyric as 15, 134–5, 152
  theater as 76, 79, 134–5

Romantic
  drama 8, 9
  lyric 10, 50, 53, 56, 63, 75, 78, 113, 157, 163–4
  genre theory 9–11
Royal Court Theatre 74, 96, 178, 202n48
Royal Shakespeare Company 60
Royal Swedish Theatre 85

Sayers, Dorothy 3, 74
  The Just Vengeance 17, 24, 30–6, 39, 41, 43, 47, 165, 185n32, 184n34
satyr play 170–3
Schechner, Richard 135
Schlegel, Friedrich 9
Second World War 17, 24–5, 30, 56, 80, 85, 185n35
Shakespeare, William 1–2, 4, 5, 9, 75, 85, 108, 155, 192n17, 192n22, 200n9
  Hamlet 57, 59, 65–6, 86, 119, 191n60
  Henry IV, Parts 1 and *2* 6, 76–7, 92
  Henry V 24
  Macbeth 138
  Measure for Measure 177
  Titus Andronicus 86
Shange, Ntozake 17, 25,
  for colored girls who have considered suicide 32, 36–43
Shaw, George Bernard 9, 102
Shaw, Robert 60, 190n44
Shelley, Percy Bysshe 9, 50–2, 78
Shuffle 178–9
Sidney, Philip 166
Snyder, Emily C.A. 1
Sophocles 23, 29
  Antigone 122
  Ichneutae 170–1
  Oedipus at Colonus 184n10
  Oedipus the King 24
  Philoctetes 43–7, 155, 187n91
  Tereus 110
Soyinka, Wole 4
Spender, Stephen 3
Stein, Gertrude 17, 19, 76, 118, 126, 175
  Byron a Play 119–20
  Doctor Faustus Lights the Lights 198n63
  Ladies Voices 16–17, 176, 198n63
  The Mother of Us All 157–62, 173
Stendhal (Marie-Henri Beyle) 7
Stevens, Wallace 145

Index

Stewart, Susan 19, 134, 140, 155–7, 173
Swinburne, Algernon Charles 9

television 92–3, 135
Templeton, Fiona 177
Tennyson, Alfred 9, 63
Theatre Workshop (UK) 74
tragédie domestique et bourgeoise 6–7
tragedy 5–8, 23–4, 76–7, 85–6, 167, 173
Troubles (Northern Ireland) 17, 25, 43–7
Turn to Flesh Productions 1

Unity Theatre 73

Valk, Kate 106, 196n16
Vawter, Ron 107–8
Vendler, Helen 49–50, 64
Victorian literature 9, 74, 80
   dramatic monologue 9, 63–64, 140

Walcott, Derek 4
   Harry Dernier 14, 17–8, 52–9, 67, 70, 139, 175, 177, 189n21, 189n22, 189n32, 189n36
   "The Poet in the Theatre" 3, 4, 8–9, 163
Webster, John 86, 195n82

Wesker, Arnold 3
Whitelaw, Billie 141–5, 201n42
Whitman, Walt 152
Wilbur, Richard 2
Williams, Charles 3, 24, 74
Williams, William Carlos 2, 76, 175,
   Many Loves 18, 89, 104, 120–6, 198n55
Wilson, Wils 157, 162–7, 173, 205n43
Wooster Group, 118, 126, 135, 196n10
   Nayatt School 18, 104–9
   Rumstick Road 104–5, 107
   Sakonnet Point 104–5, 107
   Since I Can Remember 197n16
Wordsworth, William 113, 164

Yeats, Anne 150
Yeats, William Butler 2, 4, 14, 73, 99, 163–4, 175, 193n29
   At the Hawk's Well 77–9, 193n34
   "The Circus Animal's Desertion" 148
   "Man and the Echo" 58
   On Baile's Strand 76–7, 92, 192n23, 192n24, 192n26
   On the Boiler 202n60
   Purgatory 18, 133, 135, 145–54, 171, 202n60, 202n63, 203n75, 204n99